ANCIENT EGYPTIAN JEWELRY

CAROL ANDREWS

HARRY N. ABRAMS, INC., PUBLISHERS, NEW YORK

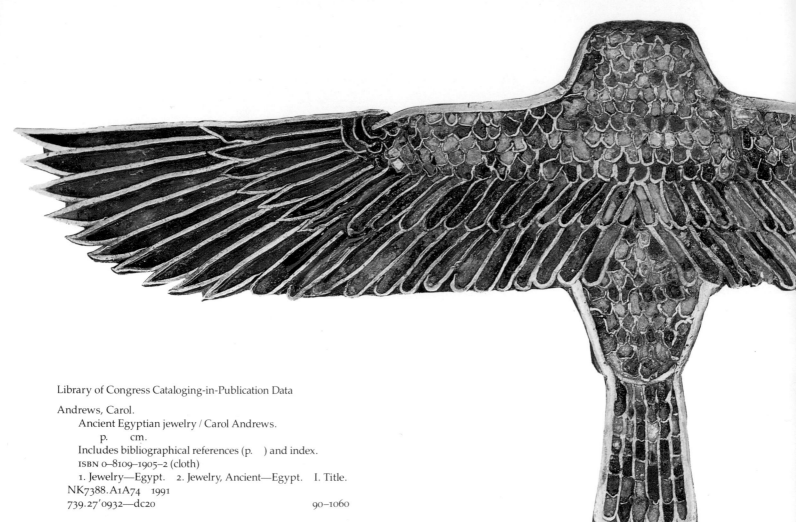

Library of Congress Cataloging-in-Publication Data

Andrews, Carol.
  Ancient Egyptian jewelry / Carol Andrews.
      p.   cm.
  Includes bibliographical references (p.   ) and index.
  ISBN 0–8109–1905–2 (cloth)
  1. Jewelry—Egypt.   2. Jewelry, Ancient—Egypt.   I. Title.
NK7388.A1A74   1991
  739.27′0932—dc20   90–1060

Copyright © 1990 The Trustees of the British Museum

Published in 1991 by Harry N. Abrams, Incorporated,
New York
A Times Mirror Company

Printed and bound in Italy

Designed by Roger Davies

Half title page Gold inlaid scarab pectoral from the tomb of
Tutankhamun (see 118).

Title page Gold-capped amethyst beads and amethyst scarab.
Middle Kingdom (*c.* 1900-1800 BC); blue-glazed composition
beads in the form of four-celled fruit. 18th Dynasty
(*c.* 1370-1320 BC); glass and hollow gold beads. 18th Dynasty
(*c.* 1340-1320 BC); gold-capped cornelian beads. Middle
Kingdom (*c.* 1900-1800 BC); solid cast gold flies and garnet
beads. 18th Dynasty (*c.* 1500-1400 BC).

This page Gold falcon pectoral, once inlaid with polychrome
glass (see 70).

CONTENTS

Introduction

Jewellery permeated every facet of Egyptian civilisation at every level of society. In life it might be worn as a sign of rank or office, as a military or civil award, to be amuletic and protective, or to be merely decorative. All such pieces could be taken to the tomb with their owner for use in the Afterlife, and the mummy itself was in addition bedecked with prescribed funerary jewellery made specifically to give amuletic protection during the fraught passage to the Other World.

Among the most spectacular and renowned jewellery surviving from ancient Egypt is that from Tutankhamun's tomb in the Valley of the Kings and from the royal burials at Tanis and Dahshur; together with famous pieces from Abydos, Thebes and Saqqara, these are now in the Egyptian Museum, Cairo. In New York the Metropolitan Museum of Art boasts the jewellery of a 12th Dynasty princess from Lahun, that of a contemporary noblewoman from Lisht, and most of the pieces which once belonged to three minor wives of Tuthmosis III. But the achievements of the jewellery-maker's craft over three millennia are represented not just by these royal treasures, but also by individual items of outstanding workmanship and beauty. Many superb pieces are now housed in the Egyptian collection of the British Museum, but also in museums in Paris, Berlin, Munich, Boston and Brooklyn, Edinburgh, University College London, Oxford, Cambridge and Manchester, Leiden, Hildesheim and Philadelphia. Often these are of unknown provenance, their owners' names long forgotten, or else they give us a tantalising glimpse of the one time richness of burials despoiled long ago. Furthermore, since everyone from the meanest peasant to pharaoh himself could and did wear jewellery, and took it to the tomb for use in the Afterlife, a far greater proportion of jewellery has survived from humble burials than from those of the great. In many ways the jewellery of ordinary Egyptians, too often ignored, can be as striking as that of their rulers, and perhaps more instructive.

The beginnings of Egyptian jewellery-making can be traced four thousand years before the birth of Christ, when men of the Badarian culture wrapped around their hips massive girdles of bright-green glazed stone beads, and shaped bangles of ivory and amulets of shell. Even before the beginning of the 1st Dynasty in 3100 BC craftsmen of the Naqada II Period had progressed to making beads from highly coloured semi-precious stones and precious metal, skilfully combined in a diadem for a non-royal female. Less than a hundred years later, when four superb bead bracelets were made for a queen of Djer, the jewellery-maker's skill was fully fledged. For the next three thousand years, until the twilight of the Graeco-Roman Period, the products of the jewellery-maker's workshop delighted the living and afforded amuletic protection for the dead.

It is fortunate that the Egyptians were pleased to be depicted wearing

1 Pectoral and girdle of Sithathor. The gold openwork pylon-shaped pectoral (**a**) is inlaid with lapis lazuli, cornelian and turquoise, currently strung with beads of turquoise, lapis lazuli, cornelian and gold. Above a cartouche containing the prenomen of Sesostris II are hieroglyphs reading 'the gods are content' – the king's Horus-of-gold name. Appropriately, the two flanking falcons wearing the double crown stand on the sign for 'gold'. H 4.9cm

The girdle (**b**) is composed of hollow gold cowries, strung with acacia-seed beads of gold, feldspar, lapis lazuli and cornelian. L 70cm

From the cache of Sithathor, Dahshur. 12th Dynasty (reign of Sesostris III, *c.* 1850 BC)

2 Limestone relief from the tomb of the king's priest Iry, showing the deceased wearing a curious, leaf-shaped pendant strung on a cord between two barrel beads. He also wears plain bangles. H (total) 95cm

From Saqqara. 4th Dynasty (c. 2550 BC)

3 Sheet-gold circlet, originally fastened at the back by cords. It is studded with rosettes imitating marguerites, inlaid with cornelian and decayed blue and green glass or glazed composition. The two hollow gold gazelle heads perhaps denote the lesser rank of its owner, who was a royal harim lady and not the Great Royal Wife. L 43cm

From the burial of the three wives of Tuthmosis III, W. Thebes. 18th Dynasty (c. 1465 BC)

Far right 4 Map showing the principal sites mentioned in the text.

their prized possessions, whether on statues, in reliefs and paintings, in papyrus vignettes or on coffins. Sometimes jewellery forms have survived only in representations, like the curious, large, leafy pendant prominently worn by the 4th Dynasty priest Iry in relief panels from his tomb. No pendant in this form has survived and there are many other such instances where, were it not for the pictorial representation, the jewellery form would be unknown. Various types of jewellery were also depicted on tomb walls as funerary goods and as royal gifts and awards, on temple walls among the spoils of war and offerings to the gods and in Middle Kingdom coffins and later in funerary papyrus vignettes as prescribed protection for the dead. Even in literary sources, such as lists of temple treasures and autobiographical accounts of awards from pharaoh, the nature of the Egyptian scripts ensured that the word for a specific type of jewellery was determined by a pictorial representation of it.

It is of even greater importance that, because of their religious beliefs, the Egyptians covered the walls of their tomb chapels with scenes of daily life, for it is only thus that depictions have survived of workers in precious metal and jewellery-makers at their crafts, casting, burnishing, boring, polishing and threading. There are even scenes of the arrival of the raw materials from which they fashioned the jewellery, brought as tribute or trade from Nubia, Syria and Asia Minor.

It is because it first appears during Egypt's earliest prehistory, exhibits so many of the techniques and skills known to her craftsmen, was worn at every level of her society, and is so numerous in both survival and depiction that of all the products of ancient Egyptian civilisation her jewellery is perhaps the most characteristic.

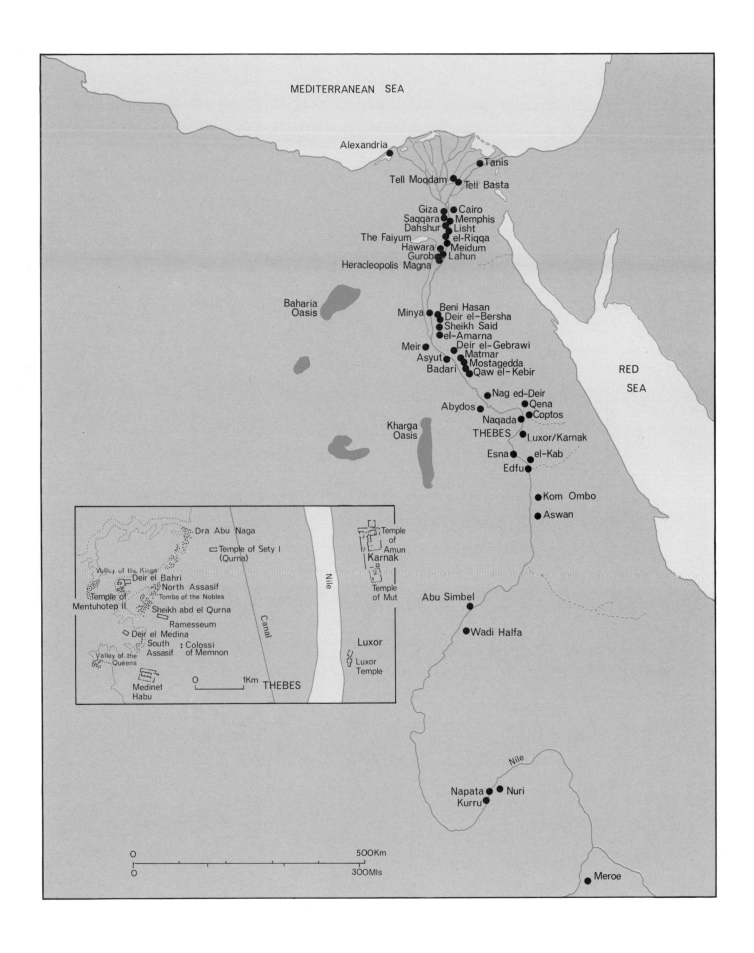

MEDITERRANEAN SEA

Alexandria

Tanis

Tell Moqdam
Tell Basta

Giza   Cairo
Saqqara   Memphis
Dahshur   Lisht
The Faiyum   el-Riqqa
Hawara   Meidum
Gurob   Lahun
Heracleopolis Magna

Baharia
Oasis

Minya   Beni Hasan
Deir el-Bersha
Sheikh Said
el-Amarna
Meir   Deir el-Gebrawi
Asyut   Matmar
Badari   Mostagedda
Qaw el-Kebir

Nag ed-Deir
Abydos   Qena
Naqada   Coptos
THEBES
Luxor/Karnak
Esna   el-Kab
Edfu

Kharga
Oasis

RED
SEA

Kom Ombo
Aswan

Abu Simbel

Wadi Halfa

Napata   Nuri
Kurru

Meroe

Dra Abu Naga
Temple of Sety I
(Qurna)

Valley of the Kings
Deir el Bahri
North Assasif
Temple of   Tombs of the Nobles
Mentuhotep II
Sheikh abd el Qurna
Ramesseum
Deir el Medina
South   :Colossi
Assasif   of Memnon
Valley of the
Queens
Medinet
Habu

Temple
of
Amun
Karnak

Temple
of Mut

Luxor

Luxor
Temple

Nile

Canal

0   1Km   THEBES

0
0   500Km
300MIs

Nile

9

CHAPTER ONE

Rediscovering ancient Egyptian jewellery

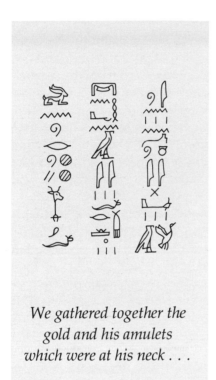

We gathered together the gold and his amulets which were at his neck . . .

5 *Shebyu*-collar of Psusennes I, part of an honorific decoration. The solid gold ring beads are strung tightly on cords whose knots are hidden by the sheet-gold clasp which bears on both faces the king's nomen and prenomen cartouches. The inscription on the upper face is inlaid with lapis lazuli, that on the underside is merely incised. D 30cm; WT 6315g

From the burial chamber of Psusennes, Tanis (tomb III). 21st Dynasty (*c.* 1039–991 BC)

When Tushratta, King of Mitanni, wrote to King Amenophis III in about 1370 BC, querying the non-arrival of promised valuable gifts, he justified his impatience with the words: 'in the land of my brother gold is as abundant as dust'. He exaggerated a little, yet the fact remains that two thousand years earlier, even before the beginning of the 1st Dynasty in 3100 BC, the Egyptians already had access to this most evocative of precious metals, and throughout the Dynastic Period they acquired it in ever increasing quantities, at first from the Eastern Desert and Nubia, later too as tribute and spoils of war from Syria and the north.

The Egyptian craftsmen used these enormous amounts of gold in many and varied ways – to gild lesser materials, to plate wood and stone, solid casting it into small statuary, hammering and cutting sheets of it into elements of religious and ceremonial furniture and funerary equipment. However, its most widespread use was in the production of jewellery, both that worn by the living and, in particular, that made expressly for the adornment of the corpse. Egyptian funerary beliefs required that the mummified body be bedecked with the finest products of the jewellery-maker's art and, whether for amulet or collar, pectoral or diadem, the first choice of material, indeed the prescribed material according to some of the funerary texts, was gold. Consequently, it was the valuable metal on and about the mummy which the ancient robbers sought, for, once stolen, it could be broken up or recast. Indeed, it has been suggested more than once that it was the black economy in recycled precious metal robbed from the dead that allowed Egyptian civilisation to flourish as long as it did. Had the prodigious quantities of gold, electrum and silver taken to the tombs of kings and nobility remained there undisturbed, the economy would have collapsed under the strain of constantly needing to replenish stocks.

Two excerpts from ancient texts are very revealing. The Amherst Papyrus, dated almost certainly to year 16 of the reign of King Ramesses IX of the 20th Dynasty (*c.* 1116 BC), contains a tomb-robber's verbatim account of the ransacking of the burial of King Sobkemsaf II, a Theban ruler of the late 17th Dynasty (*c.* 1590 BC), and his queen Nubkhas.

A great number of *udjat*-eyes and ornaments of gold were at his neck; his head covering was of gold. The noble mummy of this king was entirely overlaid with gold; his coffins were bedecked with gold, inside and out, inlaid with every kind of precious stone. We collected together the gold which we found on the noble mummy of this god and his *udjat*-eyes and ornaments at his neck [and] the coffins in which he rested. We found the queen likewise; we collected together all that we found on her also. We set fire to their coffins; we stole their equipment which we found with them, consisting of articles of gold, silver and bronze. We divided them amongst ourselves: we made this gold which we found on these two gods and their mummies, *udjat*-eyes, ornaments and coffins, into eight shares.

Interestingly enough, in the list of tomb-robbers which follows the first to be named is a jewellery-maker.

The second text is on the recto of P.BM 10068, again dated to the reign of Ramesses IX but on this occasion to year 17. It contains a list of 'the gold and silver . . . which the thieving workmen of the necropolis were found to have stolen when they were discovered to have violated this Place of Beauty on the west of Thebes'. Each section begins with the words 'found in the possession of the thief, the great criminal', continues with the man's office and his name and then the words 'as his share' with the size of his haul. Including the proceeds recovered from tradesmen and inhabitants of eastern and western Thebes which they had received from the thieves, the grand total of pure gold, white gold and silver stolen from tombs in the Theban necropolis by a single gang amounted to just over 283 *deben*. Since it has been calculated that at this period a *deben* weighed 91 grams, over 25.5 kilograms of precious metal was involved. Moreover, the eight tomb-robbers named in this papyrus are not the same eight who had carried out the robberies recorded in the Amherst Papyrus only one year earlier.

These texts give a clear indication of how widely spread and profitable tomb-robbery was in the Theban area during the late Ramesside Period. They also explain the anomoly of the survival from long-plundered burials of funerary goods such as *shabti*-figurines, papyri and amulets in their thousands, whereas only a few individual items of precious-metal jewellery have come down to the present from this source. An almost unique survival of this type is the gold-mounted green jasper heart scarab of King 65d Sobkemsaf II, stolen by the robbers who confessed to their crime in the Amherst Papyrus but discovered near the scene of the robbery just under three thousand years later, in the early part of the nineteenth century. Whether it was dropped or deliberately hidden by one of the ancient thieves, the heart scarab of Sobkemsaf is one of the handful of individual pieces of jewellery to have survived to the present day from a burial robbed in ancient times. The vast majority of the most outstanding and best-known examples have been recovered from intact burials and caches, but given the activities of the ancient tomb-robbers the odds against their survival were a million to one, as the history of their discovery shows.

One of the earliest important finds of jewellery stems from the very end of the Pharaonic Period at the furthest fringes of Egyptian influence. In mid-1834 Italian physician Giuseppe Ferlini and a fellow traveller arrived at the site of the ancient city of Meroe in Sudan. It was here, beside their new capital, that the successors of the Kushite 25th Dynasty were buried beneath pyramids unlike any seen in Egypt. Meroitic pyramids, although built of stone, with a funerary chapel at the east face, are small and have steeply angled sides; the burial chamber lies beneath the superstructure and is reached by a staircase which was blocked after the interment. Until modern times it was difficult for Europeans to visit the Sudan, so the royal pyramids which Ferlini found at Meroe were virtually intact. He and his

6 One of a pair of hinged gold armlets of Queen Amanishakheto. It is decorated with applied wire and granulation and inlaid with fused red, dark- and light-blue glass. Around the central band are seven panels separated by feathering, the central containing a modelled frontal bust of a male god, the others crowned goddesses. At the hinge is Mut wearing a vulture head-dress and double crown, standing on a lotus. H 4.6cm

From the pyramid of Queen Amanishakheto, Meroe. Meroitic Period (late 1st century BC)

companions began to demolish them in their search for treasure. The destruction wrought is recorded in Ferlini's own words:

I decided to make a last attempt on one of the large [pyramids] situated at the end of the hill and in particular on one I had noticed was almost intact . . . It is pointless to expound on this fine monument which is generally so well known. Mounting to the summit of the pyramid with four workmen to begin work I discovered at first sight that the demolition would be very easy seeing that the monument was already collapsing through age.

Almost at once a room was uncovered which contained funerary goods, including a bronze vessel full of superb gold and semi-precious stone jewellery and other pieces lying on the floor, all of which Ferlini managed to remove and hide. It took his workmen twenty days in all to complete the demolition to ground level and though another room (presumably the burial chamber) was found, it contained only two bronze vessels. When word reached him of a proposed attack by local inhabitants, who suspected he had found treasure, he dug it up and fled by night. On his safe return to Europe Ferlini published a catalogue of the treasure from the pyramid of Queen Amanishakheto; the jewellery, which dates to the late first century BC, remains among the finest of Meroitic origin. Most of the pieces are now in the Egyptian collections of East Berlin and Munich, although some were lost as a result of World War II.

As the usual location of the burial chamber was beneath Meroitic pyramids, the room in which Ferlini claimed to have found the hoard may have been made later to house the cache. At all events, it was a rich

6

assembly of jewellery which included amuletic collars, a necklace, pendants, amulets, armlets, earrings, eight shield rings and no fewer than sixty-four signet-rings, mostly in gold. Excavations conducted by George Reisner between 1916 and 1933 on behalf of Harvard University and the Boston Museum of Fine Arts at the Kushite pyramids of Kurru and Nuri, near the earlier capital of Napata, and at Meroe too, salvaged some superb individual pieces of jewellery, but the Meroitic cache discovered by Ferlini remains unique in its range and number of objects.

The activities of the Frenchman Auguste Mariette in the mid-nineteenth century laid the foundations of the modern Egyptian Antiquities Organisation. In 1850 Mariette, on his first visit to Egypt, was commissioned by the Louvre to purchase Coptic manuscripts. Instead, his interest aroused by what appeared to be an avenue of sphinxes at Saqqara, he used his purchase money to fund an excavation at the site. His reward was the discovery of the Serapeum, vast underground catacombs in which the Apis bulls, earthly manifestation of the god Ptah of Memphis, were interred like animal pharaohs over a period of more than thirteen centuries. The earliest burials date back to the reign of Amenophis III but it was on the bodies of the bulls Mariette dubbed Apis 2 and Apis 4 of the reign of Ramesses II, that he found jewellery which can be taken to represent contemporary royal craftsmanship. 7

Mariette saw the first season of operations of the newly founded Egyptian Antiquities Service in 1859 crowned by the uncovering of the coffin and mummy of Queen Aahhotep at Dra Abu Naga on the Theban West Bank. Unfortunately, no proper record of the find was made and the mummy was destroyed, but the Cairo Museum displays the personal jewellery of this Theban queen, whose son Ahmose expelled the Hyksos 8 from Egypt and founded the 18th Dynasty. From the very beginning Mariette had a fight to ensure that the treasure found its way to the Museum. Before his instructions arrived in Luxor, directing that the find should be sent at once to Cairo, the coffin was opened by a local governor, who broke up the mummy to secure the jewellery which he then sent off to the Khedival Palace in the capital, intent on gaining the good graces of Egypt's ruler by presenting him with the newly found treasures. Mariette, realising that the chance of all these valuable pieces reaching their final destination was minimal, raced up the Nile in a steamer and waylaid the

7 Sheet-gold rigid vulture pectoral holding *shen*-signs in its claws, its back a mass of cloisons inset with cornelian, lapis lazuli and turquoise. The fan-shaped extension beneath its chin is a decorated broad collar. w 13.7cm
   From the Serapeum, Saqqara. 19th Dynasty (reign of Ramesses II, *c.* 1250 BC)

8 Rigid hinged bracelet of Queen Aahhotep, the earliest known example of this type, made from two interlocking semicircular gold bands which are closed by pins, one of them retractable. The chased relief gold figures and text, set against an inlaid lapis lazuli background, show part of the coronation ritual. In two separate scenes King Ahmose kneels, protected by Geb enthroned; in one the god wears the red crown of Lower Egypt, in the other the double crown. H 3.4cm

From the burial of Aahhotep, Dra Abu Naga, W. Thebes. 18th Dynasty (reign of Ahmose, c. 1540 BC)

vessel with the jewellery on board. He recovered it by a combination of the misuse of a government order allowing him to stop the shipment of antiquities and outright threats of physical violence. Fortunately, the Khedive was sufficiently amused by Mariette's account of his exploits to make no claim on the jewellery, in spite of its worth, but allowed it to pass intact into the Museum, though only after he had borrowed the gold chain with scarab for a short while for his favourite wife to wear. Curiously enough, Mariette had to employ his persuasive skills on one more occasion to retain these treasures for Egypt: in 1867 the Empress Eugénie tried to acquire them after they had been displayed in France during the Paris Exhibition. It is interesting that no piece of Aahhotep's jewellery bears her name, only that of Ahmose.

In the later part of the nineteenth century another French Director of the Egyptian Antiquities Service was responsible for some memorable finds at Dahshur, north of the Faiyum. It was to this region that the kings of the 12th Dynasty had moved their capital, now known as Lisht, but called in Egyptian 'Seizer of the Two Lands', for it lay in an extremely suitable position for maintaining control over Upper and Lower Egypt. Their pyramids were built in the surrounding area, in a line running from Dahshur through Lisht to Hawara and Lahun, and it was at the first site, where seven centuries earlier Sneferu had built the first true pyramid, that Ammenemes II and Sesostris III chose to locate their tombs. Middle Kingdom pyramids, however, were not constructed of stone like their Old

78

Kingdom counterparts; they had a brick core with only an outer facing of stone. When the fine casing had been stripped away the mud-brick rubble filling was soon ruined and spread its debris over the surrounding area. Such was the situation which confronted J. de Morgan when he began excavating at Dahshur in 1894 in the angle of the enclosure wall to the north-west of the pyramid of Sesostris III. On 26 February one of his test trenches penetrated a poorly cut shaft with unfinished walls; although it did not suggest the entrance to an underground burial-place, all the evidence pointed to it not having been disturbed since ancient times, for it was still full of original blocking material. De Morgan's hopes were further raised when an intact burial of 26th Dynasty date was found a little below the surface of the shaft. Two days later the opening to a low corridor was uncovered which led into a gallery with four burial chambers opening off it; all had been robbed in antiquity. Indeed, it became clear that the way by which de Morgan had entered had been made by the ancient robbers. The fact that their pit had been sunk so exactly to meet the underground gallery and had been filled in to disguise its entrance only proved that there must have been collusion between the robbers and the priests who served the burial-place. Removal of the extensive debris in the gallery eventually revealed the original entrance; it also uncovered a lower level containing eight sarcophagi, but they too had been robbed. However, as the debris within the lower chambers was being cleared to bedrock, a workman's foot broke through into a cavity in the floor at the foot of one of the sarcophagi. The wooden box once hidden in it was long decayed but its contents, the personal ornaments of Princess Sithathor, daughter of Sesostris II, had survived and are now in the Cairo Museum. Unfortunately, although de Morgan found a great number of loose beads of various shapes and materials, no record was made of their exact positions. However, some reconstruction has been possible subsequently, after reference to the Lahun treasure (see below).

Only a few days after this discovery de Morgan found a second cache in an identical location at the foot of one of the other sarcophagi. The owner on this occasion was a queen called Mereret. Some of the jewellery dates to the reign of her father Sesostris III, other pieces to that of his successor Ammenemes III. The find included numerous outstanding pieces, such as a superb openwork inlaid gold pectoral with the name of Sesostris III, amulets and many clasps, beads and other elements which had once formed necklaces, bracelets and anklets.

During this first season at Dahshur de Morgan also excavated an area within the enclosure wall of the pyramid of Ammenemes III and was rewarded by the discovery of the underground tomb of the 13th Dynasty pharaoh Hor at the bottom of a double shaft. This secondary burial had been robbed in antiquity, but some of the royal jewellery remained. Shortly afterwards he uncovered only a few metres away a second, intact underground burial-place belonging to a contemporary princess; she was named Nubhotepti the Child, even though examination of her body proved she was at least forty-four when she died.

It was during his second season at Dahshur, however, early in 1895, that one of the sondages sunk in the area within the enclosure wall north-west of the pyramid of Ammenemes II struck a large rectangular pit which still contained its original blocking. Six metres down de Morgan uncovered the fine limestone blocks which formed the roof of a subterranean monument. He was even more excited when he came across a pit dug by robbers which had been sufficiently deep to reach the entrance of the substructure yet had missed it, by being located two metres too far to the north. As a result, the two burials within the massive stone-built substructure were intact. Each burial chamber was built to fit exactly the huge sandstone sarcophagus, which must have been put in position at the time of construction; at the interment the sarcophagus lid was closed and roofing blocks set in place above it.

The first burial opened by de Morgan belonged to a princess called Ita. Her mummy, like that of all Dahshur royalty, was in a dreadful state of decay, but on and about it had survived a ceremonial bronze dagger with decorated gold handle, a ceremonial mace and the remains of various pieces of jewellery, including a mass of loose cornelian and glazed composition beads.

But this small treasure gave de Morgan only a hint of what was to come, for the second intact burial belonged to a princess called Khnumet, the daughter of a king and the wife of a king. Her spectacular jewellery is among the finest ever made by Egypt's goldsmiths and lapidaries, and included openwork diadems, collars, granulation pendants on chains, necklaces with amuletic clasps, bracelets, anklets and a girdle. However, even after reconstruction there remained a mass of loose beads which

9 Jewellery from the treasure of Khnumet.

a (*top*) Three gold amuletic 'motto' clasps, inlaid with cornelian, lapis lazuli and turquoise, originally worn on the chest as pendants. The first wishes the wearer 'joy'; the second depicts the *mes*-apron; the third spells out 'all life and protection are behind (her)'. H (central amulet) 3.3cm

b (*centre*) String constructed from gold, turquoise and lapis lazuli beads and a row of gold drops inlaid with the same semi-precious stones.

c (*bottom*) Openwork collar composed of heraldically opposed gold amulets inlaid with cornelian, lapis lazuli and turquoise, strung with gold discs between inlaid solid gold falcon-headed terminals.

From the tomb of Khnumet, Dahshur. 12th Dynasty (reign of Ammenemes II, *c.* 1895 BC)

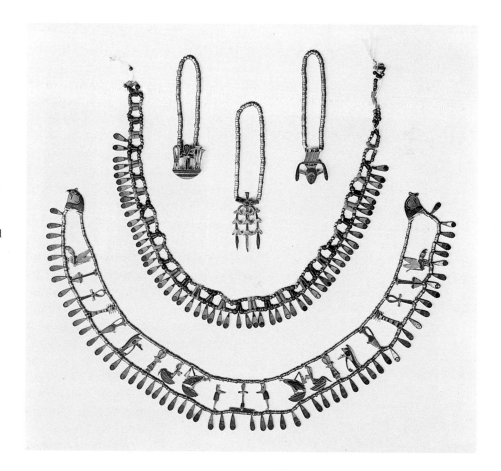

9

could not be attributed to any particular item, including over five hundred of lapis lazuli, over six hundred of turquoise and more than fifteen hundred of cornelian, and hundreds of large gold beads, many gadrooned, some with imitation granulation, others in fancy shapes.

As de Morgan continued excavating southwards two further substructures were uncovered. The first, which had contained the burials of a queen called Qemanub and a high official, had been robbed in antiquity but the second was intact. Unfortunately, de Morgan's account of the jewellery he found on the body of Princess Itaweret, one of the two royal daughters buried there, is incredibly perfunctory: 'At the wrists and ankles she wore various bracelets made of gold and hard stone beads. On her neck was a large collar composed of beads and gold ornaments, held by two gold clasps.' Cairo Museum currently exhibits Itaweret's restrung jewellery, and that of the Dahshur royalty.

Further south at Abydos, site of Egypt's first royal cemetery, the British Egyptologist W. M. Flinders Petrie was re-excavating in 1901 the great royal tombs of the earliest dynasties; they had been plundered in ancient times and ravaged even more recently by treasure-seeking, modern excavators. Totally unexpectedly, while clearing the tomb of King Djer, his workmen came across a hole in an inner brickwork wall into which had been stuffed an arm wrapped in linen. Beneath the wrappings it still wore four bracelets of gold, lapis lazuli, turquoise and amethyst; unusually for 10 ancient jewellery, the order of their stringing was certain, for the elements were held in place by the bandages. These bracelets are our sole representatives of royal jewellery of about 3000 BC; they are now in Cairo Museum.

How had they survived the original robbery of the tomb and the subsequent tidying-up by a commission piously appointed for that task in the mid-18th Dynasty, when it became a place of pilgrimage as the supposed tomb of the god Osiris? How, indeed, had the arm and its glint of gold been missed by the thousands of pilgrims passing by its place of concealment to make offerings? Petrie's theory was that when the ancient robbers first entered the tomb, the body was already hidden beneath sand which had drifted through the decayed wooden roof. They might even have stood on the mound which concealed the corpse when they poked holes at the top of the walls in their search for hidden treasure. The body was probably found and broken into pieces by the labourers who cleaned up the tomb during the 18th Dynasty and it was one of their number who hid the arm and its treasures in a hole made by the original robbers. For some reason he never returned for his booty. Was he caught by the authorities but avoided revealing the cache, or was he killed by a fellow thief who was unaware of his victim's secret? The mystery of the bracelets' concealment is as great as the miracle of their survival.

Only two years later the American archaeologist George A. Reisner discovered material which provides a fascinating complement to that found in the tomb of Djer. Reisner, who was destined in later years to make one of Egyptology's most perplexing discoveries, was working in 1903 at Nag ed-Deir, on the Nile north of Abydos, in a cemetery of the Archaic Period which had been extensively plundered in ancient times. Yet in the burial chamber of a tomb which showed in its other rooms every

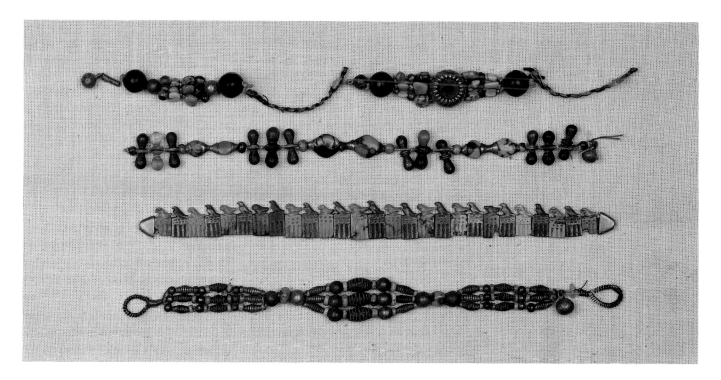

10 Four bracelets found *in situ* on a wrapped arm in the tomb of King Djer. They are made from elements of gold, lapis lazuli, turquoise and amethyst and strung on gold wires and animal hair plaited together. The falcon-crowned plaques of the second bracelet represent a *serekh* containing the royal Horus-of-gold name. The lapis lazuli beads on the fourth bracelet are grooved to imitate the markings of the spiral gold wire ones. L (*serekh* bracelet) 15.6cm

From the tomb of Djer, Abydos. 1st Dynasty (*c.* 3000 BC)

sign of disturbance he found an intact set of jewellery, much of it of gold, on a female corpse which had been crushed beneath the collapsed superstructure and had thus, presumably, escaped the attentions of the ancient robbers. The skull was still encircled by a band of sheet gold, and scattered in the vicinity were a considerable number of beads and pendants of various stones, glazed composition and gold. Clearly a number of strings were involved but the beads were in such confusion that little attempt could be made to restring them in their original order. In addition to stone and metal bangles, the remains of a cylinder-seal and two gold foil finger-rings, the burial also contained ten gold barrel beads with markings imitating reed bundles, twenty-four gold collar elements in the shape of mollusc shells with suspension loops at top and bottom and three large gold amulets.

This jewellery, now in Cairo, was dated by Reisner to the 1st Dynasty (*c.* 3000 BC), so it is roughly contemporary with the bracelets from the tomb of Djer, and gives some indication of the quality of non-royal material of the Early Dynastic Period. These two finds represent virtually all that has survived to illustrate the best of the jewellery-maker's art during the formative years of Dynastic civilisation.

In late September 1906 the great mounds of earth surrounding Tell Basta in the Delta were being removed by the Egyptian Railways Administration with the agreement of the Antiquities Service. Although this was the site of ancient Bubastis, chief cult-centre of the cat-goddess Bastet, nothing of any great importance had so far been brought to the attention of the authorities but now rumour spread that buried treasure in the shape of gold and silver vessels had indeed been discovered and dispersed. By the time the houses of the suspects were searched only a few pieces were left, but they were enough to convince the authorities that a close watch

11

needed to be kept on the earth-shifting operations. Less than a month later, on 17 October, a second hoard was uncovered. It was a strange mixture of finely fashioned precious-metal vessels and jewellery mixed up with pieces of mostly unworked silver. Perhaps everything came from a goldsmith's workshop; most pieces were probably of Ramesside manufacture, and almost certainly the collection was deliberately hidden in ancient times. The cache included many beads and pendants of gold and cornelian, silver bangles and finger-rings, and earrings of gold and silver, but the most spectacular item was without doubt a pair of richly ornamented 67 gold bracelets bearing the name of Ramesses II.

Towards the end of the nineteenth century de Morgan had made impressive discoveries of 12th Dynasty royal jewellery at Dahshur. Ammenemes I, the dynasty's founder, had his tomb at northern Lisht, but nothing has been recovered from his burial. Moreover, the cemetery of his courtiers around the royal pyramid had been systematically plundered in ancient times, probably within a few years of the king's interment. Consequently, when the expedition working on behalf of the New York Metropolitan Museum of Art began clearing the tombs west of the pyramid at the beginning of 1907 they had no indication that they would find untouched the jewellery of a high-born lady called Senebtisy, a member of the family of the vizier Senusret. Indeed, her tomb showed every sign of having been entered by robbers. Even her outer coffin had been stripped of its gold leaf, but that was as far as the thieves had penetrated and someone, perhaps her relatives, had reblocked the entrance to the burial chamber and refilled the shaft.

Senebtisy's body lay within three gilded wooden coffins, the innermost anthropoid with amuletic string, broad collar and a matching chest panel 12

11 Gold jewellery from the burial of a woman of the Early Dynastic Period. The collar elements in the shape of mollusc shells (**a**) and the two pendants were made by beating into a mould, although the pendants have in addition a flat back-plate bearing two small suspension tubes. The oryx pendant (**b**, *left*) wears a Girdle Tie of Isis amulet and the bull pendant (**c**, *right*) a *Bat*-amulet. L (mollusc shells) 1.5cm
    From Nag ed-Deir. 1st Dynasty (*c.* 3000 BC)

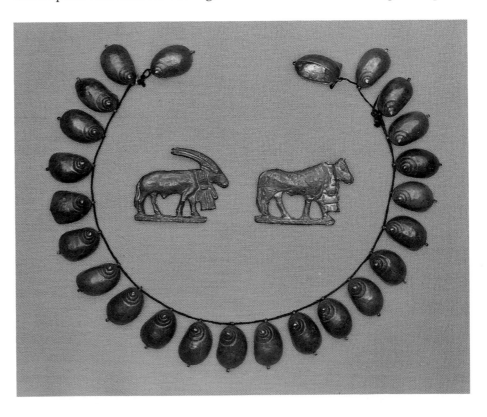

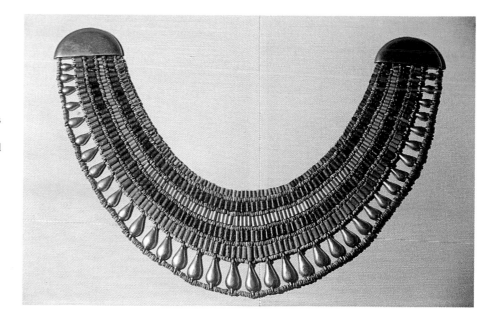

12 Broad collar of Senebtisy. The beads and drop-shaped pendants are of turquoise, blue glazed composition and gold leaf on plaster, strung between terminals also of gold leaf on plaster. There is no means of suspension nor a counterpoise, which, coupled with the use of fragile gold leaf, shows that this collar was purely funerary in function, intended to be laid on the chest of the mummy. w (max) 25cm

From the burial of Senebtisy, Lisht. 12th Dynasty (reign of Ammenemes I, c. 1975 BC)

made from real beads and pendants inset into the wood. A mass of molten resin had been poured over the wrapped mummy as it lay in the coffin and to an extent this had helped to maintain the relative order of the jewellery elements. However, it was the painstaking work of Herbert Winlock and Arthur Mace which allowed the accurate reconstruction of so much of Senebtisy's parure. All of Senebtisy's jewellery is now in the Metropolitan Museum of Art in New York.

At the beginning of 1908 the expedition sponsored by the American Theodore Davis began digging in the Valley of the Kings, just around the corner from the tomb of Ramesses VI in an area south-west of its entrance. It is a sobering thought for Egyptology that, had they diverted their attentions to the corresponding area at the north-west of the entrance, they might have discovered the tomb of Tutankhamun. At the northern side of the defile, at whose end only a month later the entrance to the tomb of Horemheb would be uncovered, work began on removing water-borne debris. Four metres down was encountered the mouth of a shaft which descended vertically for six metres until a doorway was reached in its north wall; this opened into an irregularly shaped rock-cut chamber. The shaft had been completely filled with debris washed in by the fierce torrents of rain which periodically lash the valley, and the floor of the chamber was buried under the same material, up to a depth of a metre at some points. As the debris was cleared vessels and fragments of vessels made of pottery, glazed composition and alabaster came into view, then a mass of gold leaf, still backed by plaster, and a collection of precious-metal jewellery. Apart from Ramesses II, all the cartouches on objects named the 19th Dynasty pharaoh Sety II and his wife and successor Tausret; this, coupled with the discovery of a pair of small hollow silver hands from a coffin and the sole of a child's silver funerary sandal, suggested that these remnants were all that survived from the burial of a child of Sety II and his wife. It appears that the tomb was not watertight and the water which had seeped in had deposited silt on the funerary goods and caused the decay

13

of everything organic. Somehow the location of the burial became known; everything visible above the silt was robbed and the despoiled chamber left open. It was subsequently filled by the larger water-borne debris which also blocked the shaft. Although known officially as pit tomb 56, the jewellery recovered from it has led to its nickname of the Gold Tomb.

During the season 1908 to 1909 Petrie was also operating on the Theban West Bank, excavating on behalf of the British School of Archaeology in Egypt in the foothills of Dra Abu Naga, just to the north of the road which leads to the Valley of the Kings. Although papyri containing accounts of the trials of tomb-robbers prove that the tombs in the area had been systematically rifled during the 20th Dynasty some three thousand years earlier, Petrie uncovered in a shallow trench the intact burial of a late 17th Dynasty woman. Pottery jars, still held in their net carriers, two stools, a chair and a linen box, bowls of ancient food (one *dom*-fruit still bore teeth marks) and a basket containing personal articles were crammed in around a roughly hewn gilded wooden coffin of the kind called *rishi* – the Arabic word for feather – because of its characteristic feathered patterning. Although the corpse had been swathed in copious bandages and shrouds, on unwrapping it proved to have been reduced to a skeleton, but still wearing all its jewellery, which is now in the Royal Scottish Museum in Edinburgh.

In December 1912 Reginald Engelbach, also working on behalf of the British School of Archaeology in Egypt, began excavating an extensive

14

13 Circlet formed from sixteen gold flowers, some of red gold, attached to a sheet-gold band. Each flower has ten petals formed by shaping foil into a mould and five bear the cartouches of Tausret and Sety II. They are attached by wire through rings behind the central domed button. D 17cm

From the Gold Tomb (tomb 56), Valley of the Kings, W. Thebes. 19th Dynasty (reign of Sety II, *c*. 1200–1194 BC)

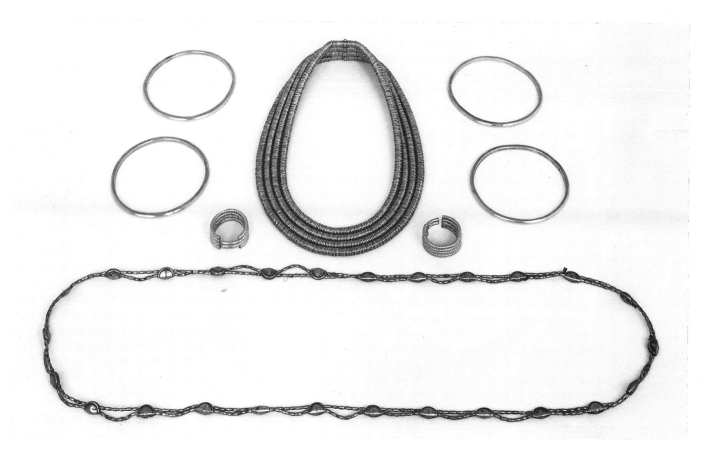

14 A full set of jewellery found on the body of a woman of the late 17th Dynasty. The *shebyu*-collar (**a**) – the earliest known – has four rows of tightly strung gold disc beads closed by inserting a pin through interlocking rings. The earrings (**b**), the earliest recorded example of this type from Egypt, were intended for pierced ears. The girdle (**c**) is composed of electrum barrel and wallet beads. The bangles (**d**) are gold rods of semicircular section, bent into a circle and soldered. D (bangles) 6cm

From Qurna, W. Thebes. Late 17th Dynasty (*c.* 1560 BC)

provincial cemetery of Middle Kingdom date at el-Riqqa on the west bank of the Nile at the mouth of the Faiyum. He was disappointed to find, however, that most of the tombs had been plundered in ancient times; indeed, most of the robberies appeared to have been carried out shortly after interment, since the corpses were still flexible when they were unceremoniously dragged from their coffins and stripped of any valuable jewellery. The robbers were almost certainly the very guardians appointed to protect the cemetery: only those tombs which had contained valuables had been plundered; if a burial had been left untouched it was because it contained nothing of value and the robbers knew it. Thus Engelbach's surprise can be imagined when, on clearing shaft tomb no. 124 in cemetery A, which showed distinct evidence that robbers had entered the burial chamber, he discovered not only a corpse still wearing valuable jewellery but the remains of a robber, buried under a massive roof-fall as he plundered his victim. His fellow thieves had obviously decided against trying to recover his body and, lest their activities be discovered, had refilled the tomb shaft. Because of this four-thousand-year-old accident the Manchester Museum now exhibits jewellery of a royal courtier who chose to be buried in his provincial cemetery.

Alone of the kings of the 12th Dynasty, Sesostris II located his pyramid at Lahun, but like all his predecessors he buried his family about him, and when the British School of Archaeology in Egypt under Petrie began excavating their pillaged tombs late in 1913 a hoard of royal jewellery as splendid as anything found at Dahshur unexpectedly came to light.

15 Gold pectoral of Sithathoriunet, inlaid with cornelian, lapis lazuli and turquoise, and currently suspended from beads and drops of gold, cornelian and turquoise. The cartouche contains the prenomen of Sesostris II. All the inlaid details are repeated by chasing on the underside. H 4.5cm

From the tomb of Sithathoriunet, Lahun. 12th Dynasty (reign of Ammenemes III, c. 1830 BC)

Indeed, the Lahun treasure in one way surpasses anything from the other site since its discovery was painstakingly recorded and all the disparate jewellery elements scrupulously collected and correctly reconstituted by Guy Brunton.

Tomb 8, as it was known, lay like all the others south of the pyramid, but it was the most roughly constructed of the four. Moreover, it had been thoroughly robbed in antiquity: the sealing wall at the bottom of the pit was destroyed, the antechamber beyond was littered with debris and the sarcophagus in the burial chamber held nothing but scraps of gold foil from the wooden coffin it had once contained. Only the canopic jars had been left intact and they revealed that the tomb-owner had been Princess Sithathoriunet. There was no reason, therefore, to suspect that anything lay beneath the thick layer of mud which almost filled a recess cut into one side of the antechamber, but as it was being cleared on 10 February 1914 the first gold beads were uncovered. For the next five days and nights Brunton worked lying on the floor resting on his elbows, since the recess was too low for him to kneel, as he slowly scratched away at the mud with a penknife to reveal piecemeal the contents of two long-decayed jewellery boxes. Every scrap of mud was subsequently washed so that not a single bead, however tiny, can have been missed. Why this selection of jewellery, which had all been worn in life, should have been placed in open view in an unsealed recess is far from clear. As for the ancient robbers missing it, perhaps the sealing wall they demolished inwards effectively covered it. Fortuitously, the mud and debris which subsequently washed into the open chamber only served to bury it deeper. All the Lahun treasure is in the Metropolitan Museum of Art in New York, except for those pieces specifically said to be in Cairo. In spite of the care taken in reconstructing this jewellery, a number of gold and turquoise ball beads remain that cannot be attributed.

In the summer of 1916 one of the violent rainstorms which periodically lash the Theban West Bank produced a waterfall in the precipitous cliff face at the back of the gorge in a secluded valley west of the better known Valley of the Queens. When a group of inhabitants of nearby Qurna set out to look for anything the floods might have exposed, they noticed that the cascading water vanished into a large crack halfway down the sheer cliff, only to reappear over thirty metres away. The only way to investigate was to let down from the cliff top into the depths a heavy rope with one of their number on it, all in the strictest secrecy. The results, however, far exceeded their labours and fears, for within the crack, at the end of a

15

16

16 Pair of Sithathoriunet's bracelets, formed from alternating sections of cornelian and turquoise discs between gold multiple bead spacers. The plain gold end-plates are grooved to take a sliding clasp cut into a T-shape at each side. Each clasp bears a cloisonné inscription inlaid with decayed blue material on a cornelian ground naming Ammenemes III. A matching pair of anklets was also found in the tomb (see 143). H 8.1cm

From the tomb of Sithathoriunet, Lahun. 12th Dynasty (reign of Ammenemes III, c. 1830 BC)

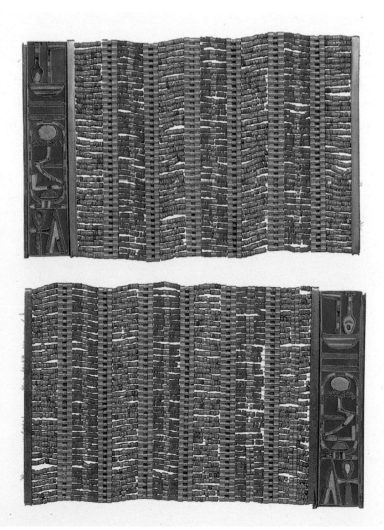

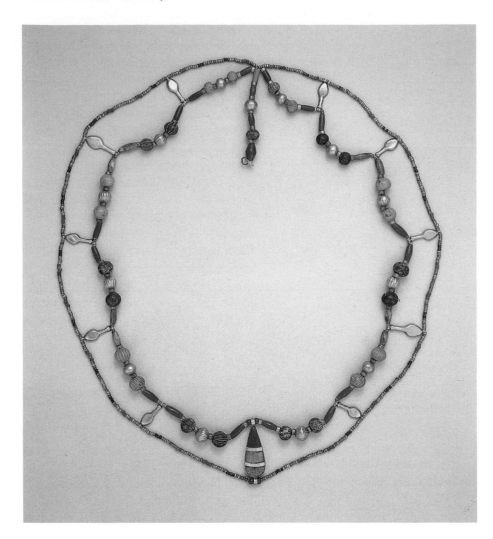

17 Loose jewellery elements, currently strung as a necklace. Seven of the gold *nefer*-signs still contain decayed inlay; the remainder are hollow with plain fronts. The large gold drop is inlaid with cornelian, green glazed steatite and decayed green or blue glass or glazed composition. The beads, a number ribbed nasturtium-seed shapes, are of red jasper, cornelian, lapis lazuli, feldspar, gold and glass. L (outer row) 65.5cm

From the burial of the three wives of Tuthmosis III, W. Thebes. 18th Dynasty (*c.* 1465 BC)

sloping passage, lay a chamber which contained the intact burial of three minor wives of King Tuthmosis III. Although hieratic graffiti on the cliffs below showed how close the ancient inhabitants of Deir el-Medina had been to discovering it, the royal ladies with the foreign names of Menwi, Merti and Menhet had slept undisturbed in their secret tomb for thirty-four centuries. Since the interment of all three seems to have taken place at the same time, they may have died during an epidemic; less probably they were executed after a harim conspiracy. A *terminus ante quem* is provided for the date of the burial by the presence on a pair of bracelets and on a scarab finger-ring of the prenomen cartouche of Hatshepsut, the aunt and stepmother of Tuthmosis III. Although at first Hatshepsut reigned legitimately as his co-ruler, she soon assumed total power; when eventually she died Tuthmosis destroyed all evidence of her reign. It is not likely, therefore, that he would have left these inscriptions untouched had the harim ladies been buried during his sole reign.

Although the organic material had suffered terribly from the damp, three complete sets of jewellery lay on the bodies. Unfortunately, the stringing had not survived, so that it was as a mass of loose beads and elements that much of it eventually came onto the market. As a result, the

17

order of elements in some pieces, even their original number, is still debatable. Over the next few years the contents of the burial chamber, which, in addition to jewellery, contained gold-banded cosmetic containers, stone vessels, silver mirrors, bowls, goblets and containers of gold, silver and glass, gold funerary sandals, toe- and finger-stalls and sets of stone canopic jars, all in triplicate, were dispersed abroad, some to be lost forever. The efforts of Herbert Winlock, however, ensured that the Metropolitan Museum of Art in New York acquired many of the pieces as they became available and, in particular, most of the jewellery elements, which he painstakingly reconstructed.

During 1919 to 1920 the excavations of the Metropolitan Museum at Deir el-Bahri, also on the Theban West Bank, uncovered the tomb of the 11th Dynasty chancellor Meketre, containing superb painted wooden models illustrating daily life on a great estate in Egypt four thousand years ago. By the end of the season it only remained to clear the tomb's entrance portico but these operations unexpectedly revealed the intact burial of one of Meketre's subordinates, an estate manager called Wah. The wrapped mummy was such a superb example of the bandager's art that no attempt was made to investigate what might lie among the layers of linen. Indeed, Wah's lowly office and the simple nature of his burial did not suggest that he might have owned valuable funerary jewellery. Consequently, for fifteen years the mummy was on exhibition in New York before x-ray equipment revealed Wah's wealth: a funerary collar with matching pairs of bracelets and anklets of glazed composition, five necklaces worn

18

18 Wah's broad collar, made from beads, pendants and terminals of bright blue-green glazed composition, still on the original threads. The semicircular shape of the collar and its depth are characteristic of the period. Depth 39.4cm

From the burial of Wah, W. Thebes. 11th Dynasty (reign of Mentuhotep II, c. 2020 BC)

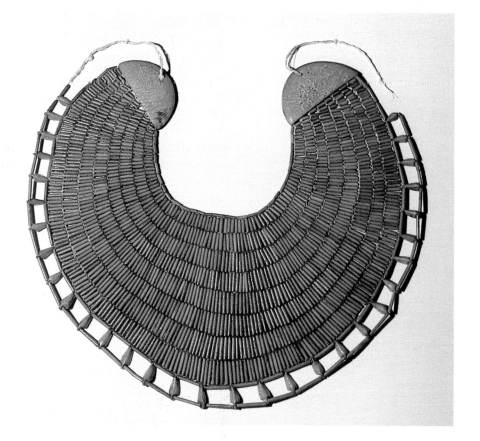

19 The mummified arms of Tutankhamun, still wearing seven bracelets between the elbow and wrist of his right forearm and six on the left. Some are rigid and hinged, others openwork and hinged; others still are of flexible beadwork. See 139

Far right 20 Gold openwork pectoral, possibly once part of Tutankhamun's coronation regalia, inlaid with chalcedony, calcite in coloured cement, lapis lazuli, turquoise, cornelian, obsidian and polychrome glass. The barque contains an *udjat*-eye surmounted by a gold crescent and silver moon-disc with applied gold figures of the king blessed by Thoth and Horus. Uniquely, the king is also crowned by lunar elements. The scarab holds in his bird's claws not only *shen*-signs but also an 'Upper Egyptian lily' and three lotus-heads. From the base-bar hang inlaid floral elements. H 14.9cm
   From the tomb of Tutankhamun (Treasury), Valley of the Kings, W. Thebes. 18th Dynasty (*c.* 1336–1327 BC)

during Wah's lifetime and, most spectacular of all, two large solid silver scarabs, the bigger bearing the names of Wah and Meketre.

The discovery of the tomb of Tutankhamun in the Valley of the Kings in November 1922, after six seasons of fruitless digging by a team led by Howard Carter and sponsored by Lord Carnarvon, is so well known as to require no retelling. Although the tomb had been entered by robbers on two separate occasions in antiquity, the mummy and all the jewellery on it was intact; however, portions of necklaces dropped by the thieves were found in the burial chamber and it has been estimated that some 60 per cent of the contents of the caskets in the Treasury, mostly jewellery, was stolen.

Encircling the wrapped head, beneath the gold mask, was a gold diadem, and around the neck a sheet-gold falcon with counterpoise. Among the objects over the chest were three other winged sheet-gold collars, two with counterpoises, and a broad collar with falcon-headed terminals. Beneath them in a lower layer of the bandages was a flexible inlaid falcon and another sheet-gold collar with falcon-headed terminals. Lower on the chest were amuletic bangles with capped bead bezels and one with an iron *udjat*. In the eighth layer a very large sheet-gold winged cobra collar with a counterpoise covered a flexible inlaid golden 'Two Ladies' collar and another of Nekhbet alone. In the eleventh and twelfth layers around the neck, suspended by plaque straps, was a rigid inlaid gold vulture; still lower on the chest was a pectoral composed of three scarabs side by side, one wearing a crescent and full moon, above a frieze of pendant floral elements attached by bead strings to an inlaid counterpoise containing the figure of Heh. Immediately below this piece were three more gold inlaid pectorals, one a rebus of the king's name, incorporating a winged scarab and attached by a gold chain to one heart-shaped and two floral pendants. The second takes the form of a rigid inlaid solar falcon on a gold chain; the third is an inlaid *udjat* suspended by strings of beads ending in an openwork inlaid counterpoise containing amulets. At the lowest layer was an unframed composition *udjat* pectoral.

Over and above the wrists were thirteen finger-rings of gold and

semi-precious stones and two gold bangles hung with amulets. Both forearms were stacked with massive braclets, seven on the right, six on the left, and on two fingers of the left hand over the gold finger-stalls were two gold stirrup-shaped rings. Encircling the hips was a ceremonial girdle and in the hollow of the groin was a gold inlaid anklet; four other narrower pairs were found over the abdomen and legs. Between the thighs lay four cloisonné gold collars, each with small falcon-headed terminals and a matching *menkhet* counterpoise.

In the Treasury the ransacked caskets only held the residue of the jewellery they had once contained, to judge from their dockets: a necklace, some pectorals, a few bracelets, some earrings and ear-studs and a finger-ring were all that survived. From the cartouche-shaped casket came jewellery which had been worn in life; from the marquetry casket with a vaulted lid came jewellery from more than one source, having been scooped up and crammed inside when an attempt was made before the tomb's final resealing to restore some order to the confusion left by the robbers. Much of it, however, appears to have an other-worldly theme. Most of the pectorals with a funerary theme came from compartments within the shrine topped by the black jackal of Anubis. Most of the finger-rings, still wrapped in the robber's kerchief, had been replaced in a box in the Antechamber.

Another royal burial containing jewellery was discovered on 9 February 1925 at Giza, just east of the Great Pyramid, when the tripod of a photographer working for the joint Harvard–Boston Expedition struck a patch of plaster which was found to mask a cutting packed with small limestone blocks. Twelve steps led into a rock-cut tunnel, which in turn penetrated the wall of a vertical shaft whose mouth had been filled with rough limestone to resemble the natural surface of the plateau. As the clearing of the shaft continued the remains of a sacrifice for the deceased's *ka* suggested that a burial lay at its end; however, it was not until a depth of about twenty-seven metres, far deeper than any contemporary shaft, that a chamber was discovered. It had been filled with furniture and wooden boxes which had decayed so that the contents spilled out; the metal bindings or inlays of the wooden objects had collapsed onto the contents and the metal, stone or pottery objects standing on the perished pieces had fallen onto the heap. A large alabaster sarcophagus lay amid all this ruin but it could not be opened until the decayed inlaid panels, gold-encased wooden poles and canopy beams lying on its lid were removed.

The task of clearing the debris, which took nearly a year, was in the capable hands of George Reisner, whose painstakingly detailed work made it possible later to reconstruct the personal possessions and grave-goods of the queen whom inscribed objects named as Hetepheres, wife of Sneferu and mother of Khufu. She had taken to the tomb two wooden armchairs, one completely cased with sheet gold and with an inlaid back panel, and a carrying chair in which she must have sat with her knees under her chin. Her lion-footed bed would have been used inside a tent formed from gold- and copper-cased wooden poles and beams hung with material to form a canopy; an empty wooden box for the curtains was nearby. The smaller objects were just as spectacular: alabaster toilet vessels, a copper ewer and basin for her ablutions, gold razors and knives

19,139

138

20

21

for her depilation, a gold manicure instrument for her nails, gold utensils and the royal jewellery case. The latter had taken the form of a gold-cased box fitted with two removable tapering rods for the storage of twenty silver bangles. Some are now in the Boston Museum of Fine Arts; the remainder are in Cairo.

Although intact, the burial was to pose a number of problems. When the sarcophagus was opened in March 1927 it was empty, although there must once have been a body since the alabaster canopic chest, still containing the remains of the queen's embalmed internal organs, was later discovered in a plastered-up recess. Moreover, pieces of plaster were found mixed up with the contents of the boxes which, furthermore, did not correspond to their labels, just as though they had been hastily scooped up off the floor. Reisner formulated a theory that Hetepheres' original burial had been at Dahshur, near her husband's pyramid, and that it had been plundered in her son's reign. However, elaborate and secret reburial at Giza would only have made sense if the body had survived. Clearly Khufu believed his mother's body was in the sarcophagus, so Reisner reasoned that no-one dared to tell the builder of the Great Pyramid that his mother's body was destroyed, thus denying her an afterlife; the reburial thus went ahead with an empty sarcophagus and the pious deception remained undetected for forty-five centuries.

A more recent, though less romantic explanation is that the secret room had indeed been Hetepheres' original burial-place but her body, in its inner wooden coffin, was later removed, because of a revised building scheme, to a new tomb, the northernmost of the Queens' pyramids, about twenty-seven metres away. Rather than attempt to recover all her grave-goods the bulkier pieces were abandoned and she was supplied with new ones. Yet surely her internal organs would have been reburied with her, and her personal toilet articles and her precious silver bangles would not have been abandoned. Perhaps Reisner was nearest the truth, except that Hetepheres was buried at Giza originally and her body was robbed and

21 The scene inside the burial chamber of Queen Hetepheres at the foot of a shaft near the Great Pyramid of her son Khufu, as it appeared to Reisner and his assistants. The queen's jewellery box lies open, her silver bangles inlaid with butterflies still in place on the rod inside.

Right 22 Gold funerary diadem from a woman's burial, the central boss flanked by papyrus-head knots crowned by crested ibises. A ribbon, knotted to leave streamers, pulled the pierced ends of the band together. L 56cm

From Giza (mastaba 294). Late 5th or early 6th Dynasty (*c.* 2355–2335 BC)

23 *Below* Solid gold figure of Bastet, found strung on a single cord on the mummy of Wendjebauendjed. Identical inscribed amulets prove she is the cat-goddess, not Sekhmet the lioness. H 7cm

From the burial of Wendjebauendjed, Tanis (tomb III). 21st Dynasty (reign of Psusennes I, *c.* 1030 BC)

destroyed in the period between the interment and the filling of the shaft.

During the season of 1930–1 the Egyptian archaeologist Selim Hassan was also working at Giza, excavating a complex of Old Kingdom noblemen's tombs in that part of the necropolis called the Central Field which lies south of the causeway linking Khafre's valley temple with his pyramid. The identity of the owner of mastaba 294 was lost long ago, although the tomb could be dated to the late 5th or early 6th Dynasty, yet the burial chamber was found to contain a limestone sarcophagus whose lid was still in position; when it was raised it revealed the intact burial of a woman. Although the body had been reduced to a skeleton all her jewellery was there, including a diadem, two necklaces – one of them with gold beetle pendants – and several bracelets and anklets; these are now in the Cairo Museum.

San el-Hagar is the modern name for the vast moonscape of a site in the north-east Delta which the Egyptians knew as Djanet and the Greeks as Tanis. Today it is a jumble of broken obelisks, shattered colossi and ruined monumental buildings scattered within what looks like the crater of an extinct volcano which rises red and dusty above the green vegetation of the surrounding countryside. After Mariette had excavated there between 1860 and 1864, uncovering not only the famous Middle Kingdom statuary he termed 'Hyksos' but also overwhelming evidence of the presence of Ramesses II, few doubted that he had discovered in Tanis the city which had been the new capital of the Ramesside dynasties under the name Pi-Ramessu, founded on the ruins of the Hyksos capital, Avaris. By the early part of this century, however, the belief was growing that the site of Pi-Ramessu and Avaris lay elsewhere but had been the source of all the Ramesside and Middle Kingdom material now at Tanis, having been systematically plundered to furnish the new capital city founded by the pharaohs of the 21st Dynasty. Indeed, in 1928 excavations at Qantir some thirty-two kilometres further to the south-east of Tanis first suggested that Pi-Ramessu/Avaris was to be sought in that vicinity and it is now generally accepted that its location was in the area of Qantir–Qatana–Tell er-Daba. The following year the French archaeologist Pierre Montet renewed excavations at Tanis; ten years later his systematic clearing of the site was rewarded with the discovery of the only virtually intact royal burials to have survived from ancient Egypt apart from that of Tutankhamun.

Early in 1939 Montet was clearing Ptolemaic mud-brick buildings south of the monumental gateway to the main temple and adjacent to the great enclosure when he noticed a deep hole between two of the rooms. It had been made by robbers and led him to what proved to be the roof of a stone-built substructure divided into four chambers, which contained four great stone sarcophagi. Within them had lain the burials of the 22nd Dynasty pharaohs Osorkon I, Osorkon II, his son Hornakht and Takeloth II; all had been ransacked in antiquity but, as Montet was later to discover, the thieves had been unable to remove all of the prince's jewellery. Furthermore, less than three weeks later a second substructure was uncovered and this time it appeared to be intact. Again, it comprised four chambers, and the first contained the solid silver falcon-headed coffin of a previously unknown Sheshonq, now generally identified as the second of that name. When the lid was raised on 21 March 1939 the royal body within was seen for the first time in more than twenty-eight centuries. In February 1940 the intact burial chamber of the 21st Dynasty pharaoh Psusennes I was opened and in April of that year that of his successor Amenemope. It would not have been surprising if Tanis had yielded up all her secrets but six years later an architectural drawing of the Psusennes complex, as it had been called, revealed the presence of a concealed room and it proved to contain the intact burial of the king's contemporary, general Wendjebauendjed. Unfortunately, some of the jewellery reco-

24

24 One of a pair of bracelets worn by Sheshonq II, composed of two unequal segments of sheet gold, hinged and closed by a retractable pin. Two raised relief cartouches on the plain inner face show they were family heirlooms, for the names are those of Sheshonq I, founder of the dynasty. The central feature of the outer face is a cloisonné panel inlaid with lapis, cornelian and white material forming a left-facing udjat-eye. H 4.6cm

From the burial chamber of Sheshonq II, Tanis (tomb III), 22nd Dynasty (c. 890 BC)

vered by Montet is no longer extant, for the storage magazines were robbed in his absence during 1943.

In 1951 the Egyptian archaeologist Zakaria Goneim began searching the Saqqara plateau for some trace of the tombs of the later kings of the 3rd Dynasty, whom he felt sure must have been buried somewhere in the vicinity. The area is dominated by the Step Pyramid of Djoser, which is not only the earliest pyramid but also the first monumental stone building in the world, and Goneim chose as his starting point a site to the south-west of its enclosure wall. Almost at once he was rewarded by the discovery of the fine limestone palace façade panelling of an enclosure wall almost as magnificent. Within months he had uncovered what proved to be the lowest step of a pyramid whose superstructure was almost totally destroyed but whose dimensions would have rivalled those of Djoser's. Even more exciting, above and around this buried pyramid were a number of intact burials of the Ramesside Period and later, which proved the site had been undisturbed for at least thirty-three centuries.

In due course a massive descending trench was located, leading down to a blocked subterranean doorway, behind which lay a whole complex of underground corridors and chambers; these culminated some seventy-six metres from the entrance in a second blocked doorway. Beyond lay an unfinished burial chamber containing a sarcophagus on which a withered funeral bouquet still lay. Goneim had every reason to believe he had an intact 3rd Dynasty royal burial, but when the sliding panel at one end of the sarcophagus was unsealed and slowly raised it revealed an empty interior which had apparently never held a body.

The generally accepted explanation is that the sarcophagus served only for a dummy burial comparable with that beneath Djoser's so-called Southern Tomb. But even more curious is the fact that funerary goods were not totally lacking. About eighteen metres from the entrance to the substructure the corridor had been completely sealed in ancient times by large blocks of limestone to a depth of four and a half metres, and in clearing this obstruction to floor level Goneim found not only, on jar sealings, the name of the pyramid's owner–King Sekhemkhet–but also, buried in a layer of clay, an exquisite gold cosmetic container reproducing a hinged sea shell and the contents of a long-decayed jewellery box. It had held bangles, a bracelet and loose cylinder beads, over four hundred gold-covered glazed composition ball beads and a number of beads of cornelian and glazed composition. This find, which is now in Cairo, represents virtually the only jewellery to have survived from the 3rd Dynasty, but its presence in the corridor remains unexplained, for there was no burial from which it could have been robbed.

25

25 Bracelet of King Sekhemkhet, formed from nearly 400 hollow gold ball beads strung between five thin gold spacers, one of the earliest examples of a type that was extremely popular throughout the Dynastic Period. L c. 14cm

From the pyramid of Sekhemkhet, Saqqara. 3rd Dynasty (c. 2640 BC)

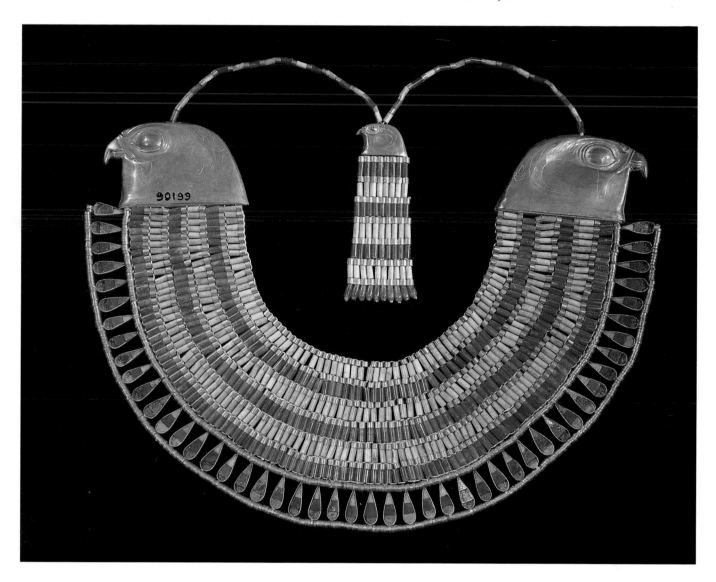

26 Broad collar of Neferuptah. Rows of cornelian, feldspar and gold beads are strung between two hollow gold falcon-headed terminals with an outermost row of gold drops inlaid with cornelian, feldspar and paste. Bead strings of the same materials join it to a matching counterpoise which was intended to lie between the shoulder-blades to counterbalance the weight of the collar and hold it in place on the chest. L 36.5cm

From the pyramid of Neferuptah, Hawara. 12th Dynasty (reign of Ammenemes III, c. 1800 BC)

In 1956 Zaki Iskander and Nagib Farag, working for the Egyptian Department of Antiquities, began excavating the remains of a small mud-brick pyramid at Hawara, lying south-east of that of King Ammenemes III of the 12th Dynasty. It proved to belong to his daughter Neferuptah and, surprisingly, her burial was undisturbed, though severely damaged by water seepage, which filled the burial chamber to half its height. The sarcophagus was completely flooded but the sludge contained jewellery elements which it was possible to reconstruct accurately by comparison with earlier royal Middle Kingdom finds; they are now in Cairo.

Although the archaeological exploration of its antiquities continues in Egypt, Iskander's and Farag's excavations in the mid-1950s are the last to have revealed a significant find of royal jewellery. This brief account of the rediscovery of Egyptian jewellery highlights the extraordinary and often improbable circumstances in which many of the finest and best-known examples have come to survive to the present day.

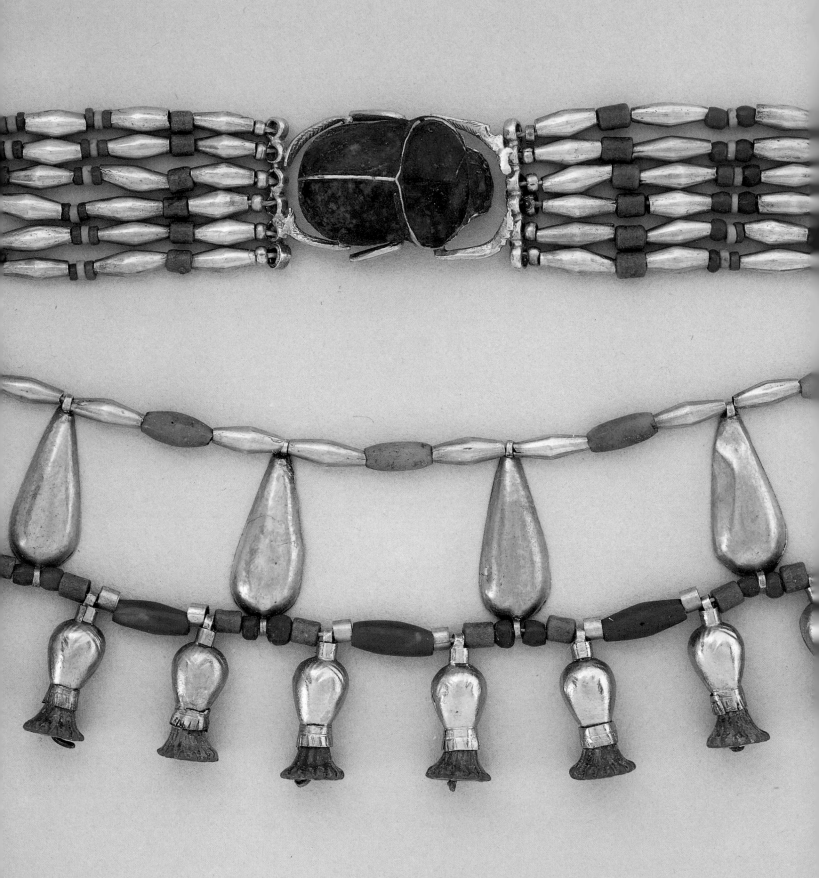

CHAPTER TWO

The jewellery-maker's materials

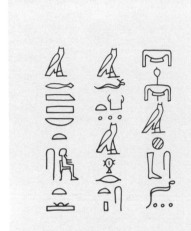

Gold and silver, lapis lazuli and turquoise, cornelian and every precious stone

27 Detail of beads, pendants and a scarab, currently strung into a bracelet and a necklace in the fashion of late 18th Dynasty jewellery. The bracelet (**a**, *top*) is composed of a lapis lazuli scarab set in gold, with six strings of gold, cornelian and glazed composition beads. The necklace (**b**, *bottom*) comprises beads of gold, green glass, cornelian, red jasper and blue glazed composition and gold drops. The pendants are in the form of cornflowers. L (scarab) 2.8cm
18th Dynasty (*c.* 1340–1320 BC)

The Egyptian jewellery-maker did not use precious stone; what he held the most valuable the modern world would consider at best only semi-precious. It is, perhaps, even more surprising that some of the most characteristic and pleasing effects were obtained using man-made materials, such as glazed composition and glass in imitation of semi-precious stones. Furthermore, most of the materials used were chosen not just because their colours created a particular effect, but because colours for the Egyptians had an underlying symbolism or amuletic significance. Indeed, in the case of funerary jewellery, certain materials were strictly prescribed for the magical properties of their colouring. Thus Chapter 156 of the *Book of the Dead* required the amulet in the form of the Girdle Tie of Isis, placed at the throat of the mummy, to be made of red jasper, whose blood-like colouring would enhance the words of the spell: 'You have your blood, Isis; you have your power'.

174
32k

Green was the colour of new vegetation, growing crops and fertility, hence of new life, resurrection even. It was, in particular, the colour of the papyrus plant, which in hieroglyphs actually wrote the word *wadj* (*w3ḏ*), meaning 'to flourish' or 'be healthy'. *Wadj* was also the name for the emerald-green mineral malachite when it was employed as Egypt's principal green pigment for painting and as the main constituent of green eye make-up. But the green stone most favoured by the Egyptians was turquoise – *mefkat* (*mfk3t*) – whose Egyptian name in the Late Dynastic Period was used as a synonym for 'joy' and 'delight'. Apart from turquoise (and green glazed composition and glass in imitation of it), the principal green stones employed by Egyptian lapidaries were green jasper, green feldspar (also known as amazon stone), prase, chrysoprase, olivine, serpentine and, in the Graeco-Roman Period, beryl and peridot.

Dark blue was the colour of the all-embracing, protective night sky, of lapis lazuli – and of the deep-blue glazed composition and glass made to imitate it. Curiously enough, *khesbed* (*ḥsbd*), the principal word for lapis lazuli, was used in the Late Dynastic Period, like the word for turquoise, as a synonym for 'joy' or 'delight'. It is difficult to believe that the Egyptians could not really distinguish between blue and green, yet the suggestion that the usage arose because of the linking over a long period of the materials turquoise and lapis lazuli is not very convincing.

Red was the colour of blood with all its connotations of energy, dynamism, power, even life itself. But it was also the colour of the evil-tempered desert-god Set, patron of disorder, storms and aridity, and

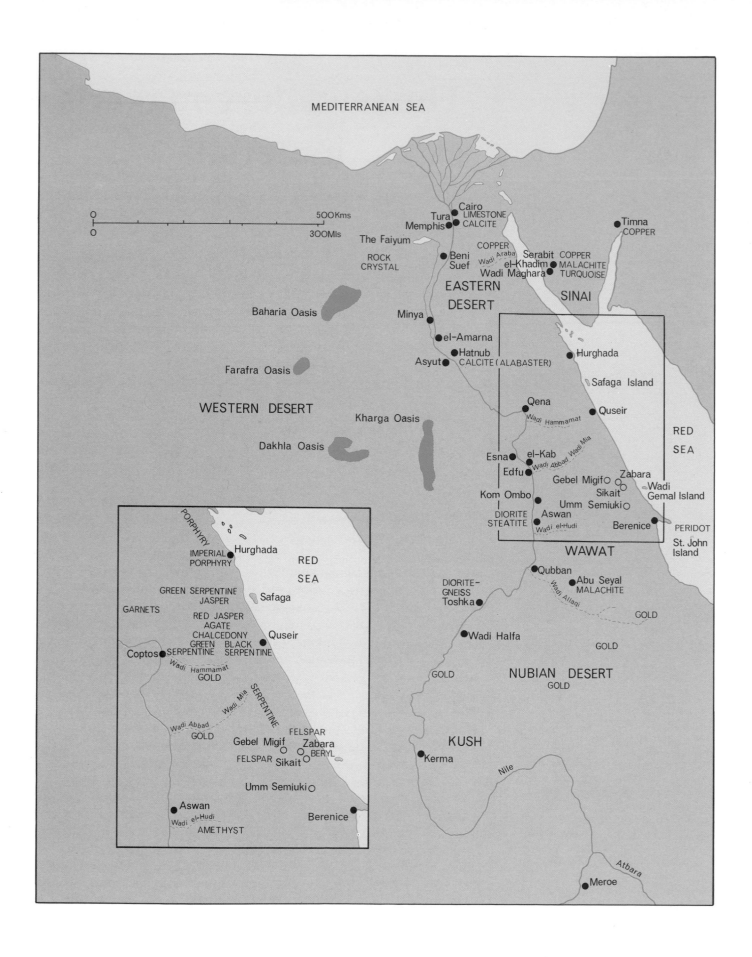

MEDITERRANEAN SEA

500 Kms
300 Mls

Cairo
Tura   LIMESTONE
Memphis   CALCITE
Timna
COPPER

The Faiyum

COPPER
ROCK   Beni   *Wadi Araba*   Serabit   COPPER
CRYSTAL   Suef   el-Khadim   MALACHITE
                                             Wadi Maghara TURQUOISE
                              EASTERN
                              DESERT   SINAI

Baharia Oasis

Minya

el-Amarna   Hurghada

Hatnub
Asyut   CALCITE (ALABASTER)   Safaga Island

WESTERN DESERT   Qena
                                            Quseir
Kharga Oasis   *Wadi Hammamat*
                                            RED
Dakhla Oasis   Esna   el-Kab *Wadi Mia*   SEA
                         Edfu *Wadi Abbad*
                                            Zabara
                              Gebel Migif○   Wadi
                              Sikait○   Gemal Island
                         Kom Ombo   Umm Semiuki○
                                    Aswan
                         DIORITE   *Wadi el-Hudi*
                         STEATITE   Berenice   PERIDOT
                                                            St. John
                              WAWAT   Island

IMPERIAL
PORPHYRY Hurghada
          RED
          SEA
GREEN SERPENTINE
JASPER
GARNETS   Safaga
RED JASPER
AGATE
CHALCEDONY Quseir
GREEN   BLACK
Coptos●SERPENTINE SERPENTINE
     Wadi Hammamat
        GOLD
           Wadi Mia SERPENTINE
Wadi Abbad
      GOLD   FELSPAR
       Gebel Migif○ Zabara
              ○ BERYL
       FELSPAR Sikait
          Umm Semiuki○
    Aswan
 Wadi el-Hudi
    AMETHYST
                         Berenice

Qubban
DIORITE-   Abu Seyal
GNEISS   MALACHITE
Toshka   *Wadi Allaqi*
                              GOLD

Wadi Halfa
                    GOLD

NUBIAN DESERT
GOLD
              GOLD

KUSH

Kerma
         Nile

Atbara

Meroe

38

murderer of his brother Osiris. This curious dichotomy is reflected in the fact that *khenmet* (*ḥnmt*), the word for red jasper, was derived from the verb *ḥnm*, 'to delight', but cornelain, with its orange-red hue, was considered an ill-omened stone and in the Late Dynastic Period its name, *herset* (*ḥrst*), also meant 'sadness'. Sard was the third red stone employed by the Egyptian lapidary, and from the New Kingdom onwards all three could be imitated by red glass and glazed composition.

The Egyptian jewellery-maker made use of an amazing variety of stones, minerals, metals, man-made materials and animal products. Most were obtained locally in the hills and deserts within Egypt's boundaries and from creatures which inhabited the Nile Valley and surrounding areas, but some, most notably lapis lazuli and silver, always had to be imported from beyond Egypt's farthest frontiers. In the following treatment the principal materials used in the production of Egyptian jewellery over a period of some four thousand years are described with details of characteristic colouring or appearance, the sources from which they were obtained and their chief usage. Wherever possible the names by which they were known to the Egyptians are also supplied, for much information has been gleaned from study of Egyptian texts which list materials, their places of origin and the uses to which they were put or which accompany coloured representations of raw materials or of jewellery being manufactured. It is rather curious, however, that although the ancient Egyptian vocabulary was normally very rich – if the Greeks were supposed to have a word for everything, then the ancient Egyptians had two or three – yet the names for some of the most popular materials used in jewellery-making cannot be securely identified.

Stones and minerals

AGATE is a variety of chalcedony (silicon dioxide), coloured by irregular concentric bands or layers of red or brown, separated by gradations of white to grey. It occurs plentifully in Egypt, usually in pebble form, although at least one source in association with jasper has been identified in the Eastern Desert about seventy kilometres north-west of Quseir. Agate drop pendants and beads have been found in burials of the Predynastic Badarian Period (*c.* 4000 BC), and small numbers of beads and amulets continued to be produced until the end of the Dynastic Period, but the use of agate in jewellery was always limited. The Egyptian name for it is still in doubt, although it has been plausibly suggested that the material known as *ka* (*k3*), with both light and dark varieties – in Egyptian *hedj* (*ḥḏ*) and *kem* (*km*) – might be agate and onyx. This material is depicted in oval lumps, coloured white and brown or red, in the tombs of the high officials Puyemre, Kenamun, Rekhmire and Menkheperresonb at Thebes, all of 18th Dynasty date. The accompanying texts, however, list *ka* among the products of Punt (modern-day coastal Somalia or southern Ethiopia) and of Nubia, the ancient land now divided between southern Egypt and northern Sudan. Nevertheless, in view of the occurrence of agate with jasper in the Eastern Desert it cannot surely be purely coincidental that in the tomb of Menkheperresonb, Rekhmire and Kenamun *ka* is depicted side by side with red jasper. See also ONYX/SARDONYX.

28 Map showing the principal sources of raw materials in Egypt.

29 Bracelets currently composed of four matched pairs of hollow gold lions strung with amethyst ball beads and closed by hollow gold knot clasps with the usual tongue-and-groove closing device. The smaller lions have a single threading hole pierced through the length of the base, the four larger have two. L (largest lion) 1.7cm, (smallest) 1.3cm

From the tomb of Sithathoriunet, Lahun. 12th Dynasty (reign of Ammenemes III, *c.* 1830 BC)

ALABASTER in an Egyptian context is the lustrous white or cream calcite (basic calcium carbonate) found in a number of locations in Egypt on the east bank, although the finest quality was quarried at Hatnub, inland from el-Amarna. Since it is soft and easily carved, beads and pendants were manufactured from alabaster as early as the Badarian Period, and by the time of the first dynasties amulets were made of it too. Large alabaster bangles are characteristic of the Nubian C-Group culture, which was contemporary with Egypt's Middle Kingdom, but until the end of Dynastic history the material was used only sporadically in jewellery, for its main uses lay elsewhere. The common word for alabaster was *shes* (*šs*). See LIMESTONE.

AMAZON STONE, see FELDSPAR

AMETHYST is a translucent quartz (silicon dioxide) with a glassy sheen, and can range in colour from a deep violet to a barely violet-tinged transparency. Its chief source during the Middle Kingdom was Wadi el-Hudi about thirty kilometres south-east of Aswan, though older workings have been found about sixty-five kilometres north-west of Abu Simbel. Although a few beads in this material predate the beginning of the 1st Dynasty, the period of its greatest popularity was the Middle Kingdom, when amethyst beads were strung into necklaces, girdles and anklets, formed part of multiple-string bracelets, were capped with gold, threaded with gold beads into amulet-case shapes and carved into various amuletic forms including scarabs. Amethyst is found infrequently in New Kingdom jewellery, probably because its strong colouring did not combine easily in composite inlays, yet it continued to be used sporadically in jewellery-making until the Roman Period, when it was probably mined in the Safaga district of the Red Sea coast. The Egyptians called amethyst *hesmen* (*ḥsmn*), exactly the same word they used for natron, the naturally occurring salt compound which served as a purifier and as a dehydrating agent in the process of mummification.

BERYL is a transparent or translucent yellowish-green aluminium-beryllium-silicate with a glassy sheen; apart from a single bead from Nubia

29

40

of Predynastic date, it has been identified with certainty only in jewellery of the Graeco-Roman Period and later, when its chief source was the area of Sikait-Zabara about forty kilometres inland from the Red Sea coast opposite the tiny island of Wadi Gemal. The Egyptian name for beryl is perhaps to be seen in the *wadj en Bakh* (*w3d n B3h*) of Late Period lists of semi-precious stones, meaning literally 'green stone of the east'.

BRECCIA is a sedimentary rock in which angular white fragments are set irregularly into a red-coloured matrix. It is found in a number of locations on the west bank of the Nile near Minya, Asyut, Thebes and Esna, and also in the Eastern Desert. It was employed in jewellery only during the Predynastic Period for pendants, for its chief uses lay elsewhere. No name for it in Egyptian has been identified.

CALCITE, see ALABASTER

CHALCEDONY is a translucent bluish-white, rather waxy-looking quartz (silicon dioxide), found in a number of locations including the Eastern Desert (about midway between the valley at Qena and the Red Sea coast), Baharia Oasis, the Faiyum, Nubia (about sixty-five kilometres north-west of Abu Simbel) and Sinai. It was employed for pendants and beads, later amulets and inlays, from the Predynastic Period until Roman times. The Egyptians called it *herset hedj* (*hrst hd*), thus acknowledging its kinship with cornelian and sard.

149c

CHERT, see FLINT

CHRYSOPRASE is a translucent apple-green variety of chalcedony (silicon dioxide) employed between Predynastic times and the Roman Period for a few beads, pendants and amulets. The Egyptians' word for it may have been *perdjen* (*prdn*). See also PRASE.

CORNELIAN is a translucent form of chalcedony (silicon dioxide), ranging in colour from red-brown or orange to a barely red-tinged transparency. It was found in considerable quantities in the Eastern Desert and Nubia, yet it was considered sufficiently precious to be mentioned beside silver, lapis lazuli and turquoise in the list of valuable New Year gifts made to the vizier Antefoker and recorded in his tomb at Thebes in about 1950 BC. Its main use from Predynastic times until the end of Dynastic history was in the production of beads and amulets, later finger-rings and ear ornaments, and as inlay. Indeed, during the New Kingdom, when glass and glazed composition inlays were usually preferred in inlaid jewellery, cornelian almost alone of semi-precious stones continued to be used for that purpose. Sometimes it was even imitated by inlays of translucent quartz on a background of red cement. The Egyptians called cornelian *herset* (*hrst*). See SARD.

DIORITE, a speckled black and white hard igneous rock obtained in the vicinity of Aswan, was used for pendants during the Predynastic Period and on a few occasions during the early Dynasties for beads; its chief uses, however, lay elsewhere. It may have been known to the Egyptians as *mentet* (*mntt*).

FELDSPAR or AMAZON STONE is an opaque, green or blue-green potas-sium-aluminium-silicate, found principally in the Eastern Desert in the

30 Unmounted green feldspar heart scarab, suspended by gold rings and a tube from an articulated chain made from long gold cylinders, including one curved for the neck. Its underside is inscribed with Chapter 26 of the *Book of the Dead*, but not for its owner, general Wendjebauendjed. Instead, one of the Ramesside pharaohs is named, suggesting the piece was a royal heirloom, a gift from the general's royal master Psusennes. L (scarab) 5cm

From the burial chamber of Wendjebauendjed, Tanis (tomb III). 21st Dynasty (reign of Psusennes, *c.* 1030 BC)

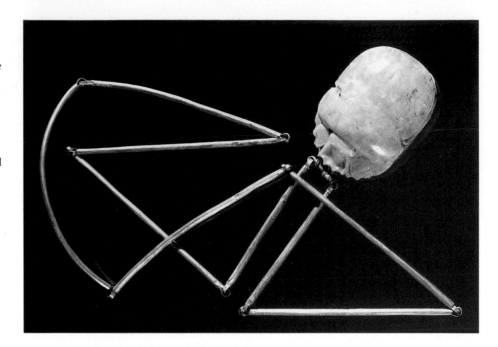

region of Gebel Migif, about eighty kilometres inland from the Red Sea coast north-west of Wadi Gemal island. Another source of feldspar, worked extensively in ancient times, has been located in the Libyan mountains north of Tibesti on the Tropic of Cancer. Although it is still uncertain whether this was the origin of any Egyptian feldspar, it has been suggested that it was the loss of this source which led the Egyptians of the Predynastic Badarian culture to glaze their steatite beads green in imitation of the green stone to which they no longer had access. Feldspar was one of the six stones considered most precious by the Egyptians and was frequently listed with lapis lazuli and turquoise. It was used in Predynastic times to make beads, and later for amulets and inlays; it was especially popular during the Middle Kingdom. Chapters 159 and 160 of the *Book of the Dead* prescribed it as the material for papyrus amulets and it was sometimes used as an alternative green stone for heart scarabs. The Egyptians called green feldspar *neshmet* (*nšmt*) and often appended the adjective 'true' (*maa, m3ˁ*), showing that it was frequently imitated by green glazed composition and glass.

FLINT (and its impure form, chert) is an opaque chalcedony (silicon dioxide) which ranges in colour from a dark grey or black to pale yellow; chert is more often coloured light grey to light brown. Flint was mined in a number of locations in the Eastern Desert, being found in the form of nodules and layers in limestone, but it could also be picked up from the surface, having been released by weathering. Although a hard stone, it is brittle and breaks easily to give sharp edges, a property exploited from earliest times to fashion primitive tools and implements. Virtually the only occurrence of flint and chert in jewellery is in roughly shaped bangles and pendants of Predynastic and Early Dynastic date. The Egyptians distinguished between the various colours of this material by terming it *des hedj* (*ds ḥḏ*), *des kem* (*ds km*) and *des tjehen* (*ds ṯḥn*), that is 'light', 'dark' and 'bright' or 'gleaming flint'.

36

30

FLUOSPAR is a translucent to transparent green or yellow calcium fluoride, found in association with quartz, calcite, dolomite and galena. It has been identified as the material used for a few Predynastic beads.

GARNET is a translucent red iron- or magnesium-aluminium-silicate with a violet or brown tint. It occurs plentifully in Egypt near Aswan at the same locality from which the Egyptians obtained much of their amethyst, in the Eastern Desert inland from Quseir and north-east of Qena, and in Sinai. Garnet beads were manufactured as early as the Badarian Period and continued to be produced until the end of the New Kingdom, although not in the quantities that might be expected for so attractive a material. This may have been in part because of the generally small size of the stones. During the Middle Kingdom, when garnet was at its most popular, it was occasionally employed for individual inlays, but, like amethyst, its strong colouring did not lend itself easily to composite inlaying. The Egyptian word for garnet was almost certainly *hemaget* (*ḥm3gt*): small regularly shaped oval lumps of dark-red material with this name are depicted among tribute from Nubia in the Theban tomb of Rekhmire, vizier of Tuthmosis III (*c.* 1425 BC).

HAEMATITE is an opaque black or black-grey iron oxide with a metallic sheen. During the Late Period it was certainly worked in the Eastern Desert, but earlier it may have been obtained in Sinai and near Aswan, locations reflected in the adjectives *meh* (*mḥ*) and *shema* (*šmˁ*), that is 'of the

31 Diadem composed of beads and chips of turquoise, garnet and malachite separated by sections of tiny gold ring beads, made by turning up strips of metal (only a few are soldered). It was found in place on the head of a woman still holding a piece of cloth like a veil over the face. L 31. 2cm
From Abydos. Predynastic Naqada II Period (*c.* 3200 BC)

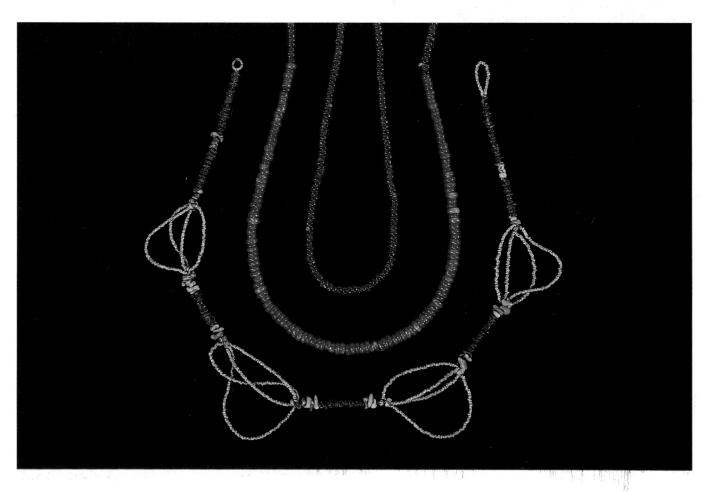

32 Group of funerary amulets; **a** glazed composition hand, conferring dexterity. L 3.1cm; **b** haematite head-rest (*weres*), to raise the head of the deceased in resurrection. W 3cm; **c** glazed composition papyrus sceptre (*wadj*), to confer new life. L 5.6cm; **d** cornelian snake's head, to give refreshment to the throat. L 4.4cm; **e** haematite plummet, to grant perpetual equilibrium. W (at base) 1.8cm; **f** haematite carpenter's square, to grant eternal rectitude. H 1.5cm; **g** glazed composition staircase, representing the dais for Osiris' throne. L 1.9cm; **h** cornelian leg with foot, conferring movement. H 2.1cm; **i** glass heart (*ib*), if the real one perish, H 5.3cm; **j** obsidian two fingers, representing the embalmer's skill. H 8.5cm; **k** red jasper Girdle Tie of Isis (*tit*), to grant the goddess's protection. H 6.5 cm

Old Kingdom – Ptolemaic Period (*c.* 2300–100 BC)

north' and 'of the south', which were often applied to it in Egyptian. From the Predynastic Period haematite was shaped into beads and later amulets, especially those in the shape of the head-rest, architect's plummet and carpenter's square. Its Egyptian name was almost certainly *bia* (*bỉȝ*), the same as the word for iron, doubtless a reference to its metallic appearance.

32b,e,f

ICELAND SPAR is a transparent colourless form of calcite (calcium carbonate) found in the Eastern Desert near Asyut and el-Amarna. Apart from a cylinder-seal of Old Kingdom date, its only certain use is in beads of the New Kingdom and Third Intermediate Period. No Egyptian word for this material has been identified; perhaps the same confusion existed in antiquity as in modern times between Iceland spar and rock-crystal.

JADE, see NEPHRITE

JASPER is a hard opaque, often mottled red, green or yellow form of quartz (silicon dioxide). The red variety is found in a number of localities in the Eastern Desert, notably in an area of hills and wadis west and north-west of Quseir, beginning about sixty-five kilometres inland from the coast, where there are signs of ancient working; green and yellow jaspers occur naturally alongside or even within layers of red. The latter, called by the Egyptians *khenmet* (*ḥnmt*) or *mekhenmet* (*mḥnmt*), is depicted as small, roughly oval red-coloured pieces of material among tribute from Punt in the tomb of Rekhmire and as rather larger lumps among tribute from Nubia in the tomb of Iamunedjeh; both were high officials of King Tuthmosis III (*c.* 1450 BC) and were buried at Thebes. It was the red stone *par excellence*, prescribed by Chapter 156 of the *Book of the Dead* as the material for the Girdle Tie of Isis amulet; it was employed as early as the Predynastic Period for beads, later too for amulets, scarabs, inlays and, in particular, for penannular earrings of New Kingdom date. The yellow

32k

33

33 Wall-painting from the tomb of Sobkhotep, showing Nubians bringing tribute from the south to Pharaoh. The figure at the front carries interlocking gold rings over one arm; the man behind bears ebony logs on his shoulder and a giraffe's tail in one hand. The third figure carries a leopard skin and a basket full of chunks of red jasper; a monkey perches behind his head. All three wear earrings. H 74cm

From W. Thebes (tomb 63). 18th Dynasty (reign of Tuthmosis IV, *c.* 1395 BC)

34 Openwork gold cloisonné pectoral found on the mummy of Psusennes I. The theme is funerary: the central winged lapis lazuli scarab is flanked by Isis and Nephthys; the cartouche names Psusennes. The articulated frieze below comprises alternating *djeds* and *tit*-amulets. The inlays of the pectoral, and of the gold *menkhet*-counterpoise and the bead strings joining them, are cornelian, lapis lazuli, feldspar and red jasper. L (pendant) 13.8cm

From the burial chamber of Psusennes, Tanis (tomb III). 21st Dynasty (*c.* 1039–991 BC)

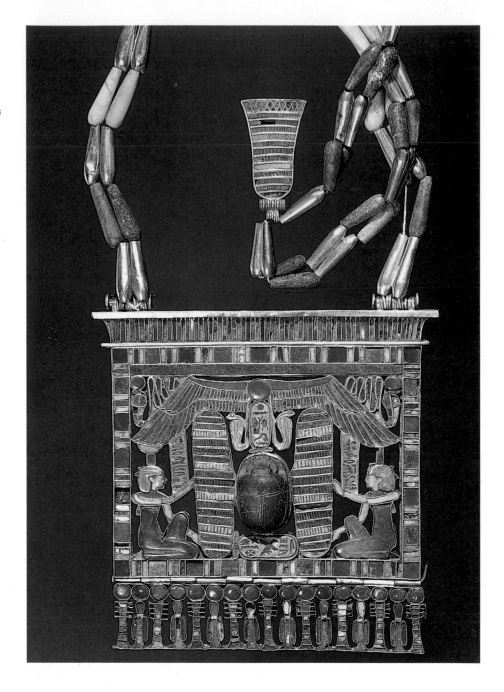

variety, which seems to have borne the same name as the red, was not used at all before the New Kingdom, and not for jewellery until the Roman Period; even then it was only used sporadically. It is depicted as both small and large yellow-coloured, irregularly shaped lumps among the offerings made to Amun at Karnak by Tuthmosis III. Green jasper was first employed as early as the Badarian Period and is found in the form of beads, pendants, amulets, ring bezels and, in particular, scarabs. Its Egyptian name is not certain; it might be *nemehef* (*nmḥf*), the green stone prescribed by Chapter 30 of the *Book of the Dead* as the material for the heart scarab, which was intended to help its deceased owner meet with success when his heart was weighed in the balance to ascertain his worthiness to enter the Egyptian equivalent of the Elysian Fields. Although a heart probably needed only to balance against the feather of Maat, perhaps one full of virtue would actually pull the pan down, hence the literal meaning of *nemehef*, 'it does not float'. Yet *nemehef* might just as well be the word for other green stones from which heart scarabs were manufactured, such as serpentine or even basalt, in which case green jasper is possibly to be equated with *sehert* (*shrt*), the green material prescribed for heart-shaped amulets by Chapter 29B of the *Book of the Dead*.

LAPIS LAZULI is an opaque dark-blue mineral (a sulphur-containing sodium-aluminium-silicate), often streaked with white and flecked with gold impurities, which takes a lustrous polish. The Egyptians prized it most highly of all their semi-precious stones, nearly always placing it immediately after gold and silver in lists of valuable materials. As the principal blue stone it was so often imitated by glazed composition and later glass that the adjective *maa* (*m3ʿ*), that is 'true', was frequently appended to its name in an effort to distinguish the real stone from its cheaper imitations, which were also known as lapis lazuli (*khesbed*) but usually with the additional description *iryt* (*îryt*) or *wedeh* (*wdḫ*), that is 'manufactured' or 'artificial'. Lapis was in use from the Predynastic Period, at first for beads and pendants, later for amulets, scarabs and inlays, and it remained popular until the Late Period, yet at all times it had to be imported into Egypt, almost certainly from Badakhshan in northeast Afghanistan. Indeed, it has been suggested that *khesbed* (*ḥsbd*), the name by which it was known to the Egyptians, retains a memory of its place of origin, the consonants transposed by the process of metathesis. There can at least be no doubt that *tefrer* (*tfrr*), the less common word for lapis, is named from the region of Tefreret, which probably lay south of the Caspian Sea. Lapis is also listed among tribute and gifts from Assyria, Babylon, the Hittites, Syria and Palestine, even Punt and Meroe far to the south in the modern Sudan, but in all these instances the material can

35 One of Psusennes' two magnificent necklaces, made from a double row of graduated lapis lazuli ball beads, with four gold spheres strung at the centre. The flat underside of the gold box-clasp bears the name of Psusennes, and on one of the stone beads is a three-line cuneiform text; its presence on the string has never been satisfactorily explained. L 56cm

From the mummy of Psusennes, Tanis (tomb III). 21st Dynasty (c. 1030–991 BC)

have been obtained originally only from a source in Afghanistan. In the temple of Ramesses III at Medinet Habu it is depicted in rectangular blocks, whereas at Karnak, among the offerings made to Amun by Tuthmosis III, it is shown in large round, and small irregularly shaped blue lumps.

LIMESTONE is an easily worked opaque calcium carbonate with small admixtures of other materials which cause it to vary widely in quality and to range in colour from cream through yellow and pink to black. Although the hills which border the Nile Valley from Cairo as far as Esna are of limestone, the finest quality, which the Egyptians called most simply *iner hedj* (*ỉnr ḥḏ*) or 'white stone', was quarried from the time of the Old Kingdom at Tura, in the cliffs behind what was to be the site of Cairo. Its use in jewellery, however, was strictly limited. It was the black variety, found in the Eastern Desert, which was carved into beads and pendants as early as the Badarian Period. Pink limestone, which occurs in the Western Desert near Edfu and between Asyut and Kharga Oasis, was used for beads from the Early Dynastic Period and for amulets from the time of the Old Kingdom. See MARBLE.

62d

MALACHITE is a soft, opaque, emerald-green basic copper carbonate with a silky sheen, exhibiting characteristic light and dark concentric zones of colour. Since it is found in or near copper ore deposits, the Egyptians obtained it from the same localities as the metal itself, in particular Serabit el-Khadim and Wadi Maghara in Sinai, but also from Nubia and the Eastern Desert, to judge from representations of it brought as rough unworked lumps in the tombs at Thebes of Rekhmire and Menkheperre-sonb, both high officials of Tuthmosis III (*c.* 1450 BC). Beads were manufactured from malachite even before the beginning of the 1st Dynasty and it was occasionally used for amulets and inlay until the end of the New Kingdom, but its main employment was as a green pigment. As a semi-precious stone the Egyptians certainly called malachite *shesmet* (*šsmt*), but it was probably also known as the general word *wadj* (*w3ḏ*), literally 'green', which was applied to other similarly coloured stones.

31

MARBLE is a crystalline limestone (calcium carbonate) found at various locations in the Eastern Desert; depending on the admixtures of other materials, it can have almost any colouring. The Egyptians employed it mostly for stone vessels and statues. Virtually its only occurrence in jewellery is in large bangles of Early Dynastic date. The name by which it was known is uncertain but it might have been *ibhety* (*ỉbhty*) or the variant form *behet* (*bht*).

MICA is a pearly white potassium-aluminium-silicate with admixtures of iron and magnesium. It splits easily into wafer-thin transparent sheets and is found in a number of localities. It was used sporadically from the Predynastic Period, at first for beads and later for pendants and attachments, particularly by the Kerma culture in Nubia during the Middle Kingdom. Its Egyptian name is unknown, unless it was *paqt* (*p3ḳt*), which can also mean 'eggshell', or, as has also been suggested, *irqeb* (*ỉrḫb*). See, however, QUARTZ.

NEPHRITE, better known as jade, is an opaque green calcium-magnesium-iron-silicate, capable of taking a high polish. Although often recorded as a material used in Egyptian jewellery-making, it can be securely identified in only a single instance, a double-bezel ring belonging to Tutankhamun. The material would have been obtained from sources in Turkestan or possibly Kashmir. 149a

OBSIDIAN is a translucent shiny black, naturally formed volcanic glass which was used from the Early Dynastic Period for beads, and later for amulets (especially scarabs) and inlays. It is not found in Egypt, however, its probable source being Ethiopia. The name by which it was known to the Egyptians is uncertain, unless it was *menu kem* (*mnw km*), literally 'dark quartz', a general term also applied to other dark-coloured stones. 146g

OLIVINE is a translucent glassy olive-green (hence its name) magnesium-iron-silicate, found in many locations in Egypt. It was used even before the beginning of the 1st Dynasty to make beads, amulets and pendants and continued to be employed during the Dynastic Period. A number of pieces formerly identified as beryl have proved subsequently to be olivine. The name by which it was known to the Egyptians has not been identified, unless it was *perdjen* (*prḏn*). This word, however, which occurs only once in a Late Dynastic text, has been equated with other similarly coloured materials. Perhaps olivine was confused with, or not clearly distinguished from, other green stones, as has certainly been the case far more recently. See PERIDOT.

ONYX/SARDONYX are varieties of chalcedony (silicon dioxide) with regular concentric bands or layers coloured respectively black or dark brown and reddish-brown or red, separated by gradations of white to grey. Although onyx beads are known from the Predynastic Period, these materials were most popular from the time of the 22nd Dynasty and, in particular, during the Graeco-Roman Period, when they were used for intaglios, cameos and settings for rings and earrings. It was then that onyx was even imitated in glass. Although the Romans obtained their onyx and sardonyx from India, there must have been a local Egyptian source, though none has been securely identified. See AGATE.

PERIDOT is the transparent green or yellow-green gemstone variety of olivine found on the island of St John in the Red Sea. However, apart from a possible instance of its use for a scarab, rather doubtfully dated to the 18th Dynasty, it does not seem to have been exploited in jewellery before the Ptolemaic Period, when it was used for intaglios. It may have been known to the Egyptians as *berget* (*brgt*) or possibly *perdjen* (*prḏn*), both of which occur only once in a text of Late Dynastic date.

PORPHYRY is the term applied to various igneous rocks which comprise a single-coloured matrix embedded with scattered differently coloured crystals. A black variety with white crystals, used as early as the Predynastic Period for pendants and later for beads, was almost certainly obtained from a range of hills near the Red Sea coast, about fifty kilometres north-west of Hurghada. The famous purple imperial porphyry, however, which was much exported into Italy during the early centuries of the Christian era, was used for only a handful of amulets and pendants during the Predynastic Period and for some small vessels during the early

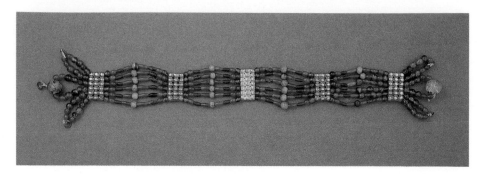

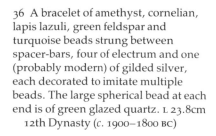

36 A bracelet of amethyst, cornelian, lapis lazuli, green feldspar and turquoise beads strung between spacer-bars, four of electrum and one (probably modern) of gilded silver, each decorated to imitate multiple beads. The large spherical bead at each end is of green glazed quartz. L 23.8cm
12th Dynasty (c. 1900–1800 BC)

Dynasties. Although the Romans quarried it at a locality in the Eastern Desert about sixty-five kilometres inland from Hurghada, the Egyptian objects could well have been made from loose pieces of porphyry found lying on the surface. Not surprisingly, the Egyptian name for this material has not been identified.

PRASE is a leek-green quartz (silicon dioxide), used extremely rarely during the Dynastic Period for beads. It is yet another material for which the word *perdjen* (*prḏn*) has been suggested as the Egyptian equivalent.

QUARTZ (MILKY) is a hard, opaque white variety of silicon dioxide. Two sources of it were probably in Nubia near the Toshka quarry, and a few kilometres north of Aswan, although, if the Egyptian name for it has been correctly identified, it was also brought as tribute from Syria. It is highly probable that the Egyptians called it *menu hedj* (*mnw ḥḏ*), that is 'white quartz', a term which also embraced rock-crystal but distinguished both from *menu kem* (*mnw km*) or 'dark quartz', which could also be applied to obsidian as well as to coloured quartz. Another word, *irqebes* (*ìrḵbs*), which occurs only once in a list of Nubian products, has also been tentatively identified as quartz. The milky variety was first used during the Early Dynastic Period for pendants, and during the Middle Kingdom for inlays and beads, which were sometimes glazed. A number of the red inlays in Tutankhamun's jewellery have subsequently proved to be quartz or rock-crystal on a bed of red-coloured cement imitating cornelian. See ROCK-CRYSTAL.

36

47

ROCK-CRYSTAL is a hard, glass-like transparent colourless quartz (silicon dioxide), which was first used during the Predynastic Period for beads, and later also for inlays. Found particularly in an area to the west of the Nile Valley between the Faiyum and Baharia Oasis and in Sinai, it was probably known to the Egyptians as *menu hedj* (*mnw ḥḏ*), 'white quartz', the same term used for milky quartz.

SARD is a translucent red-brown variety of chalcedony (silicon dioxide) which is almost indistinguishable from cornelian except for being generally darker in colour. This kinship was recognised by the Egyptians, who called it *herset* (*ḥrst*) like cornelian but added the adjective *desher* (*ḏšr*), meaning 'red'. Although obtainable from a number of locations in the Eastern Desert, sard has been identified with certainty in only a few instances as a material used for jewellery, notably scarabs and scaraboids of New Kingdom date and an openwork plaque of the reign of Amenophis III. See CORNELIAN.

SERPENTINE is an easily carved opaque to semi-translucent basic magnesium silicate which is often mottled, hence its name of 'snake-like'; it can range in colour from dark green to almost black. Serpentine is found in a number of locations in the Eastern Desert, notably one which lies south-west of Hurghada and north-west of Quseir, also midway between the Nile Valley and the Red Sea in a line running from Esna to Kom Ombo and in Nubia, just north of the Tropic of Cancer; no ancient quarry, however, has been identified. As early as the Badarian Period it was employed for beads, later also for pendants, cylinder-seals, amulets, scarabs and, in particular, heart scarabs. Its name in Egyptian is not certain: perhaps it was *sehert* (*shrt*), the green stone prescribed for heart amulets by Chapter 29B of the *Book of the Dead*, but only if green jasper is *nemehef* (*nmhf*). See STEATITE.

SLATE is an easily split opaque metamorphic rock, rich in silica; it ranges in colour from black through blue to green and is found in various localities in the Eastern Desert in the vicinity of the Wadi Hammamat, which joins the Nile Valley to the Red Sea coast at Quseir. Although slate was employed by the Egyptians as early as the Predynastic Period, its use in jewellery-making was restricted to the Early Dynastic Period for simple small rings, presumably for the fingers, and large bangles. It was probably known as *bekhen* (*bhn*), a term the Egyptians seem to have applied to more than one green stone.

SOAPSTONE, see STEATITE

STEATITE (SOAPSTONE) is a very soft, easily carved basic magnesium silicate characterised by a greasy or soapy feel (hence its name); it ranges in colour from white or grey to black. It occurs in a number of locations in the Eastern Desert, from just north of the Wadi Hammamat to as far south as Wadi Halfa and, in particular, in the vicinity of Aswan. It was a stone exploited extensively and early by the Egyptians, who by the Badarian Period carved it into beads which they often glazed green; this technique 37 was to be frequently applied to steatite during most of the Dynastic Period, especially in the case of scarabs. In spite of its prevalence, no word has yet been identified as the Egyptian word for steatite.

TURQUOISE is an opaque, pale sky-blue or blue-green copper-containing basic aluminium phosphate which the Egyptians obtained alongside copper ore at Wadi Maghara and Serabit el-Khadim in Sinai. Today the best-quality turquoise is considered to be the blue, which is less highly

37 Detail of a girdle made from rows of bright-green glazed steatite beads, found over the knees of a male corpse. The bone spacers are among the earliest known. Such girdles are typically male ornaments during this period. L (total) 131.5cm
From Mostagedda (grave 592). Predynastic Badarian Period (*c.* 4000 BC)

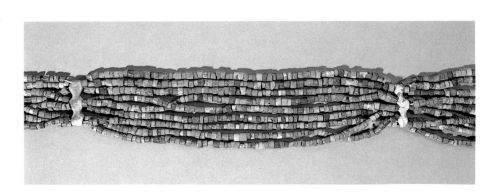

38 Openwork gold diadem of Khnumet. The design, inlaid with lapis lazuli, turquoise and cornelian, comprises units formed from rosettes and 'lilies of Upper Egypt' alternating with single rosettes. The sheet-gold vulture at the front has chased feathering and obsidian-inlaid eyes. D 20.5cm

From the tomb of Khnumet, Dahshur. 12th Dynasty (reign of Ammenemes II, c. 1895 BC)

prized when exposure to light has faded it to green, yet the Egyptians preferred the green variety, valuing turquoise as the green stone *par excellence* and bracketing it with lapis lazuli in lists of valuable materials. In his *Admonitions* bewailing the state of Egypt, Ipuwer alternates turquoise with gold, lapis lazuli and silver. In the temple of Ramesses III at Medinet Habu both turquoise and lapis lazuli are represented as rectangular blocks; at Karnak, however, among the offerings made to Amun by Tuthmosis III, turquoise is depicted as very large oval and smaller round green lumps. The word for turquoise, long misinterpreted by scholars, was *mefkat* (*mfk3t*), to which the adjective *maa* (*m3ˁ*), 'true', was often appended in order to distinguish it from the glass and glazed composition by which it was frequently imitated. The Egyptians used turquoise as early as the Badarian Period, at first for beads and pendants, later for amulets and, during the Middle Kingdom in particular, for inlays. It was still employed in a few pieces of inlaid jewellery from the tomb of Tutankhamun and the royal burials of Tanis, even when other green inlays were of glass.

Metals

GOLD. In the Amarna Letters, the court correspondence written to Amenophis III and his son Akhenaten by the contemporary rulers of the neighbouring Near Eastern kingdoms, the constant theme is the desire for Egyptian gold. 'As for gold, send me what you have to hand as quickly as possible', requests Burnaburiash, King of Babylon. 'I want gold; send me gold', demands the brother of the King of the Hittites. 'Send me great quantities of gold, more gold than was sent to my father, for in the land of my brother gold is as abundant as dust': thus writes Tushratta, King of Mitanni. Even today the treasures of Tutankhamun and the pharaohs of Tanis have ensured that, for the public, the most abiding image of ancient Egypt is reflected in gold, the material of the flesh of the gods, the colour of divinity.

Even before the 1st Dynasty gold was being made into simple beads of sheet metal or foil over a core; within a few centuries Egyptian goldsmiths had become skilled in virtually every known goldworking technique and applied most of them in the production of jewellery of every description: amulets, pendants, diadems, pectorals, bangles, earrings, finger-rings, anklets, torques, elements of collars, girdles and bracelets were all manufactured from the precious metal. Indeed, certain chapters of the *Book of the Dead* demanded that prescribed amulets and funerary jewellery be made of gold.

Almost certainly, in the earliest period, the Egyptians obtained the small quantities of the metal they required as alluvial gold, whether in the form of tiny nuggets visible to the naked eye in water-washed gravel or sand or left lying on the beds of desert wadis after gold-bearing rock had been worn away by running water which had long since dried up. Soon improved extraction was achieved by digging up this gold-containing material and washing it; this process, called 'panning' – well-known to the forty-niners of the Californian gold-rush – separated the heavier metal fragments from the lighter sands or gravels surrounding them. Larger-scale extraction was possible with the use of sloping tables or channels for the washing; they were inset with grooves or depressions or hung with cloth or skins to catch the particles of gold. But it eventually became necessary to mine into hard, gold-bearing quartz if the metal was to be acquired in sufficient quantities. The Greek author Agatharchides, whose writings have been transmitted by Diodorus Siculus, has left an eyewitness account of how the Egyptians mined gold ore during the second century BC and the procedures he describes had almost certainly been in operation for millennia.

First of all, the gold-bearing rock in the mine was broken down with fires so that it could be broken up with picks and hammers. The ore-bearing chunks of rock obtained in this way were then brought out into the open to be crushed between heavy stone mortars and were even further reduced by hand-held grinders. Finally, the particles were washed and the metal gathered. However, it is possible that not all of these processes were carried out at the same site. The nature of the terrain from which the Egyptians obtained their gold was not such as to provide the considerable quantities of water required for the washing of the crushed ore, and there is little evidence of washing areas or furnaces for smelting at the sites from which the metal was extracted. In some private Theban tombs of the New Kingdom the high-ranking owners are shown supervising the arrival of gold among various raw materials, and the metal is not depicted just in the form of dust or granules tied up in leather bags, but as rough nuggets fused from granules or even heavy rings or moulded hide-shaped ingots, which must have been produced under better-equipped conditions than those available at the site of extraction.

Although gold is found in a number of locations in the area between the Nile Valley and the Red Sea, as far north as east of the Wadi Qena and as far south as the Fifth Cataract, the Egyptians obtained it from three regions in particular, which they termed 'the upland of Coptos', 'Wawat' and 'Kush'. The first and northernmost source clearly refers to the town of that name on the Nile north of Luxor which seems to have acted as a collection point for metal obtained from a number of sites to the east, running in a line southwards from Wadi el-Gidami and Wadi Hammama. Inscriptions left in the area by expeditions date the earliest extraction of gold in the vicinity to the 5th Dynasty and the First Intermediate Period, and it was obtained there again during the New Kingdom. Indeed, the only map to have survived from ancient Egypt, drawn on a scrap of papyrus now in Turin, shows the central area of the Wadi Hammamat, where there were gold mines as well as stone quarries.

Sources in an area around the Wadi Allaqi, north-east of Wadi Halfa, produced the gold of Wawat, the Egyptian name for Lower Nubia (from Aswan to the southern end of the Second Cataract), which was annexed to Egypt during the Middle Kingdom. The 12th Dynasty fortress of Qubban on the Nile then became the entrepôt for local gold, but inscriptions make it clear that the metal was extracted in the vicinity from at least the 6th Dynasty, and in particular during the 18th and 19th Dynasties. Between the areas designated the 'Upland of Coptos' and 'Wawat' lay other gold-producing regions. East of el-Kab the Wadi Abbad, which leads to the gold mines of the Wadi Mia, has an inscription of 1st Dynasty date, although the mines themselves were particularly exploited during the reigns of Amenophis III, Sety I (who excavated a rock temple there) and Ramesses II. It was to aid the extraction of gold from this area that Sety I sank a well 'that he might sustain the weary and refresh the heart that is burnt up in summer' and recorded the deed in his temple in the Wadi Mia. According to some inscriptions in the Wadi el-Hudi south-east of Aswan, gold was mined there along with amethyst during the Middle Kingdom. However, it is not at all clear whether these sources belonged to the 'Upland of Coptos' or 'Wawat', although it has been suggested that everything north of Aswan was part of the 'gold of Coptos'. Kush, the third main gold-producing area, was the Egyptian name for Nubia south of the Second Cataract, and gold has indeed been found in numerous locations in the Eastern Desert between Wadi Halfa and Kerma but there is no clear evidence for any workings of ancient Egyptian date.

The Egyptian word for gold was *nub* (*nbw*) and in it may lie a romantic, though perhaps linguistically indefensible explanation for the name applied to the area immediately south of Aswan, comprising the southern part of modern Egypt and the northern part of modern Sudan. It was the Greek historian Strabo, writing in the first century BC, who first called it Nubia; before that it had been known to the Greeks as Ethiopia, the land of (sun)burnt faces. The prosaic explanation for its new name is that in Strabo's time the region was inhabited by a tribe called the Nobae. Yet throughout Dynastic history the chief product of the area, named in texts and depicted on tomb and temple walls, was gold, whether as dust, nuggets, rings or ingots. Hence Nubia would mean 'gold land', which, for the Egyptians, it had always been.

ELECTRUM, which the Egyptians called *djam* (*ḏ'm*), is both a naturally occurring and an artificially produced compound of which the main constituents are gold and silver. Indeed, since most ancient Egyptian gold is impure, containing by nature various proportions (up to 20 per cent) of silver, it is often difficult to be sure whether the metal in question is to be

39 Amuletic jewellery of the 12th Dynasty (c. 1900–1800 BC). The girdle elements (a) are strung with hair ornaments, pendants, amulets and beads. The hollow cowrie shells, the beard and fish pendants and the Heh-amulet are of electrum; the lotus pendant is silver inlaid with polychrome glass and cornelian; the beads are of cornelian, amethyst, lapis lazuli, green feldspar and electrum. L 46.3cm

The gold openwork bangle (b) is inset with a frieze of amulets and animals alternately of gold and silver. This procession – comprising a snake, a turtle, *udjats*, two fingers, *Bats*, *ankhs*, hares, baboons, *djeds*, falcons and two draughtsmen – is similar to those found on contemporary amuletic ivory wands. D (external) 8.3cm

considered low-grade gold or electrum: the division drawn between the two is often very arbitrary. Pliny defined electrum as gold which contained 20 per cent of silver; modern authorities have termed electrum any gold–silver alloy containing between 20 and 50 per cent silver and thus ranging in colour from deep yellow to pale yellowish-white. The Egyptians depicted it coloured yellow, just like gold, but also white, like silver, and even red. In the tomb of Rekhmire at Thebes it is brought as tribute from Nubia and Punt in the form of rings and nuggets and as dust in leather bags just like gold; indeed, in every reference to its acquisition, the sources are located to the south of Egypt. Because electrum is rather harder than gold it was particularly suited to withstand the daily wear and tear imposed on jewellery, and from the earliest dynasties it was made into amulets, beads, bangles and various settings for inlay.

39a

SILVER was at first called by the Egyptians *nub hedj* (*nbw ḥḏ*), later just *hedj*, which means literally 'white gold', clearly showing that they distinguished between the two metals merely on the basis of colour. In fact, all ancient gold contains silver to a greater or lesser degree and recent research has suggested that most so-called silver objects which predate the Middle Kingdom are actually manufactured from naturally silver-rich gold which the Egyptians presumably obtained from their gold mines. Indeed, they might have utilised this as one of the main sources of silver had they been able to separate the two metals, but the process does not seem to have been in use before the Graeco-Roman Period. The commonest source of ancient silver, metal-bearing ore, does not occur in Egypt. Consequently, from at least the time of the Middle Kingdom silver was imported into the country and was therefore always more highly prized than gold, which was so much more readily obtainable. Until the time of the Middle Kingdom silver regularly precedes gold in lists of precious materials, and until the Graeco-Roman Period the ratio between it and gold remained constant at 1:2. However, silver objects were rather more numerous in Egypt than the pieces which have survived might suggest: unlike gold, silver can corrode away beyond restoration leaving little trace behind.

By about 3000 BC the method of extracting the metal from ore, known as cupellation, was well established in Asia Minor and that was the source from which the Egyptians obtained the bulk of their silver during most of the Dynastic Period. Shaped into rings, bars, nuggets and hide-shaped ingots or already fashioned into vessels, statuettes and small luxury articles, it was depicted in the tombs of great officials of the New Kingdom at Thebes and on temple walls among offerings to the gods. According to the texts, silver was always obtained as booty or tribute, often brought by the inhabitants of Retenu (Syria) or by the Minoans, later Mycenaeans, presumably from a Cypriot source, although undoubtedly peaceful trade was just as often involved. In Ptolemaic times, when the Greek mines at Laurion were being exploited, a new word referring to the metal *arqur* (ʿ*rḫwr*) appears in demotic texts, obviously a phonetic rendering of *arguros*, the Greek word for silver.

Symbolically silver was linked with the moon and was often employed as the material for representations of the lunar disc; it was also held to be the stuff from which the bones of the gods were made. Although it was always used more sparingly than gold, from as early as Predynastic times silver was employed in the manufacture of beads, bangles, diadems, finger-rings, amulets, pendants and, occasionally, torques and earrings.

39,49

COPPER was the first metal known to the Egyptians and as early as the Badarian Period it was being made into beads. Bangles and finger-rings were fashioned from it even before the 1st Dynasty and by the end of the Old Kingdom it was being used, frequently gilded, for circlets, diadems and belts, but it was never as common in jewellery-making as precious metals. Unusual examples of copper jewellery include an inlaid roundel

87b

49d

from a headband dating to the First Intermediate Period, solid copper broad collars of Middle Kingdom date and a pair of spiral earrings from a Second Intermediate Period burial. The addition of tin to copper produces

40

bronze, which not only is harder and stronger than the basic metal but also melts at a lower temperature. However, like copper before it, bronze had only a limited use in jewellery-making for its chief employment lay in the production of tools and implements, weapons, vessels, ritual objects and statuettes. From the Middle Kingdom bronze was occasionally used for bangles and bracelets with push-fit ends, later for signet-rings and the shanks of rings with stone bezels.

The earliest copper jewellery produced during the Predynastic Period was almost certainly made from native metal which required nothing more than hammering into shape. During the New Kingdom, however, the Egyptians imported much of their copper and bronze in the form of bars and hide-shaped ingots from Syria, Cyprus and Asia Minor, and, though it is usually depicted in the tombs of great officials at Thebes as

40 Bronze collar counterpoises (*menkhet*). They depict (**a**, *above*) Hathor as a goddess, a sistrum fetish and a cow and (**b**, *right above*) the Hathor fetish as a sistrum handle above a scene inlaid with polychrome glass showing the goddess as a cow. 40a is incised with the name of Amenophis III. H (**b**) 18cm

a: 18th Dynasty, *c.* 1370 BC; **b**: late New Kingdom, *c.* 1100 BC

booty or tribute brought by vassal peoples, peaceful trade must also have been an important source. Earlier the Egyptians' chief sources were the copper ores of Sinai and the Eastern Desert. In Sinai copper was certainly mined at least from the time of the Old Kingdom at Timna and possibly also at Wadi Maghara and Serabit el-Khadim, although at the latter sites the workings were primarily for turquoise. In the Eastern Desert there were three main ancient sources. The ores of Wadi Araba, running inland from the Gulf of Suez and lying almost due east of Beni Suef on the Nile, were worked from at least the 19th Dynasty. Umm Semiuki, about sixty-five kilometres inland from the Red Sea coast almost due east of Aswan, has extensive ancient workings, some of them underground. In Nubia at Qubban there are slag heaps of Middle Kingdom date but no local source; it is generally supposed that the ore smelted there came from Abu Seyal to the south-east, which was certainly mined in antiquity.

At first, when copper ores were obtained from surface deposits, primitive flint tools would have been sufficient for extraction, but as shafts had to be cut to follow veins underground metal chisels became essential. After it was extracted and crushed the simplest method of smelting the ore was to mix it with charcoal and heat it, either piled in a heap on the ground or inside a shallow pit. The burning often took place on a hillside or in a valley to achieve maximum utilisation of the prevailing winds. A further improvement in the technique came with the introduction of closed furnaces. The rough lumps of impure metal thus obtained could be further refined by hammering and remelting in clay crucibles before being cast into bars or ingots for ease of handling and transportation. The Egyptian word for copper was *hemt* (*ḥmt*) and for bronze *hesmen* (*ḥsmn*).

Man-made materials

GLAZED COMPOSITION, also known less accurately as faience, is perhaps the most characteristic of all ancient Egyptian materials. It consists of a sandy core, ideally but rarely pure powdered quartz, with a vitreous alkaline glaze on its surface which can be given any colour, depending on the colorant added to the glazing mixture. The body material was, in fact, far more often raw sand, not only that but dirty sand, with the result that the core of faience objects is rarely white but rather grey or brown or even yellow or red depending on the prevailing colour of local sand sources. Research has suggested that there were three methods by which the all-important surface glazing, essentially a sodium- or potassium-calcium-silicate, could be achieved and the oldest was certainly practised as early as the Badarian Period to coat steatite beads (and later amulets) with green glaze in imitation of a semi-precious green stone. By one method, known as applied glazing, the raw materials in powdered form were mixed with water (a compound known as slurry) and applied to the stone or faience body material by dipping, pouring or painting, with the result that the glaze formed on the surface during firing. For the best results the raw materials in the slurry were prefired and ground down before being mixed with water. This process is characterised by the unevenness of the glaze produced, which often shows drips and flow lines, and some authorities believe that it was the earliest employed by the Egyptians. However, a self-glazing process known as cementation, certainly in use at least as

41

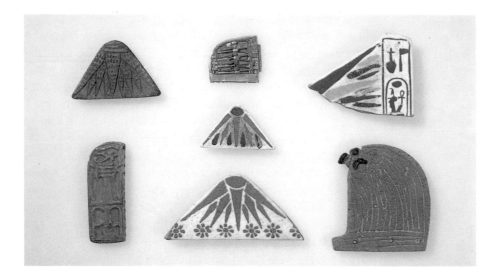

41 A selection of collar terminals:
a blue glazed composition lotus-head;
b hinged gold, with polychrome glass inlays; **c** polychrome glazed composition lotus-head, naming Amenophis III; **d** polychrome glazed composition lotus-head; **e** glazed composition, with moulded scene of Heh below a *djed*, an *udjat* and a *nefer*-sign. H 6cm; **f** two-coloured glazed composition lotus-head. W 8.3cm; **g** blue glazed composition falcon-head, with black details. H 6.2cm
    New Kingdom (*c.* 1370–1180 BC)

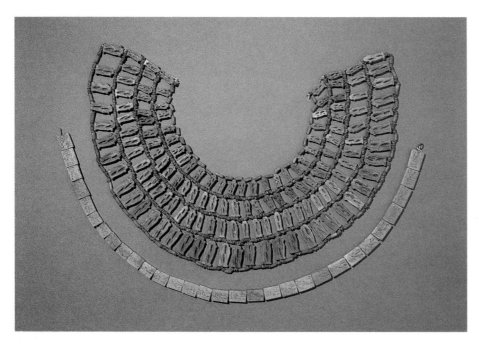

42 Blue glazed composition jewellery.
    a (*top*) Openwork collar of beads and amulets, each of the latter a shrine containing a standing goddess holding a papyrus sceptre. From a child's burial at Matmar (grave 779). L 39cm. 3rd Intermediate Period (*c.* 945–700 BC)
    b (*bottom*) String of tubular beads incised on one face with the name Psamtek (Psammetichus). Saite or later (after 650 BC)

early as the Middle Kingdom, has also been put forward. By this method the stone or faience object was enveloped in the glazing mixture, which might be in a wet or dry state; the mixture melted during firing to form a glaze on the surface and excess material could just be crumbled away. The third method, another self-glazing process, which could only be used to glaze objects with a faience body, entailed the mixing of the glazing materials with that of the body. During drying the glazing salts rose to the surface and coated it by a process known as efflorescence; firing melted the surface salts to form the glaze. Appropriately, the Egyptians called glazed composition *tjehnet* (*ṯḥnt*), literally 'that which gleams', which well describes its shiny, glass-like appearance.

In the Predynastic Period only green and blue glazes occur; black, white and purple are used sporadically from the Old Kingdom onwards and yellow and red were added to the palette during the 18th Dynasty. Glazed

43 Openwork gold pectoral of Mereret, inlaid with cornelian, lapis lazuli and polychrome glazed composition. Below the vulture Nekhbet are the prenomen cartouches of Ammenemes III flanked by hieroglyphs reading 'the good god, lord of all lands and foreign countries'. At each side the king is about to dash the brains of an Asiatic. All the inlaid details are chased on the reverse. The suspension string is of beads and drops of cornelian, lapis lazuli and gold. W 10.4cm

From the cache of Mereret, Dahshur. 12th Dynasty (reign of Ammenemes III, *c.* 1810 BC)

44 Miniature mosaic glass slice, in a 19th-century gold mount. It may have once functioned as a pendant and depicts a *ba*-bird with the unusual detail of a wide-open mouth, as though shrieking. 1.3cm sq.

1st–2nd century AD

composition was extremely versatile, for it could be moulded or modelled into almost any shape. Because of this malleability and its ability to imitate almost any stone, it was one of the Egyptian jewellery-maker's favourite materials. As early as the Badarian Period it was formed into beads, and by the end of the Old Kingdom into amulets and multi-coloured pendants too. By now beads had assumed fancy shapes, and could also be decorated with spiral patterns or crumbs of another colour. During the remainder of the Dynastic Period glazed composition was employed in jewellery-making for ring bezels in the form of scarabs and scaraboids, for stirrup-shaped finger-rings which aped those in metal, for those made in two parts with circular shank and fancy bezel and for those in the form of openwork bands with intricate designs, for bangles and bracelets, for the terminals, spacer-bars and flat-backed moulded elements which were threaded into collars, for pectorals and ear-studs, even for headband rosettes, and in particular for inlays in imitation of semi-precious stones. Glazed composition jewellery elements could even be inlaid with glazed composition of a different colour.

GLASS as manufactured by the ancient Egyptians and the glaze of glazed composition are basically the same material – an alkaline calcium silicate. The difference lies in how they were employed: if the raw product was to form glass it was used independently; if it was to form glaze it was provided with a core of a different material. It is generally believed that glass was discovered by accident when the necessary raw materials were unknowingly heated. Certainly Egyptian glass required a far lower temperature for fusion than modern glass. The other basic difference is that ancient Egyptian glass was never blown – that process only came into use during the Roman Period. Rather it was formed from rods and canes of material which, in the case of large objects, were built up around a core

59

Right 46 Flexible vulture collar of gold inlaid with dark-blue, red and green glass, found on the mummy of Tutankhamun. There is a small matching *menkhet*-counterpoise. This collar, known as the Nekhbet collar, was prescribed by Chapter 157 of the *Book of the Dead*. H 39.5cm.

From the tomb of Tutankhamun, Valley of the Kings, W. Thebes. 18th Dynasty (*c.* 1336–1327 BC)

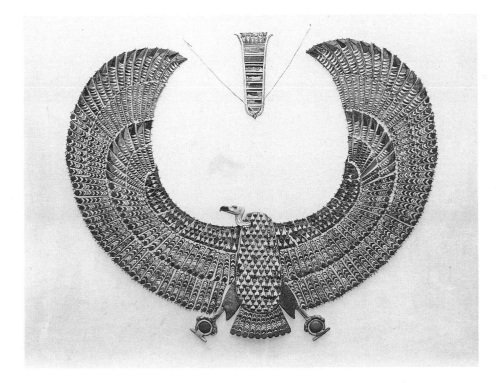

Left 45 Selection of amuletic glazed composition finger-rings. The designs are: **a** solar falcon-headed gods seated around an *ankh* and Hathor. H 2.8cm; **b** column of Bes figures standing on each others' heads; **c** aegis of Bastet; **d** galloping oryx; **e** *udjat*-eye; **f** aegis of Mut wearing the double crown, over a papyrus-head; the counterpoise forms part of the shank; **g** massive, stirrup-shaped, with cartouche bezel naming Amen-Re with epithets. H 6.8cm; **h** cartouche bezel naming Amenophis III, protected by a crowned uraeus; **i** seated goddess in barque; **j** inlaid openwork bezel; **k** stirrup-shaped, moulded bezel of baboon and feather under crescent and full moon; **l** falcon-headed aegis wearing sun-disc over a lotus-flower; part of the shank is formed by the counterpoise. H (bezel) 3.5cm. From Matmar (grave 745); **m** stirrup-shaped, with the name of Tutankhamun's wife.

18th Dynasty–3rd Intermediate Period (*c.* 1470–750 BC)

which was subsequently removed. However, for beads, amulets, pendants and inlays, which represent the chief uses of glass in Egyptian jewellery-making, the molten material was either modelled in an open mould so that the resultant piece had a flat back, pulled into shape at the end of a mandril, cast in a closed mould rather like metal, or, in the case of beads, wound around a central rod which was later withdrawn. Individual miniature mosaic glass slices were made by bundling together tiny coloured rods and canes into the desired pattern, visible at each end of the bundle. These were then heated until they fused, and the pattern was then miniaturised by being drawn out. Mosaic glass slices may well have served as jewellery inlays or, when mounted, as pendants. Appropriately, the Egyptian name for glass was *iner en wedeh* (*inr n wdh*) or *aat wedhet* (*'3t wdḥt*), both meaning literally 'stone of the kind that flows'.

Individual beads are known from the time of the Old Kingdom and there are some isolated scarabs of Middle Kingdom date, but glass was not produced in any quantity until the New Kingdom, and in particular from the time of Amenophis III onwards (*c.* 1390 BC). Depending on the colorant added, glass might be blue, green, red or yellow, less often white or black, and its ability to imitate semi-precious stones, which were far harder to model and carve, meant that during the New Kingdom and later it was often substituted for beads and inlays which at earlier periods would have been manufactured from lapis lazuli, turquoise, feldspar, cornelian and jasper. Indeed, much of Tutankhamun's jewellery is little more than magnificent costume jewellery: most of it consists of precious-metal settings for glass and glazed composition elements.

Recently the date of the first appearance of colourless glass in Egypt has been put back from the reign of Tutankhamun by more than a hundred years to the time of Queen Hatshepsut with the identification of two beads

44

46
47

Left 47 Inlaid counterpoise, attached by articulated straps (made from plaques of four different designs) to a pectoral, part of Tutankhamun's coronation regalia. Inside a kiosk the king is offered the sign of life by a winged Maat. The materials employed are quartz in coloured cement, red, green, dark-blue and light-blue glass, gold, electrum and silver. H 8.4cm

From the tomb of Tutankhamun (Treasury), Valley of the Kings, W. Thebes. 18th Dynasty (*c.* 1336–1327 BC)

Below 48 Ear ornaments of Tutankhamun.

a (*inner*) An elaborate pair of earrings with much granulation decoration, for pierced ears. The front studs are open flowers of red and yellow gold. The large pendant ring is formed from dark resin and hollow gold beads. Gold beads and seed pods hang from the gold and blue glass bead tassels. H 10cm

b (*outer*) Pair of small gold ear-studs inlaid with glass and adorned with uraei. D 2.5cm

From the tomb of Tutankhamun (Treasury), Valley of the Kings, W. Thebes. 18th Dynasty (*c* 1336–1327 BC)

bearing the name of the royal favourite Senenmut as glass. During the New Kingdom and later glass was made into beads and amulets, earrings, ear-plugs and finger-rings and inlays for collars, bangles, bracelets and pectorals.

EGYPTIAN BLUE is the name given to an artificially produced frit consisting of a calcium-copper-silicate used essentially as a blue pigment but also, from the time of the Old Kingdom, made into beads and amulets. Superficially it can be mistaken for glazed composition which has lost its shiny appearance, but unlike composition, where the glaze is only on the surface, the colour is uniform throughout. Experiments have shown that after a single firing Egyptian blue is coarse in texture but a dark blue in colour. However, if the material is broken down, moulded and then fired for a second time, it becomes much finer textured, but the colour is correspondingly paler. The Egyptian term for this frit is *shesyt* (*šsyt*).

Organic materials and animal products

AMBER could have been obtained from an ancient source now identified in the Lebanon but there is no definite evidence that it was ever employed in Egypt before the Late Period. Earlier identifications of this fossil resin have subsequently proved to be erroneous or at least extremely doubtful. On the other hand, true resins from coniferous trees of the same area of the Levant were certainly employed, at first for beads, later for finger-rings, scarabs and earrings as early as the Predynastic Period.

BONE, not only that of animals and birds but of fish too, was carved into hoop finger-rings, bangles with convex outer faces, spacer-bars, beads,

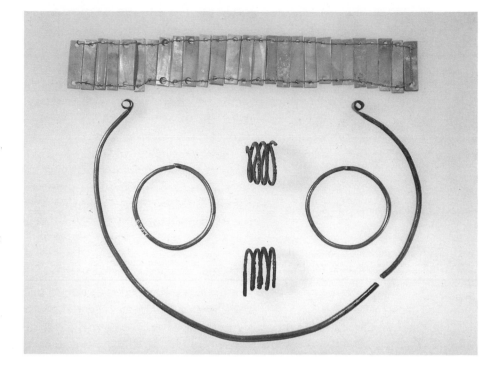

49 The pair of hoop-shaped silver wire earrings (**a**), found at the ears, and the silver wire torque (**b**) are from the burial of a woman. Like the bracelet composed of mother-of-pearl plaques (**c**), they belong to the Nubian Pan-grave people, who settled in Egypt during the late 2nd Intermediate Period. A pair of contemporary Egyptian earrings (**d**) are of spiral copper wire. L (bracelet) 16.7cm

a & b: From Mostagedda (grave 3120); **c**: from Hu (grave x 58); **d** Mostagedda (grave 2639), 2nd Intermediate Period (*c.* 1650–1540 BC)

pendants and amulets even earlier than the 1st Dynasty and its use in simple jewellery-making continued sporadically throughout the Dynastic Period.

CORAL, which consists of the skeletons of marine organisms, is found in various distinctive forms. The white and the red branching varieties (*Corallum nobile* and *Corallum rubrium* respectively), although both native to the Mediterranean, were rarely employed in Egyptian jewellery before the Ptolemaic Period. However, red 'pipe' or 'organ' coral (*Tubipora musica*), which is found in the Red Sea, was turned into simple beads as early as the Badarian Period.

FLAX FIBRES, often elaborately knotted at intervals along their length, were usually used for threading Egyptian jewellery. During the Predynastic and Early Dynastic Periods, however, rather more unusual materials such as animal hair and reed sometimes occur.

HAIR, in at least one case ox hair, has been identified as the material of bangles dating to the 1st Dynasty and First Intermediate Period; it was also used for bangles belonging to the Nubian Pan-grave people, who were contemporary with Egypt's Second Intermediate Period.

HORN was shaped into flat bangles, plain finger-rings and beads during the Predynastic and Early Dynastic Periods.

IVORY can be obtained from the tusks of elephants or hippopotamuses, but there can be little doubt that it was from the latter that bangles, some with knobs, hoop-shaped finger-rings, pendants, amulets and fancy beads were shaped during the Predynastic and Early Dynastic Periods: of the two animals only the hippopotamus is represented on contemporary painted pottery, formed into theriomorphic vessels, carved into slate palettes and shaped into amulets. However, it is no coincidence that *abu*

(*3bw*), the Egyptian word for 'elephant' and 'ivory', was also the name borne by the ancient town at Egypt's southern border which the Greeks called Elephantine, opposite modern Aswan. To it were brought luxury goods from the south and among the panther skins and living apes, gold and jasper, incense and ebony, were always depicted elephant tusks, at least from the time of the Old Kingdom. During the New Kingdom elephant ivory was still imported chiefly from Nubia and Punt, although an additional new source was Syria; here herds of wild elephants still ranged free in the Orontes Valley, where they were hunted by King Tuthmosis III in person. As his general Amenemheb records in his tomb at Thebes around 1445 BC: 'He hunted 120 elephants for the sake of their tusks'. During the New Kingdom ivory was also carved into earrings and ear-studs, stirrup-shaped finger-rings and scarabs and, occasionally, into shapes for inlaying.

MOTHER-OF-PEARL (NACRE) is the lining of the shell of the Red Sea oyster (*Pictada margaritifera*), which does not produce pearls. Indeed, pearls were unknown in Egypt before the Ptolemaic Period. During the Middle Kingdom actual oyster-shells inscribed with the name of the reigning pharaoh were worn on the chest, apparently as military insignia, and were imitated in gold, silver and electrum to serve as amulets. Mother-of-pearl bangles and finger-rings were popular in Nubia as early as the time of the A-Group people, who were contemporary with the Late Predynastic and Early Dynastic Periods in Egypt, and they were still popular fifteen hundred years later with the Nubian Pan-grave people, who settled in Egypt during the Second Intermediate Period. It was this culture which produced very characteristic armlets formed from rectangular plaques of 49c mother-of-pearl pierced at top and bottom and strung together vertically.

OSTRICH-EGGSHELL was employed as early as the Badarian Period for disc beads, pendants and amulets, and it remained a popular material for jewellery-making among the Nubians until the early 18th Dynasty.

SHELLS were among the earliest materials used by the Egyptian jewellery-maker, whether whole, sliced or shaped into beads, amulets, bangles or rings. It is interesting that the commonest varieties found in strings of the Badarian culture – conus, ancillaria, natica and nerita – are native not to the Nile Valley but to the Red Sea, suggesting farther-reaching contacts than might have been expected at so early a date. Sliced nassa shells, again of Red Sea origin, are particularly characteristic of the Old Kingdom and First Intermediate Period. Cowrie shells were amuletic in nature, worn to ward off the evil eye from pregnant women. Not only were actual cowries used as components of girdles, but they were also imitated in precious metal and semi-precious stones. The rather poetic name by which the Egyptians called shells was 'stone of the water's edge' or 'stone of the shore' (*inr n r* or *inr n spt mw*).

TORTOISESHELL was first carved into flat bangles during the Predynastic Period, and these were still popular with the Nubians of the Pan-grave culture fifteen hundred years later. It probably came from the Red Sea turtle, not any of the species of land and fresh-water turtles known to the Egyptians.

CHAPTER THREE

The craftsmen and their techniques

Every labour of the craftsmen's workshop

In Egypt the great workshops attached to the temples and palaces where fine-quality jewellery was produced were under the control of high officials; it is their names which have survived and in their tombs that the manufacture of jewellery was depicted. Far less often are known the names of the craftsmen who actually shaped semi-precious stones into inlays, delicately tapped and chased precious metal into jewellery elements or strung beads into intricate collars, and most of those named are goldsmiths – the Egyptian term is *neby* (*nby*). Although part at least of the jewellery-maker's art involved working with precious metal (indeed, it is no accident that the activities of precious-metal workers and jewellery-makers are always depicted side by side), still remarkably few of the skilled craftsmen who called themselves *neshdy*, earlier *mesneshdy* (*nšdy/ msňsdy*), are known. This word is best translated as 'jewellery-maker', although it actually means something more like 'worker in semi-precious stones'. However, the ability to shape a hard stone into an inlay to fit snugly within a cloison or to form an intricately detailed amulet from a pebble was the essence of the Egyptian jewellery-maker's art, far more than the craft of the 'bead-maker' – *iru weshbet* (*ìrw wšbt*) – or 'stringer together of a collar' – *seti nub* (*stì nbw*). Nevertheless, a recent study has identified less than thirty named men who bore the title over a period of fifteen hundred years, from the early New Kingdom to the end of the Ptolemaic Period, and no tomb of a *neshdy* has ever been discovered.

Although sculptors might become acquaintances of pharaoh, it would appear that the social standing of jewellery-makers was not high. One suspects that because of their close working contact with gold- and silversmiths the occupations were bracketed together, and the antisocial nature of metalworkers' activities was well known. Misleading reference has sometimes been made to goldsmiths who held court positions and owned splendid tombs, but without exception these men were noblemen

50 A broad collar (*wesekh*) of glazed composition beads and pendants, some of a dark purple colour from oxide of manganese, unusual before the 18th Dynasty. The terminals are pierced along the flat edge by six holes for the threads. Depth 18.3cm
From Deir el-Bahri, W. Thebes (pit 3). 11th Dynasty (*c*. 2020 BC)

or high-ranking officials whose other titles make it clear that the office of Chief of Goldsmiths was purely supervisory and administrative. A more accurate view of the metalworker's standing from the viewpoint of a privileged official is provided by the literary text known as the *Satire on Trades*, one copy of which is now in the British Museum (EA 10182). It was composed during the early 12th Dynasty by the scribe Khety son of Duauf, who pours scorn on all occupations except his own. He writes: 'I have seen the metalworker at his task at the mouth of his furnace. His fingers are like a crocodile's and he stinks more than fish roe'. It is highly probable, too, that an exquisite piece of jewellery, produced in a hot, dirty and noisy workshop, was quickly transferred from supervisor to supervisor, each appropriating the credit for its manufacture, until by the time it reached the great official in charge the identity of its maker was lost.

Barely a score of scenes of jewellery-making have survived from nearly three thousand years of Dynastic history and most of them come from tombs dating to the Old and New Kingdoms, with a single example each from the Middle Kingdom and Saite Period. Between them, however, they serve to illustrate just about every stage in the production of jewellery, either pictorially or through the graphic nature of the accompanying hieroglyphs. Even when the same activity is represented in more than one source, there are always subtle differences in detail. In almost every instance, too, the craft is practised alongside the working of precious metal.

One of the earliest undamaged illustrations of jewellery-makers at work, now in the Cairo Museum, is a painted low relief from the tomb of Kaemrehu at Saqqara; it dates to the 5th Dynasty (*c.* 2400 BC). Here are depicted all the daily activities which the tomb-owner would have witnessed in life and which he would have wished to be perpetuated in the Other World in order to recreate his supervisory office of Director of the Palace; among registers of baking and brewing, sculpting and metalworking two dwarfs work at a low table, threading beads onto a string to form a collar. Three completed examples of their work lie on another table. Amusingly, one of the dwarfs appears to be sucking the end of the thread in a gesture well-known to anyone who has had trouble threading a needle. Lest there be any misunderstanding, the hieroglyphs which accompany the scene describe their activity as 'stringing together a collar' – *seti nub* (*stì nbw*). Interestingly, the word *nbw*, as has been seen, actually means 'gold', but because gold was the choice material for collars, the word for the material from which the object was made has become a synonym for the object itself.

Even if the scene had been damaged, the mere presence of dwarfs would have been an immediate indication that jewellery-making was depicted, for in every Old Kingdom workshop where precious metal was shaped into personal adornment dwarfs are always on the roster of craftsmen. Perhaps it was to stress the link with the god Ptah, patron of craftsmen, who, according to Herodotus, could assume the form of the dwarfish patakoi. Perhaps, more prosaically, it was to ensure that these workers in precious metal would be easily caught if they chose to steal and try to run away on their short legs. Curiously, they no longer appear in scenes of metalworking after the Old Kingdom. What is noteworthy, however, is that in all European traditions workers in precious metal have a weakness in their lower limbs. According to classical mythology, Hephaestos, the divine smith, and his Roman equivalent Vulcan were both lame; in Teutonic legend the goldworkers *par excellence*, the Nibelungen, were dwarfs. Perhaps the origin of them all lies in ancient Egypt.

In the tomb of Khafre's son Nebemakhet at Giza, which dates to the end of the 4th Dynasty (*c.* 2500 BC), the deceased and his wife review another seated dwarf and his kneeling companion at work stringing a collar. Again, completed pieces of jewellery are depicted above them. To the left, however, a new activity is illustrated; unfortunately the scene is badly damaged. Two craftsmen face each other over a work-table. Only a leg survives of the figure on the left but the one on the right is intact. He sits on a stool with one foot on the ground and the other up on the table as though bracing himself; his right elbow is held high and pointing up. What he is working on is lost but it must have been a collar, for to the left another craftsman holds up a finished one for inspection to a supervisor who stands with folded arms, but what stage in its manufacture might he have been executing? The only task left between stringing beads and completion was the drawing together of the strings through a terminal at each end of the collar; however, the last thing needed for such an operation would have been force. There may just be some significance in the fact that this is the earliest known scene of jewellery production, and the activity depicted might have been dropped from the later repertoire; otherwise the scene remains unexplained.

The attachment of terminals to a collar is apparently depicted in the tomb of Nefer at Saqqara, which dates to the mid-5th Dynasty (*c.* 2400 BC). Below two dwarfs, one standing and holding up a collar while his squatting companion carefully adds beads to the other end of the string, squat two equally small craftsmen, their noses to the collar they hold between them as they carefully fit a falcon-headed terminal to each end of the string. Unusually, no metalworking is depicted anywhere in the tomb.

One of the more detailed and amusing scenes of jewellery-making during the Old Kingdom is found at Giza in the tomb of the high official Wepemnefret, dating to the later 5th Dynasty, just after 2400 BC. At the left of the lowest register, after scenes of metalworking, brewing, carpenting, sculpting and baking, four dwarfs are shown at work, and their conversations are recorded in the accompanying hieroglyphs. Two squat at a work-table, each holding the string of a collar onto which they are threading tiny, fancy-shaped beads; the end strings of collars were often decorated in this way with tiny bell or flower shapes. The one of the left says: 'Make haste with the collar to finish it'. His companion soothes his impatience: 'As Ptah loves you, I want to finish it today [too]'. The pair beyond them perch on high stools, their feet well off the ground. They are preparing stringing thread from two strands which they hold taut between them. The figure on the left speaks crossly to his fellow worker: 'Hold tight the stringing thread which is in our hand. You are delaying work which made a good start'. He is angry because his workmate is watching what the others are doing, his head turned back at an angle of 180 degrees, a posture possible only in Egyptian art. But the only answer he gets is: 'What is the matter? I am beside you'.

All these scenes are found in tombs of great courtiers who were buried at Giza and Saqqara near the pyramids of their kings, but jewellery-making was also depicted in the tombs of provincial noblemen, far away from the capital. At Sheikh Said, north of the future site of Akhenaten's capital at el-Amarna in Middle Egypt, the high official Serekfa had carved on the walls of his rock-cut tomb a scene in which three dwarfs string collars together and a fourth presents two completed pieces to a supervisor for inspection. The date is the mid-5th Dynasty.

It is at Saqqara, however, in the tomb of the Overseers of Palace Manicurists, Khnumhotep and Niankhkhnum, dating to the later 5th Dynasty, that a new stage of production is shown. Immediately beneath a register of goldsmiths at work are three scenes of jewellery-making; none of the craftsmen is a dwarf. At the right two men daintily string beads onto a collar, as the text above them confirms. They sit on high stools with one knee up, apparently to support an elbow, and the ends of the string hang over their wrists. To the left two craftsmen hold up a collar in a more advanced state of completion, for now a row of drop-shaped pendants has been added to it. It is the next operation, however, termed 'washing the collar' (*iat nub*, *i*ᶜ*t nbw*), which has led to some differences of interpretation. One craftsman is shown holding together in one hand the two ends of a completed collar, supporting it with the other over a wide-necked container; this catches liquid poured by his companion over the collar from a spouted vessel. It has been suggested the liquid is water to shrink the stringing threads and thus make the whole collar hang together more compactly but in that case immersion of the piece would have been more efficient. Gilding by the pouring of liquid gold can also be discounted; in any case that is depicted elsewhere, among scenes of metalworking, and the hieroglyphic term used is quite separate. Nor is the pouring of liquid unguent to scent the collar very likely. The only remaining suggestion is that the liquid is a dye-stuff or a means of imparting a glaze to the beads, which would thus have to be made from composition or stone rather than gold, or else it is a means of maintaining a shine on metal beads. In all these instances immersion would surely have been more effective.

In the tomb of Kairer at Saqqara, dating to the late 5th or early 6th Dynasty (*c*. 2350 BC), four dwarfs sit two by two on high chairs which leave their feet dangling. The two central figures hold up a completed collar between them while their companions raise for inspection two beaded counterpoises, which were attached to collars to counterbalance their weight and make sure they sat correctly positioned on the chest of the wearer.

Two registers of jewellery-making are depicted in the tomb of the vizier Ankhmahor at Saqqara, which dates to the early 6th Dynasty, a little after 2345 BC. Yet they form only part of what was once a great tableau of workshops, for supervision of the state-controlled industries was one of the duties of this most important official. For the first time the jewellery-makers work in a recognisable location: the normal-sized craftsmen on the ground floor are in a room whose ceiling is supported by elaborate lotus-form columns, whereas the dwarfs upstairs work in a cramped space under the low roof. For the first time too, work is depicted being carried out on the counterpoises worn as a complement to the broad collar. The dwarfs, working at benches in three groups of two, put the finishing touches to two counterpoises whose large scale is out of all proportion to the collar worked on by their fellows. Although the details are difficult to see clearly, one appears to be in the process of being polished, while the other is having a final row of drops strung along its lower edge. A third, huge, completed counterpoise is draped over another table. On the ground floor four craftsmen squat at low benches while they work on the counterpoises attached to two broad collars; behind them a supervising scribe keeps a tally on his papyrus scroll.

Some of the most superbly detailed jewellery is depicted in workshop scenes in the tomb of Mereruka at Saqqara. He was vizier to King Teti during the 6th Dynasty (*c.* 2340 BC) and in his case too the jewellery-making forms only part of a great tableau of sculptors, vase-makers, carpenters and metalworkers. Beneath a register of metalworking is depicted a frieze of completed pieces of jewellery comprising two chokers, three elaborate counterpoises, a diadem with three double lotus-head ornaments and two streamers, a broad collar with falcon-headed terminals and a pectoral with curved metal pieces for suspension and a falcon-headed clasp. In the lowest register similar articles are being completed. Two normal-sized workers, one of them greatly overweight, hold up a completed broad collar with falcon-headed terminals and an outermost row of pendants. Next to them two dwarfs stand to display a choker which is supported by a high table. 'It's very beautiful, mate', remarks one. Beyond them two more dwarfs sit putting the finishing touches to another keyhole-shaped pectoral with curved supports. 'Make haste and get it done', exhorts one, as his workmate wields a chisel to chase some last detail at its lower edge.

Interestingly, the Old Kingdom scenes illustrating other stages in the production of jewellery, unrecorded earlier, are found not in the tombs of palace officials at Giza and Saqqara but in provincial cemeteries far to the

51 Drawing of a relief scene in the mastaba of Mereruka, depicting the activities of a precious-metal workshop during the later Old Kingdom. A frieze of completed jewellery divides the upper register of metalworking from a lower register of jewellery-makers at work.

From Saqqara. 6th Dynasty (reign of Teti, *c.* 2340 BC)

52 Painted limestone relief showing the daughters of the provincial governor Djehutyhotep, each wearing a diadem with lotus-form attachments and knot with streamers, a pectoral on heavy bead straps and matching bracelets and anklets.

From the tomb of Djehutyhotep, el-Bersha. 12th Dynasty (reign of Sesostris I, *c.* 1930 BC)

south of Memphis. Presumably the provincial artists who decorated these tombs did not adhere to the strict repertoire of scenes drawn upon by those who worked in the capital's cemeteries.

Ibi was a very important provincial governor and local nobleman who served King Pepy II early in his long reign (about 2250 BC), and owned a rock-cut tomb at Deir el-Gebrawi in Middle Egypt, north of Asyut. In his tomb chapel, amid scenes of agriculture and marsh life, food and drink production, funerary ritual and leisure pursuits, the deceased sits in state, 'viewing every labour of the craftsmen's workshop and the activity of every craftsman inside and out'. The obligatory dwarfs are shown two by two finishing the threading of two broad collars, as the text makes plain, although the terms *menkh* (*mnḫ*) and *seti* (*stỉ*) are employed for what looks like the same activity. Because the scenes are painted the pieces are seen to be made from strings of red and green stone beads (presumably cornelian and feldspar or turquoise); only the semicircular terminals are probably made from gold. Completed collars, counterpoises and a pectoral with curved metal suspension pieces are depicted above them, and again the colouring makes it clear that the beads and inlays are of stone. Even more important, however, is the lower register, for here in a unique scene stone beads are being bored by hand-held drills. Two craftsmen squat holding steady in one hand the shaft of the drill, which is balanced on top of a large red-coloured bead. The other hand appears to pat the top of the drill handle, which suggests the piercing was done by glancing blows rather

53

than by a turning motion. The text labels the activity as 'cornelian being bored by lapidaries'. In the next scene two lapidaries polish cornelian by rubbing the beads across an abrasive block. Immediately beyond them the activities of the goldsmiths begin.

The high-ranking provincial governor Hemre, called Isi, who held office rather late in the reign of Pepy II (c. 2200 BC), also chose to have jewellery-making depicted in his rock-cut tomb at Deir el-Gebrawi. Immediately below two scenes of metalworking and, rather amusingly, next to the scene of a cow calving, two seated craftsmen hold up a completed broad collar by its tie strings; its two semicircular terminals are in position and it has an outermost row of red and blue drop pendants. The damaged hieroglyphs which label the scene have been read as the usual 'stringing together' but also as *sesher* (*sšr*), which means 'to overspread' or 'wash (with colour)'. If this is correct, then they must have been transposed in error with those above the next scene, for there two workers are holding what looks like the selfsame collar over a large cauldron in which they have obviously just immersed it, for streams of blue liquid drip from its lowest edge. Although the accompanying hieroglyphs are damaged they do not contain the term 'washing' (*iat*, *i*ʿ*t*), which was applied to the only other example of a similar activity, depicted in the tomb of Khnumhotep and Niankhkhnum at Saqqara. They seem rather to read *menkh wesekh* (*mnḫ wsḫ*), another expression for 'stringing together a broad collar'. Because the tomb-owner viewing this tableau stands to the right, by artistic convention the scene of immersion is to be understood as having taken place before the other jewellery-making scene. This makes the intepretation even more difficult: the multi-coloured pendants on the collar mean that the liquid cannot have provided a wash of colour or a shine on metal. Perhaps, as suggested earlier, it is a process to tighten up the stringing.

In his rock-cut tomb at Meir, north of Deir el-Gebrawi, the high-ranking local official Pepyankh, nicknamed Heni the Black, who also served Pepy II, is depicted viewing 'all the work of the craftsmen'. In a new version of the activity already shown in the tomb of Wepemnefret at Giza a crafts-man is seated on the ground, his legs stretched out before him, holding one end of a taut strip of material between his toes while he twists the other end between his two flat palms. The hieroglyphs state that he is 'twisting thread with fingers for the stringing of broad collars'. Before him on low tables are a splendid completed broad collar, two bracelets with

53 Drawing of a painted relief scene in the tomb of Ibi, a Middle Kingdom provincial nobleman, showing stone beads being bored, uniquely, by hand-held drills. The two craftsmen hold steady in one hand the shaft of the drill, which is balanced on top of a large red bead. The other hand appears to pat the top of the drill handle, which suggests that piercing was done by glancing blows rather than a turning motion. In the next scene two lapidaries polish cornelian by rubbing the beads across an abrasive block.

From Deir el-Gebrawi. 6th Dynasty (reign of Pepy II, c. 2250 BC)

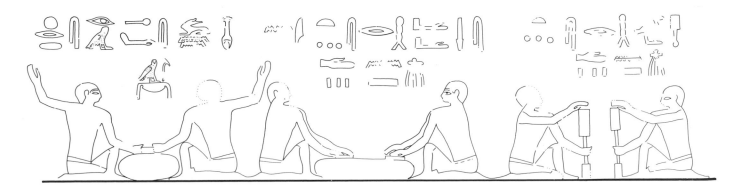

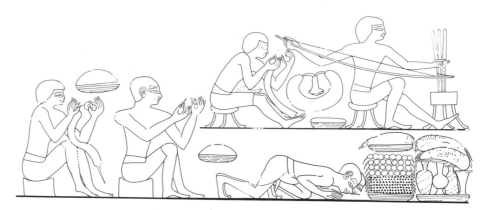

54 Drawing of a painted plaster relief in the New Kingdom tomb of the vizier Rekhmire, depicting a jewellery-makers' workshop. One craftsman sits working a triple-shafted bow-drill to perforate beads. The man behind bends to thread a bead onto a multiple string necklace. A completed broad collar with lotus-shaped counterpoise is between them. Behind are bead-stringers and at the front of the scene masses of multiple strings of beads are presented to the tomb-owner by two workmen in full obeisance.
From W. Thebes (tomb no. 100). 18th Dynasty (reign of Tuthmosis III–Amenophis II, c. 1435–1415 BC)

inlaid strips and an inlaid belt. The text reveals they are made of electrum and Upper Egyptian *wadj*, which can mean malachite but in this instance is more likely to be an unspecified green stone, such as feldspar or turquoise. Beyond, two jewellery-makers squat at a work-bench delicately stringing beads to the end of a collar, as the text confirms. Finally, two beaded counterpoises are offered to the tomb-owner for his inspection.

Although scenes of daily life abound in tombs of the Middle Kingdom, the only one to contain scenes connected with jewellery-making is that of Baqt III at Beni Hasan in Middle Egypt. He was a great provincial nobleman who supported the princes of Thebes during their struggle to defeat the Heracleopolitans and reunite Egypt at the end of the First Intermediate Period (c. 2050 BC). Here, among scenes of goldsmithing, one man works on a diadem with elaborate knots atop a tall stand; behind him a fellow craftsman works on a belt which he holds on a low bench. In both instances the hieroglyphs label the activity as *sekha* (*sẖˁ*), a word probably best translated as 'overlay with gold'.

The New Kingdom witnessed a revival in the depiction of jewellery-making. Puyemre was Second Prophet of Amun during the reign of Tuthmosis III (c. 1450 BC), an office which was particularly concerned with the administration of the workshops of the estate of Amun. In his tomb at Thebes, therefore, he had depicted the industrial activities with which he would have been well acquainted through his supervisory duties and among them is the production of jewellery. Two craftsmen, one seated on a low three-legged stool, the other perched on a box, work at a three-legged bench. Each uses a double bow-drill to perforate stone beads but, as only a single drill-head is shown, perhaps the second handle is there merely to provide a better grip. To the right a fellow worker appears to be buffing or polishing a worked object with a lump of some unspecified material. Unfortunately, the scene is damaged but the activity does seem to be related to the jewellery-making and not to the adjoining production of stone vessels. In the register above, completed pieces of jewellery include a broad collar with falcon-headed terminals, a row of drop pendants and elaborate counterpoise. Another splendid gold pylon-shaped counterpoise is joined by two strings of long beads to a pectoral in the shape of a winged scarab with a sun-disc on its head; it bears a striking resemblance to royal jewellery of the reign of Tutankhamun. Round about in baskets and boxes lie unworked lumps of green and blue material and completed single strings of ball beads which, from their colouring of red, green and blue, are presumably of cornelian or jasper, feldspar or turquoise and lapis lazuli, all interspersed with beads of gold.

As one of the viziers of Tuthmosis III, Rekhmire exercised control over all the great workshops of Egypt and duly recorded their activities on the walls of his tomb at Thebes. The construction of his tomb chapel is noteworthy for the strong upward slope of the side walls in its inner room and it is right at the top of one of them, just under the ceiling, that the jewellery-makers are shown. At their head a craftsman sits at a three- ₅₄ legged bench working a triple-shafted bow-drill. The beads he has perforated are presumably depicted in the shallow basket behind him; their greenish-blue colour indicates they are of lapis lazuli, turquoise or feldspar. Also behind him is a completed broad collar with lotus-shaped counterpoise, the work of a fellow craftsman who sits bent forward, intently threading a disc bead, its size out of all proportion so that it can be clearly seen, onto a necklace of multiple strings. A dish of beads ready for threading is balanced in his lap. Behind and below him two other bead-stringers are at work, both seated on box stools with concave tops for a snug fit. The one at the front is right at the start of his task, for he is attempting to thread the very first disc bead, which he holds delicately between thumb and forefinger. Behind him his companion has all but completed a collar of multiple strings to which he is adding a last truncated conical bead. The blue-coloured beads with which they are working are contained in two shallow baskets beside them and a third stands right at the back on a chest. At the front of the register two workmen 'sniff the ground', as the Egyptians so graphically describe full obeisance, behind various completed bored stone objects which are being presented for inspection to Rekhmire. They include three masses of multiple strings of beads coloured blue and eleven individual strings of ball beads, four of them large balls, the remainder small; all are coloured red and are therefore, presumably, of cornelian, since single strings of jasper beads are rare.

In the Egyptian collection of the British Museum is a wall-painting from a private Theban tomb of the New Kingdom which is usually identified as the tomb of Sobkhotep (TT 63), Mayor of the Southern Lake (the Egyptian name for the Faiyum) during the reign of Tuthmosis IV (c. 1395 BC). It is in two registers which come from the very top of the wall. In the uppermost ₅₅ two men sit boring holes in beads with quadruple bow-drills; at their feet, below the work-tables, are two footed goblets, one with a spatula, presumably containing an abrasive such as wet sand to aid the drilling. It has been suggested that this scene depicts not the drilling but the polishing of beads, by revolving them in the abrasive. However, that activity is clearly being carried out by the third man who sits before them, rolling the beads on a sloping wooden block. The five completed strings of beads depicted above him and those upon which he is working are all of cornelian, to judge from their red colouring. In the lower register more beads are being bored by a craftsman using a triple bow-drill and a number of finished strings are shown, the beads magnified in size so that their varied shapes can be seen: cornelian balls, conical beads and long truncated convex bicones are all identifiable. At the back a fellow worker puts the finishing touches to the stringing of an elaborate broad collar with

semicircular terminals. Behind him yet another multiple bow-drill is being
wielded. At the front of the fragment is depicted precious-metalworking:
only one complete figure survives, blowing down a pipe to raise the
temperature of the flames in the brazier around a piece of metalwork
which he holds by means of tongs. Above him are stacked completed
precious-metal objects including a silver lotus-shaped chalice, silver
dishes, gold jugs, a silver sistrum and gold *shebyu*-collars.

Amenhotepsise was Second Prophet of Amun during the reign of
Tuthmosis IV (c. 1395 BC), and, like his predecessor Puyemre fifty years
earlier, was depicted in his tomb at Thebes reviewing the activities of the
workshops of the temple of Amun, including the production of jewellery,
for which he held special responsibility. In the first such scene a craftsman
works a triple bow-drill to perforate beads of the type shown round about
him in four completed strings: they are all ball beads, some of gold, others
of a blue stone (probably lapis lazuli) and a few of red, possibly cornelian.
A new element is the small saucer balanced on the work-top; presumably
it held some abrasive. In the next scene a worker sits on a stool, leaning
slightly forward, one arm above, the other apparently supporting an
object now completely lost. At his feet stands a large footed goblet.
Depicted just above him is an elaborate necklace terminal in the shape of a
lotus-head, of a type whose details are usually picked out by means of
inlays in cloisons. A fellow worker faces him across a chest, on top of
which he holds up the top edge of a squared object. Above is depicted
a completed multi-stringed broad collar with terminals in the shape of
inlaid lotus-flowers and a matching counterpoise. The scene in

its damaged state would be almost unintelligible were it not for a virtually identical tableau in another Theban tomb which was decorated a generation later. It seems impossible that the scene in the tomb of Amenhotepsise was not used as the model for that in the tomb of Nebamun and Ipuky, who were royal sculptors during the reign of Amenophis III (*c.* 1370 BC). Was the same family of decorators responsible or did the tomb-owners unknowingly make their selection of scenes from the same master copy of tomb decoration?

In the latter tomb two craftsmen face each other over a fine chest whose colours show it was inlaid with ivory and ebony. The figure on the left, exactly like his counterpart in the tomb of Amenhotepsise, holds up the top edge of what is now seen to be the chest lid, with its characteristically sloping profile and knob at the front for the fastening cord. This enables a splendid piece of jewellery stored in the chest to become visible, for by artistic convention it appears to be standing vertically instead of lying flat as it would in reality. It takes the form of two cartouches naming King Amenophis III in brightly coloured inlays, flanking a child-like squatting figure apparently of lapis lazuli. Although no pectoral in this form has survived, the king as the new-born sun was a favourite motif in jewellery of the reigns of Amenophis III, Akhenaten and Tutankhamun. His colleague is now seen to be grinding two flat stones into inlays with the aid of the abrasive in the stemmed goblet beside him. A cloth hides from view a small dish of semi-precious stones intended for working lest their value and small size encourage pilfering in the workshop. Above are depicted completed examples of the inlayer's skill. A splendid pectoral formed from an open lotus-flower flanked by two buds, all inlaid with lapis lazuli,

56 Copy of a New Kingdom wall-painting from the tomb of Nebamun and Ipuky, depicting the weighing of gold, the grinding of stone inlays and the displaying of magnificent completed pieces of jewellery. The latter comprise broad collars with lotus-head terminals and counterpoise, a winged scarab pectoral, a lotus pendant on bead straps, an inlaid bracelet and two *mesketu*-bangles.

From W. Thebes (tomb no. 181). 18th Dynasty (reign of Amenophis III, *c.* 1370 BC)

turquoise and cornelian, is suspended from a double string of turquoise and cornelian cylinders interspersed with gold discs. Next to it is an ornament in the shape of a scarab, from its colouring feldspar, its vertical wings a mass of turquoise, lapis lazuli and cornelian inlays. Very similar pectorals date from the reign of Tutankhamun. 57

In a lower register, beyond a scene of smiths working foot bellows to stoke up a furnace, sits a craftsman who perforates stone beads using a triple bow-drill, just like his counterpart in Amenhotepsise's tomb. This time, however, the small saucer containing abrasive which stands on his work-table has a spatula for ease of application. The artisan next to him uses a weighted drill to bore a stone vessel but beyond him is another man bending intently over a collar with a curious appearance. It is perfectly semicircular and has no terminals, even though an elaborate inlaid lotus-flower example is shown above. This craftsman does not appear to be stringing beads, however, but instead is placing inlays; indeed, some small red and blue ones are shown loose in the collar's upper section, apparently awaiting setting. In this case the collar must be of solid metal – gold to judge from its colour – with inlays, a type depicted on temple walls for use in the daily ritual of the god's adornment. To the left the tomb-owner, on a superhuman scale, admires completed jewellery before it is put away in the chest waiting for it. A servant raises up a tray for inspection and on it lies a superb broad collar with alternating rows of lapis lazuli, turquoise and cornelian, separated by gold; the terminals and counterpoise take the form of an open lotus-flower with every petal inlaid. An identical collar appears in the upper register lying next to a large gold footed bowl. Also on the tray are two bangles, one of gold, the other of lapis lazuli with gold edging; they exhibit the characteristic convex profile between projecting rims, a shape well known from the monuments but surviving only in a few examples. Part of the regalia of an award, they are called *mesketu*-bangles. A third gold bracelet with bands of semi-precious stone inlay is almost identical with ones found in the burial of the minor 135 wives of Tuthmosis III.

The office of the Treasury Scribe Neferrenpet entailed the reception and listing of the products of the workshops of the estate of Amun during the reign of Ramesses II (*c*. 1250 BC), and that is exactly what the deceased is depicted doing in his tomb at Thebes. He is actually shown standing outside the workshops with his brush poised over his scribe's palette, about to make a note of the goods being brought to him. Although the tableau is damaged, two jewellery-makers can be seen drilling beads with multiple bow-drills. The one at the front, whom the hieroglyphs name as Chief Lapidary, *hery neshdy* (*ḥry nšdy*), is working a quadruple drill while his fellow worker, seated behind him, wields five drills at once, a record.

This is virtually the last depiction of the manufacture of jewellery to survive from ancient Egypt, although the Dynastic Period endured for more than a thousand years after this date. The only later example is found at Thebes in the tomb of the Chief Steward of the Divine Adoratrice Ibi, which dates to the reign of Psammetichus I of the 26th Dynasty (*c*. 650 BC), but it is in reality only a copy of a far earlier jewellery workshop depicted on the walls of the tomb of Ibi's namesake at Deir el-Gebrawi sixteen hundred years earlier.

57 Pectoral in the form of a green jasper heart scarab, from the mummy of Psusennes I. The underside is inscribed with Chapter 30B from the *Book of the Dead* to protect its owner when weighed in the balance to ascertain his worthiness to enter heaven. The vertical wings are inlaid with polychrome glass and the gold cartouche-shaped plaque above it spelling Psusennes' name with red jasper and polychrome glass. It stands on an inlaid *shen*-sign. All these details are repeated by chasing on the gold of the underside. Suspension is by a double string of drops of feldspar, red and green jasper and gold. L (scarab) 6.5cm
From the burial chamber of Psusennes, Tanis (tomb III). 21st Dynasty (*c*. 1039–991 BC)

The great tableau of industries in the Theban Ibi's tomb was originally in five registers and covered much of one of the long walls of the entrance hall. It is now badly damaged, but comparison with the copy made by J. G. Wilkinson in the early nineteenth century and what has survived to the present day shows craftsmen in exactly the same postures as those at Deir el-Gebrawi, using hand-drills to bore cornelian beads and polishing them by rubbing them across an abrasive block. Both scenes are labelled by exactly the same hieroglyphs as those used in the earlier tomb. In an upper register the four dwarfs of Deir el-Gebrawi have been metamorphosed into craftsmen of normal stature, and they now hold their two broad collars over chests rather than work-tables through a misinterpretation on the part of the later draughtsman. One change occurs in the hieroglyphs labelling the scene: whereas the original used the terms *menkh* (*mnḫ*) and *seti* (*stỉ*) for the activity of 'stringing' the collar, the copy uses only the first term, presumably because the writing of the second with its rarer hieroglyphic form was not understood. The two completed broad collars which are exhibited on a table at Deir el-Gebrawi are so stylised in the Theban version that they look more like tied-up pouches. Furthermore, a bead counterpoise in the original has become a mat at Thebes, and the pectoral, with curved neck surrounds, is now a pot with rounded base and long neck. Here it is obvious that the Theban copyist misinterpreted what he saw in the tomb in Middle Egypt.

One new detail does appear at the very top of the tableau, just above scenes of metalworking, although exactly what is depicted is not obvious. A large gold ring is handed by one small standing figure into the waiting arms of another larger kneeling figure, who bends intently over it. Behind, on a table watched over by a second kneeling figure, is a similar ring flanked by what look like two two-legged stools on their sides. It has been suggested that what is depicted on the table-top is a stack of gold rings, held in place by the stool-like supports. This would be a unique representation, but on analogy with depictions in the tomb of Baqt at Beni Hasan and an even earlier representation in the tomb of Khnumhotep and Niankhkhnum at Saqqara, it can be seen that the draughtsman was attempting to show a diadem with streamers, although again he has misunderstood his subject.

In spite of the small repertoire of scenes depicting the manufacture of jewellery, every aspect of the production of stone beads during the Dynastic Period is illustrated. Once a pebble had been selected or a suitable piece of material chipped from a larger lump, it was drilled to provide a stringing perforation, usually from top and bottom so that the boring produced is characteristically biconical, but sometimes it was drilled all the way through from one end so that a conical boring results. In Predynastic times a pointed flint or even a reed twirled between the hands, using an abrasive such as wet sand, would have been sufficient to drill soft stones. In Dynastic times, however, a drill with a copper or, later, bronze tip fed with an abrasive could bore even the hardest stones. In the only Old Kingdom representation of bead-boring, in the tomb of Ibi at Deir el-Gebrawi, the drill is hand-held and apparently used concussively. During the New Kingdom, however, stone beads are frequently shown being bored by multiple bow-drills; indeed, in one instance, in the tomb of

Neferrenpet, no less than five are depicted being wielded at the same time by one skilled craftsman. Such an operation would at first sight appear impracticable if not impossible for drilling purposes, especially as in most representations the bow-string is shown passing around the shaft not the handle of the drill and would thus provide little if any torsion. It is suggested, rather, that such scenes illustrate polishing by revolving the stones in a bed of abrasive material. However, in the wall-painting from the tomb of Sobkhotep one craftsman seated among the workers of 55 multiple bow-drills can be doing nothing other than polishing beads by hand. Indeed, his action is identical with that of bead-polishers in the tomb of Ibi at Deir el-Gebrawi who are specifically stated to be doing just this. Obviously the single hand-held percussive drill of the Old Kingdom had become a multiple bow-drill by the New Kingdom. Beads were always polished after they had been drilled not before, since during perforation they were prone to splitting, cracking or other damage and then earlier polishing would have been energy expended in vain.

The rather easier task of fashioning beads, amulets and jewellery elements from glazed composition and glass was in the hands of the craftsman called *baba* (*bˁbˁ*). Glazed composition cylinders and discs could be fashioned by cutting sections of an appropriate length from a long roll of the body material, formed around a thread or stick, which would be burned out during the firing to provide a stringing hole, or else formed around a hot wire which would contract on cooling, allowing its extraction. Barrels, balls, conical and cigar-shaped beads would entail some extra modelling between the fingers, while fancy shapes such as segmented or melon beads and amulets would need shaping with some sort of instrument. Flat-backed glazed composition amulets and, in particular, jewellery elements such as the characteristic floral pendants of the 105 Amarna period, as well as scarabs and ring bezels, were shaped by pressing into open terracotta moulds which have survived in their hundreds to illustrate pieces which are themselves no longer extant. While the body material was still soft a means of suspension was supplied by perforation or by adding a loop of composition. The well-known polychrome appearance of so many mould-made elements was achieved by painting different areas with different coloured glazes prior to firing.

None of the tomb scenes of industrial activities shows the production of glazed composition jewellery. Indeed, there appears to be only one representation of faience-makers at work and that has been identified with some hesitation. Found in the tomb of Ibi at Thebes, but without precedent in his namesake's tomb at Deir el-Gebrawi, it shows one squatting craftsman rolling a ball of material, possibly composition, in a basin while a fellow worker, perched on a cushion, works an elaborate ornament in the shape of a lily-head which, to judge from its colouring of yellow and blue, is probably to be understood as polychrome glazed composition. Moreover, behind him are four canopic jars and two *shabti*-figures which, at this period, would all have been made of glazed composition.

Glass beads were formed from a molten rod of material coiled around a wire and snapped off at the end, or by folding a thick cane, as long as the proposed bead, around a wire. Patterning could be achieved by trailing

58 Rigid gold vulture pectoral found on the mummy of Tutankhamun and certainly worn in life. Its cloisons are so closely fitted with polychrome glass inlays that it has been suggested that they represent the first example of true enamelling from Egypt. The feathering is chased on the underside. A repoussé pectoral with chain is depicted around the bird's neck. An articulated strap of alternating plaques of gold and lapis lazuli end in a clasp formed from two resting falcons in the round, the top surface inlaid with glass to imitate feathering. W 11cm

From the tomb of Tutankhamun, Valley of the Kings, W. Thebes. 18th Dynasty (*c.* 1336–1327 BC)

rods or canes of a different colour around the body material, by impressing glass of a different colour or even by forming the body material from canes of more than one colour sandwiched together. Glass amulets, fancy-shaped beads and elaborate inlays were made just like glazed composition examples, by pressing the molten material into a terracotta mould. Polychrome effects were achieved by impressing glass of different colours into the body material or pouring different coloured glasses together into the mould.

From the time of the New Kingdom inlays, which in earlier periods would have been shaped from semi-precious stones, were frequently made from glass. Indeed, in Tutankhamun's jewellery many of the inlays which appear to be red jasper, green turquoise or feldspar or dark blue lapis lazuli are actually glass coloured in imitation of these materials.

From employing glass as inlay within metal cloisons to enamelling, that is heating glass in powdered form to a point where it melts and bonds with the metal, would seem a small step. Surprisingly, though, there is no definite evidence for enamelling in Egypt before the Late Period, although the technique was employed elsewhere in the ancient world as early as the mid-second millennium BC. An attempt to identify enamelling in a single piece of Tutankhamun's jewellery, the splendid rigid vulture pectoral, has not met with general acceptance. Enamelling is, however, a feature of Meroitic inlaid jewellery.

Just about every metalworking technique known to the Egyptians was employed to fashion gold, silver, electrum, copper and bronze into beads, amulets, pendants, finger-rings, earrings, jewellery elements, applied decoration and chains. However, in tomb scenes depicting the activities of precious-metal workers, only a handful of these processes are ever illustrated and the object under manufacture is never a piece of jewellery. It is virtually only among the completed work of the jewellery-makers, who are always depicted somewhere in the vicinity, that metal jewellery appears.

A preliminary stage common to all scenes of metalworking was the weighing out of the ingots, blocks or rings of raw material before they were issued to the workers, while the scribe made a record of the tally. This was particularly important in the case of precious metal, which was undoubtedly reweighed when it had been manufactured to check that no scrap had been diverted for the craftsman's own use.

The one process which is always depicted is the melting of the metal, which involved a whole clutch of workmen, each blowing down a reed tube ending in a pottery nozzle to raise the temperature of the fire beneath a clay crucible. Because of artistic convention, however, it is often only the men nearest the fire who are shown with their blowpipes in the flames; all their fellows look rather as though they are blowing glass. There is some variation in the details of the crucibles in use during the Old, Middle and New Kingdoms. The scenes from the tomb of Kaemrehu contain a good example of the Old Kingdom type, which in this instance is supplied with air by two workmen, one of whom sits back on his heels to apply his blowpipe to the top, while his colleague goes down on one knee to blow near the foot of the flames. It has exactly the same appearance as the hieroglyph *ta* (*t3*), which has been identified as a potter's kiln but on this

59 Hinged gold armlet of Queen Amanishakheto, one of a pair, made in two sections with gold wire decoration and fused polychrome glass (enamel) inlays. The central strip has five panels on each half of the armlet, separated by horizontal feathering and containing a raised relief cobra. H 4cm
From the pyramid of Amanishakheto, Meroe. Meroitic Period (late 1st century BC)

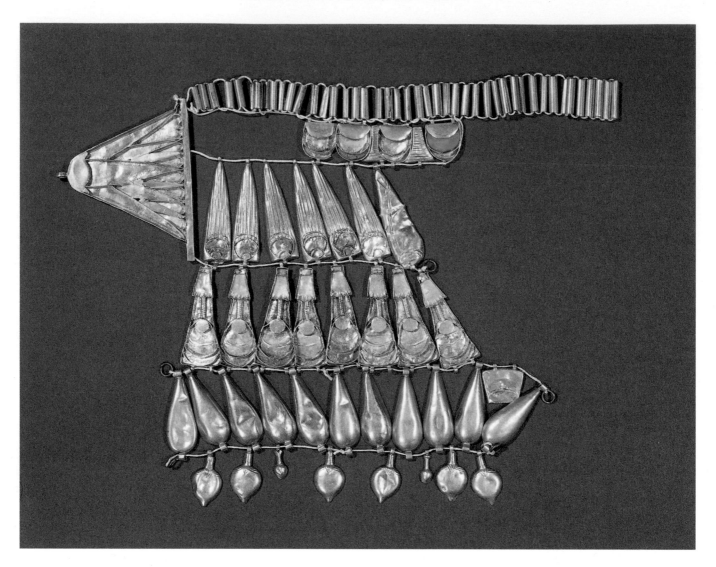

60 Part of a floral collar formed from gold inlaid elements. It illustrates the technique of cloisonné-work and the working of precious metal. The remaining inlays are of cornelian and blue glass. The terminals are in the form of a lotus, and the other shapes are folded leaves, papyrus flower-heads, leaves with mandrake fruits, buds with flowers, mandrake fruit, lotus-seed vessels and closed lotus-buds. H (as strung), 12.2cm
New Kingdom (*c.* 1370–1300 BC)

evidence is a round crucible with a side flue at the base. Scenes at Beni Hasan of Middle Kingdom date, however, show a trough-shaped crucible, as in the tomb of the nomarch Amenemhat, or else a deep-bowled crucible set within a trough-shaped hearth, such as that illustrated in the tomb of Baqt. During the New Kingdom a far shallower, dish-shaped crucible was employed in a trough-shaped hearth, but one improvement lay in the addition of a spout at its top edge to aid pouring.

The hieroglyphs which accompany metal-melting scenes in Old Kingdom tombs sometimes throw a little light on the processes involved. In the mastaba of Wepemnefret the four workmen are told to direct the air down to the base of the crucible, which is almost buried in a mound of charcoal. In the tomb of Khnumhotep and Niankhkhnum two crucibles are in use side by side, surrounded by leaping flames into which four kneeling workmen direct their blowpipes. An overseer with a stick, however, instructs one of them to get closer to the fire even though the air is hot. In the tombs of Ankhmahor, Mereruka and Isi the hieroglyphs read literally: 'It means a new pot'. Perhaps this is a reference to the constant need to replace the clay nozzles on the blowpipes; otherwise the sense is far from clear.

During the course of Dynastic history the only improvement in the process of melting metal was the introduction of the foot bellows which are depicted in New Kingdom tombs. They were operated by a workman marking time as he stood on a pair of bellows, each made from leather; a reed tube tipped with a clay nozzle passed into the flames. As the air was expelled from one leather sack the workman moved his whole weight onto the other foot and refilled the deflated bellows with air by pulling on a string attached to its top. Thus, as one bellows was filled with air, the other was emptied. Often a sole bellows worker stokes up the flames, as in the tombs at Thebes of Puyemre and the vizier Hapu, although in those of Menkheperresonb and Rekhmire two keep up their tiring tread. In the tomb of Nebamun and Ipuky, however, no fewer than four pairs of bellows are being worked to maintain the temperature of a veritable blast furnace.

When the metal had been reduced to a molten mass it was transferred in its crucible from the fire to a waiting mould. In New Kingdom representations the crucible is held between two flexible rods which appear to grip it above and below, although this is almost certainly artistic convention, for in order to have any control over the red hot bowl and its equally hot contents the rods must have gripped at each side. In Old Kingdom representations the characteristically shaped crucible is hand-held between two stones, which act as a shield from the great heat while the molten contents are poured into what, in most instances, appears to be a dish-shaped container; here, presumably, the metal hardened into a thin sheet. Where there are accompanying hieroglyphs, they usually describe the activity as *wedeh* (*wdḥ*), that is 'pouring out', but there is an interesting variant in the tomb of Pepyankh, nicknamed Heni the Black, at Meir. As the workman bends forward, pouring out the molten metal into a shallow dish, he addresses a fellow worker kneeling before him with his hand inside a pot: 'Let the water cool it', to which the other replies: 'I shall do as you wish'. Perhaps this is part of the cooling process, or it may show a first aid remedy for a burnt hand!

The most elaborate pieces of metal jewellery could be manufactured by the *cire-perdu* or lost-wax method of casting. The object to be cast was first modelled in wax and this matrix was covered with a thick mud casing. When it had dried it was pierced, the wax was heated until it melted and was allowed to run off so that it left a closed mould into which the molten metal could be poured. If the piece was to have a core to save precious metal, a more common practice with large-scale metalwork than with jewellery, the wax matrix was modelled around a mud or plaster core. This was held in place when the wax was melted by pins, which passed through the outer casing of the mould. Since the mould had to be broken open to extract the casting, the lost-wax process did not allow mass-production. One of the earliest solid-cast jewellery elements made by this process is the body of a gold falcon amulet on a necklace found in a 4th Dynasty grave at Mostagedda. Although the lost-wax casting method continued to be used sporadically in jewellery-making throughout the remainder of Dynastic history, its most characteristic employment was

62a

61 Detail of an electrum cowrie clasp, showing the tongue-and-groove closing device on the underside. See 39a for the complete string. L (clasp) 2.7cm

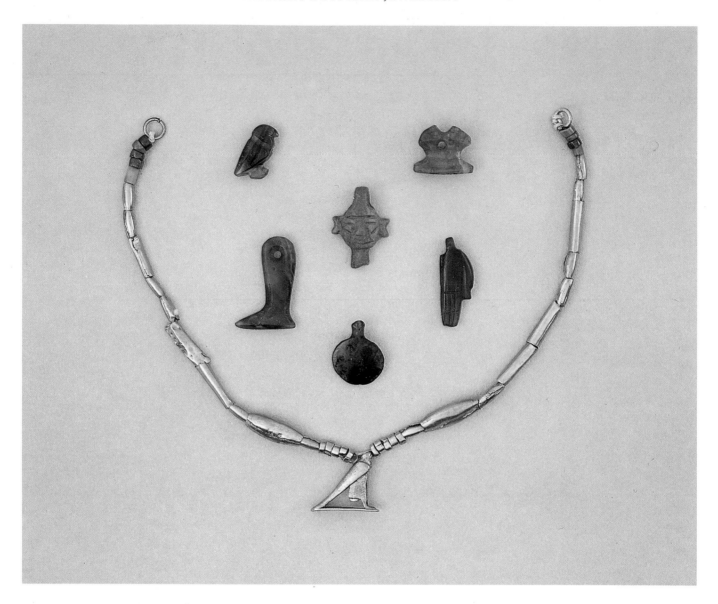

62 Group of gold and stone amulets.
   a The gold falcon amulet, with solid cast body, part of a necklace of gold and turquoise beads, was perhaps connected with Chapter 77 of the *Book of the Dead*. L 17.4cm
   b–g Amethyst falcon; cornelian double lion; pink limestone face; cornelian leg with foot; cornelian hand; green jasper turtle. They were intended to endow the wearer with their earthly faculties and confer on them the protection of powerful deities or divine powers. H 1–1.9cm
   a: From the burial of a woman at Mostagedda (grave 312), 4th Dynasty (*c.* 2550 BC); b–g: Old Kingdom–1st Intermediate Period (*c.* 2300–2100 BC)

during the New Kingdom and later in the manufacture of massive metal finger-rings in which the shank and bezel were made in one piece. Although there is no reason why open-backed moulds should not have been used to make precious-metal jewellery elements, their individual use was virtually restricted to the production of flat-backed amulets, the earliest being the gold *serekh* beads in a bracelet from the tomb of King Djer at Abydos. However, two- or even three-piece open moulds made of stone or terracotta were used to make earrings and finger-rings with separate bezels from as early as the New Kingdom. 10

If the metal was produced in sheet form, it was worked further by beating over a flat stone or wooden block with a hand-held rounded stone hammer. This activity, depicted in nearly every tomb of Old and Middle Kingdom date which contains scenes of metalworking, was usually labelled simply *seqer* (*sḳr*) that is 'striking', an apt description; sometimes, too, the metal being worked, such as gold or electrum, was named. In addition, in the tombs of Wepemnefret and Ti the conversation between the beaters is given, and both describe the metal as 'cooking', an amusing reference to the fact that intensive beating would indeed cause it to grow hot to the touch.

It was in sheet form of various thicknesses that gold, silver or electrum, less often bronze or copper, were most frequently employed in the manufacture of jewellery and jewellery elements at all periods of Egyptian history. Hollow metal bangles of circular section and, of course, beads were made by the simple process of bending the metal strips or, if necessary, shaping them around a wooden block of suitable profile. In early examples of this technique, such as the tiny gold ring beads in a Predynastic diadem from Abydos, the open ends were frequently not soldered together, but merely turned up towards each other. This was still the practice some six hundred years later, to judge from the gold cylinder and bicone beads strung with a falcon amulet. Soldering the join, however, was far more common and, indeed, indispensable when extra strips of metal needed to be attached, as in the case of the fourth face of a square-sectioned bangle or spacer-bar, or in the provision of cloisons for inlays.

At first the Egyptian goldsmith probably joined gold to gold by using as solder the compound of gold and silver called electrum; the silver would have had the effect of lowering the melting point of the compound. However, Egyptian gold naturally contains a proportion of silver (often quite high – up to 20%), so whether the solder would actually have melted before the pieces it was meant to join would have been a very hit or miss affair. Moreover, even if the join were successful, the solder was liable to be noticeably paler in colour. If copper was used in the solder though, its

63

31

62a

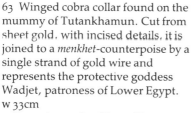

63 Winged cobra collar found on the mummy of Tutankhamun. Cut from sheet gold, with incised details, it is joined to a *menkhet*-counterpoise by a single strand of gold wire and represents the protective goddess Wadjet, patroness of Lower Egypt. W 33cm

From the tomb of Tutankhamun, Valley of the Kings, W. Thebes. 18th Dynasty (*c.* 1336–1327 BC)

melting point would not only be lowered quite drastically but the solder itself would be less pale in colour and consequently less conspicuous. By the Middle Kingdom Egyptian goldsmiths were producing solders of different colours and melting points to meet their requirements by mixing copper with gold or silver. If a flux were needed to improve the fusion of the metals then use was almost certainly made of natron, a naturally occurring sodium compound. However, by far the most common, and most successful, method of joining together metalwork jewellery was colloidal hard soldering, whereby the copper was present in a compound such as malachite which, when ground up, could be applied just to that part of a tiny and delicate piece where it was required. Moreover, if it was mixed with glue it would even hold parts in position until the metal melted. There cannot be much doubt that soldering is the very process depicted in a number of New Kingdom tomb scenes. In those of Rekh- 55 mire, Sobkhotep, Amenhotepsise, Nebamun and Ipuky and Kayiry the craftsman sits at an individual brazier holding his work in the flames by means of tongs while he directs his blowpipe to the relevant point. In other representations, however, such as those in the tombs of Puyemre and Hapu, he has to bend down or kneel to work with blowpipe and tongs in the glowing charcoal embers lying in a trough-shaped hearth.

A technique of decoration in which colloidal hard soldering played an essential role – and which in Egypt is almost unique to jewellery – is granulation, whereby hundreds of tiny gold or, less often, silver granules were attached to the surface of precious-metalwork to form patterns. The earliest examples known from Egypt occur in the jewellery of Khnumet 64 and date to the 12th Dynasty. This suggests that the technique was introduced from abroad, for granulation had first been produced in Mesopotamia more than half a millennium earlier. The patterns achieved might be simple chevrons, like those on a hollow gold cylinder amulet, 155a which, nevertheless, is extremely fine work, having no less than eight granules to each half centimetre of decoration. They might, on the other hand, be extremely elaborate, like the lozenge and rosette patterns on the duck bracelets of Ramesses II from Tell Basta. What is still not clear is how 67 such uniformity in the size of the granules was achieved before the introduction of shears to cut up metal strips into tiny pieces. It is uncertain whether the granules were formed by heating such scraps until surface tension rolled them into spheres or by dripping molten metal into water. Another incredibly time-consuming method might have involved sifting gold dust to find naturally formed grains of similar size. The applied decoration known as beaded wire is now generally believed to have been made by joining granules together before attaching them wire-like to a surface.

One of the most characteristic techniques employed by the Egyptian jewellery-maker was cloisonné, whereby inlays of semi-precious stone, glass or glazed composition were inset into metal. As early as the beginning of the 4th Dynasty the silver bangles of Queen Hetepheres were 21 inlaid with butterfly designs of cornelian, turquoise and lapis lazuli, but the technique was not true cloisonné, for the inlays are set into recesses impressed into the metal. In true cloisonné the inlays are fitted and cemented into place in openwork cells formed by soldering metal strips at

64 Detail of gold wire and granulation pendants belonging to Khnumet. The openwork star-shaped pendants are outlined with tiny gold granules and joined by wire chains to the central circular medallion, which is of blue frit painted with a recumbent cow; the whole is set into a gold frame with a rock-crystal cover. D (medallion) 2.85cm

From the tomb of Khnumet, Dahshur. 12th Dynasty (reign of Ammenemes II, c. 1895 BC)

65 Egyptian royal jewellery of the Middle Kingdom and 2nd Intermediate Period (*c.* 1795–1590 BC): **a** ajouré gold plaque showing Ammenemes IV offering unguent to Atum; **b** two bracelet spacer-bars crowned by reclining cats, with twelve threading tubes; the inscription on the base names Nubkheperre Inyotef and his wife Sobkemsaf; **c** gold finger-ring with lapis lazuli bezel, naming Inyotef on the gold funda; **d** human-headed green jasper heart scarab of Sobkemsaf II, a roughly incised verse of Chapter 30B from the *Book of the Dead* around the gold plinth. L (heart scarab) 3.6cm

Above 66 King as newborn sun on inlaid lotus; suspended from a loop-in-loop gold chain. H 7.2cm
19th Dynasty (reign of Ramesses II (?), *c.* 1279–1213 BC)

right angles to the surface of a sheet-metal base to form a series of boxes, or cloisons. Although the technique was known during the 5th Dynasty, its earliest use in jewellery-making was in the two drop-shaped pendants found in the pyramid of Queen Iput, wife of the 6th Dynasty King Teti (*c.* 2330 BC). It is the cloisonné work of the 12th Dynasty, however, which marks the apex of the Egyptian jewellery-maker's art. Notable examples are to be found in the treasures of the princesses at Dahshur and Lahun, with lapis lazuli, cornelian, turquoise and feldspar cut exactly to fit snugly in cloisons to form intricate designs and scenes. The technique was still employed extensively in Tutankhamun's jewellery and again in that of the royalty buried at Tanis, but in the former the inlays are predominantly of glass or glazed composition, and in the latter, although precious stones are employed, more often there is an over-reliance on large inlays of lapis lazuli. However, in the Late Dynastic Period there was something of a revival in the craft, to the extent that stone inlays were sometimes used as well as polychrome glass. The cloisonné technique of inlaying was also employed to set ring bezels of semi-precious stone, glazed composition or glass in a box-like funda.

Since the Egyptian goldsmith did not have shears or fine saws to cut metal, the technique of ajouré, that is cutting out from sheet metal, is found relatively rarely in an unadorned form, although it is the method used to produce the base plates of openwork metal pectorals to which

68 Gold pylon-shaped pectoral of Amenemope, made from two metal sheets with a filling between. The scene of Amenemope raising incense before Osiris is incised on one side (illustrated here), and worked in repoussé on the other. It is suspended from a loop-in-loop gold chain. H 8.9cm; TH 0.4cm

From the burial chamber of Amenemope, Tanis (tomb III). 21st Dynasty (c. 993–984 BC)

69 Openwork gold cloisonné pectoral, the inlays now lost, showing a seated Set-animal and a falcon-headed sphinx flanking a *Bat* beneath *udjat*-eyes and a sun-disc. At each side a drooping papyrus-head acts as a support. Undoubtedly the protection of Set and Horus as patrons of Upper and Lower Egypt is represented. H 3.8cm

From Dahshur? 12th Dynasty (c. 1900–1800 BC)

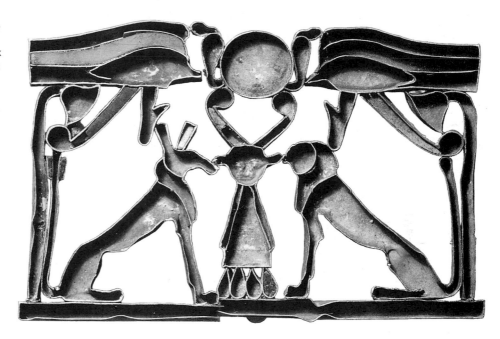

Left 67 Pair of rigid hinged gold bracelets with applied wire and granulation. The upper section, with retractable pin at one end, is inset with the lapis lazuli body of a two-headed duck. The cartouche behind it contains the prenomen of Ramesses II. The remainder of the bracelet has alternating plain and ribbed half-cylinders; the inner face is plain. D (max) 7.2cm

From Tell Basta. 19th Dynasty (Ramesses II, c. 1279–1213 BC)

cloisons and additional details were subsequently soldered. It involved the separation of the design by a chisel alone, punching out around an outline. An early example is a gold plaque showing King Ammenemes IV of the 12th Dynasty offering unguent to Atum, Lord of Heliopolis, god of the setting sun. Additional details were provided by chasing. Tutankhamun owned four red-gold ajouré buckle-shaped plaques. One depicts him enthroned, protected by Maat and being offered a sphinx by Atum. In another he and his wife take their ease in a garden setting. A third has a scene of wild bulls attacked by a lioness and the fourth depicts the king as warrior in his chariot. All owe their details to chasing and extensive granulation.

65a

73

70 Gold flying falcon in the round, its back a mass of cloisons once inlaid with polychrome glass, probably red, blue and green, but now much decayed. w 14.8cm

   Saite Period or later (after 600 BC)

Chasing is the indentation of details in metal using a blunt-edged chisel tapped by a mallet; rather importantly when precious metal is involved, it does not entail any loss of material, which is merely pushed aside. Originally, of course, this displaced metal formed a ridge at the top edges of the indentation but wear would usually erode it. This fact, coupled with a general lack of microscopic examination, has often led to confusion between chased and engraved decoration. Engraving, however, involves the gouging out and removal of material and was not practised on metal in Egypt before the introduction of iron tools during the course of the later New Kingdom. Chasing, on the other hand, and its complementary technique, repoussé, played an essential part in jewellery-making in Egypt from as early as the 1st Dynasty: both techniques were employed in the manufacture of gold amulets from Nag ed-Deir.[11]

Repoussé is the working of a design into sheet metal from the back so that the pattern appears as raised relief on the top surface; clarity of detail can be provided subsequently by chasing into the raised top surface, this time from the front. In both techniques the metal needed to rest against a yielding surface; probably just mud or plaster was adequate, although beeswax and resin were also used. At first repoussé was produced free-hand using variously shaped punches, and this was the method by which the finest-quality work was always executed. However, if a repetitive design was the aim, it was quickly realised that it was easier to make a stone or metal die into which the design had been previously incised or on

which it was already carved in raised relief or even in the round. The twenty-four gold shell-shaped pendants found in a 1st Dynasty burial at Nag ed-Deir were certainly made by hammering into a mould. On the other hand, raised relief models or formers were more a feature of precious-metal jewellery-making during the Late Dynastic and Graeco-Roman Periods: a collection of goldsmith's tools of Ptolemaic date from Galjub in Egypt contained bronze formers on which the two hollow halves of animal-headed terminals, so characteristic of Hellenistic jewellery, would have been produced.

11a

76

Even before the beginning of the 1st Dynasty the Egyptian jewellery-maker was able to make sheet gold sufficiently thin to gild other materials, yet the process of gilding is depicted in only two tombs and the production of gold leaf in only one. At Beni Hasan, among goldworking scenes in the tomb of the 11th Dynasty governor Baqt III, one craftsman sits before a curiously shaped apparatus from which he removes a strip of gold leaf and hands it to another worker who is gilding a wooden shrine. The operation is called *redit nub* (*rdìt nbw*), 'placing gold'. The equipment in which the leaf is being produced has been interpreted as a basin-shaped stone mould with a narrow groove running lengthwise down the middle. A strip of gold foil placed in the groove could be turned into leaf by the action of rocking back and forwards a hand-held stone which fitted the basin exactly. Beyond the shrine and facing away from it is another figure, this time accompanied by the hieroglyphs *redit nub er sesher* (*rdìt nbw r sšr*), 'placing gold in order to gild'. He holds his hand outstretched to two pairs of goldworkers in two registers, each sitting around what looks like a deep container with a flat base and recurved sides. If the object is indeed a container perhaps they are soaking the gold leaf in some liquid to make it adhere to the wood of the shrine. Another suggestion, however, is that the object is not a container but the characteristically shaped cavetto cornice of a lid or roof, perhaps of the nearby shrine. In this case the accompanying hieroglyphic label *sesher* (*sšr*) refers to the gilding of this object. At any rate, the same term is applied to the two craftsmen depicted

71 The reverse of the pectoral (69) illustrated on p. 91, showing the chased details which repeat the cloisonné scene of the upper face. H 3.8cm

below the maker of gold leaf who are obviously gilding a staff and sceptre. Exactly the same operation with the same hieroglyphic label is shown in the mastaba of Khnumhotep and Niankhkhnum at Saqqara over three hundred years earlier. There too a sceptre and staff are being gilded and, in addition, gold leaf is being applied with the fingers to the belt-buckle and triangular starched linen apron of the tomb-owner's ceremonial kilt. In a nearby scene two funerary diadems adorned with elaborate knots are being created, apparently from foil alone: in the accompanying hieroglyphic text they are said to be 'created' not 'gilded'.

Further scenes of goldworking in the tomb of Baqt depict a craftsman working on what is generally interpreted as two diadems with elaborate knots, atop a tall stand; behind him a colleague works on a belt which he holds on a low bench. A form of gilding is clearly involved but the text labels the activity as *sekha* (*sh'*), not *sesher*, as in the nearby scenes of overlaying with gold leaf. Moreover, it has been noted that in both instances an extraneous hieroglyph, normally the ideograph for copper, has been written immediately after the word *sekha*. Perhaps the process depicted is the gilding of copper with gold leaf by burnishing and heating, rather than overlaying with gold leaf by means of an adhesive. In fact, the latter technique, because of its poor durability, would only have been suitable for funerary jewellery and, interestingly, the jewellery being covered with leaf, according to the text in the tomb of Khnumhotep and Niankhkhnum, has just this function. On the other hand, for jewellery which was to be subjected to any kind of wear, gilding by burnishing gold leaf onto the surface of a second metal and heating gently – a technique which has been termed diffusion bonding – would have been essential. A bangle from a burial at Badari and an amulet in the shape of an ibis found in a grave at Hamamiya prove that copper was being overlaid with gold at least as early as the First Intermediate Period. A pair of bracelets of 11th Dynasty date, excavated at Deir el-Bahri, are of gilded silver tubes. 77a Presumably all were manufactured by the same diffusion bonding process, for there is no concrete evidence that the Egyptians of this period had any knowledge of fire-gilding.

A form of overlaying seems to have produced the very characteristically coloured metal known as red gold. Although Egyptian gold naturally exhibits a range of colours through impurities and chemical change, red gold was certainly an artificial creation. It can be seen most clearly in some of the flower elements forming the circlet of Queen Tausret and in the 13 winged sun-disc on the elaborate ear-plugs of Ramesses XI. Although it 94 was originally noted on a number of pieces of jewellery from the tomb of Tutankhamun, notably the ajouré plaques, it is no longer extant on all of 73 them. It is still not absolutely certain how the effect, which is caused by a surface film of iron, was obtained, although it has been duplicated by heating and hammering gold mixed with iron sulphide, that is iron pyrites or 'fool's gold'.

Another decorative use of precious metal, almost exclusive to jewellery of Middle Kingdom date, is the shaping of gold or silver foil into caps for beads. Either the metal was wrapped around the perforations and glued into place, as in the case of the gold caps on strings of cornelian and amethyst convex bicones now in the British Museum or else the metal foil 74

72 Pectoral of Queen Kama, comprising a large inlaid lapis lazuli plaque carved with a ram-headed Amen-Re crowned by a gold sun-disc, squatting above an inlaid lotus-head flanked by two standing gilded silver goddesses in repoussé. The same details are repeated by chasing on the gold of the underside. H 11.7cm

From the burial of Kama, Tell Moqdam. 23rd Dynasty (reign of Osorkon III, *c.* 760 BC)

73 One of Tutankhamun's red gold ajouré plaques with chased and granulation details. It depicts the king in his chariot protected by the vulture Nekhbet and winged cobra Wadjet and preceded by Nubian and Semitic captives. In the scene below the sign for unification is flanked by a bound Semite and Nubian and the floral symbols of Upper and Lower Egypt. L 8.5cm

From the tomb of Tutankhamun, Valley of the Kings, W. Thebes (*c.* 1336–1327 BC)

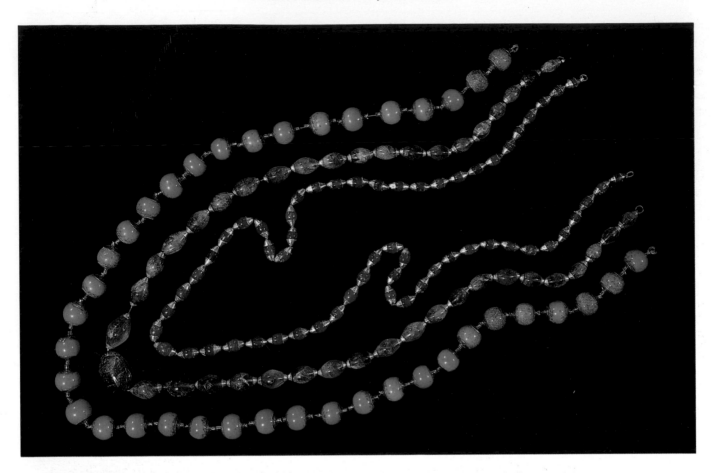

74 Strings of metal-capped beads of Middle Kingdom date (*c*. 1900–1800 BC); **a** bright-blue glazed composition, capped with silver; **b** graduated amethyst beads capped with gold, with an uninscribed amethyst scarab; **c** graduated cornelian beads capped with gold. L (**c**) 74cm

was soldered onto a tube which fitted into the perforation: this is the method used for the silver caps on a string of blue glazed composition ball beads.

There is no evidence that the Egyptians knew how to draw wire. Hammering would certainly have produced wire which was roughly circular in section but to have made wire of regular circular section from metal strips the techniques of strip-twisting or block-twisting were employed. By the first method a ribbon of metal cut from a sheet was coiled into a hollow tube in the manner of a drinking straw; the spirals would then be compressed into a solid rod by rolling between two flat surfaces, although more often than not strip-twisted wire remained partly hollow. If examined under a microscope wire made by this method has a single spiral seam. In block-twisting the original ribbon was first twisted on itself like a barley-sugar stick before being rolled into a solid rod. This form of production is characterised by a double spiral seam. To make wire of regular square section the technique of swaging was used by which a metal rod was struck between two grooved metal or stone blocks.

The gold or silver wires manufactured by these methods were employed in a variety of ways. During the 12th Dynasty, even in royal jewellery, an individual wire threaded through a scarab could form the plainest of shanks for a finger-ring. In the New Kingdom plain wire passed through the loops of glass earrings provided a means of suspension for use with pierced ears. A bangle in a burial of the First Intermediate

96

75 Openwork gold wire circlet and hair ornaments of Senebtisy. The hair ornaments consist of ninety-eight gold rosettes imitating marguerites, made by beating into two different moulds. Some have a bar soldered at the back, others are pierced by two holes for a thread. All were attached to individual tresses. D (rosettes) 1.1cm

From the burial of Senebtisy, Lisht. 12th Dynasty (reign of Ammenemes I, *c.* 1975 BC)

76 Three metal bangles of the Graeco-Roman Period (*c.* 100 BC–AD 100); **a** cast silver with lion-head protomes. D (max) 6.5cm; **b** gold, made from two sheet-metal strips twisted together, with additional wire. D (max) 8.3cm; **c** gold, made from wire coiled around a core, with snake-head terminals. D (max) 7.2cm

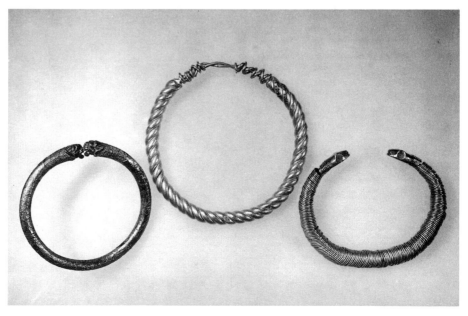

Period at Mostagedda was made from two gold wires looped into a reef 77c
knot. In a more sophisticated example of 11th Dynasty date from Deir
el-Bahri, two silver wires, soldered together for part of their length, were
provided with push-fit ends. In the Graeco-Roman Period wire was coiled
around a core to form characteristic bangles with hollow animal-headed 76c
terminals.

Plain wire also formed a distinctive element in the attachment of the
bezels in two-part finger-rings. Usually it had an essential function, for it
passed through the bezel and was wrapped around either end of the
shank, thus securing the two elements together but allowing the bezel to
rotate on its axis so that the ring might function as a seal. Sometimes,
however, wire that appears to have been added was in fact hammered out
from one end of the shank, passed through the bezel and wound around
the opposite end of the shank. For decorative purposes simple gold or
silver wire could be applied to a precious-metal surface in the technique
known as filigree. This was the method used during the 12th Dynasty to
decorate a gold oyster-shell amulet with the prenomen of Sesostris III and
an electrum example with that of Ammenemes III, his successor. The use
of plain wire, often of different diameters, was also the essential feature of
ajouré filigree work, exemplified by the elaborate openwork beads and
cornflower pendants on a necklace of Queen Tausret, found in tomb 56 in 110
the Valley of the Kings.

A far more frequent decorative use involved plaiting together two wires
into a rope, which was then employed as a decoration for the rims of ring
bezels and bangles or to mask the seam on metal earrings. Two such ropes
laid side by side formed the even more elaborate and characteristic
rope-braid applied decoration. A type of beaded applied wire which first
occurs during the New Kingdom was probably made by soldering the
granules together to form a strip which was then attached to the metal
surface. However, it has also been suggested that it could have been made
mechanically by notching with a suitably shaped tool.

77 Metal bangles of the First
Intermediate Period and 11th Dynasty:
a (*top*) a pair of silver-gilt tubular
bangles, closed by a push-fit device; **b**
(*bottom*) a second pair of bangles, each
formed from two tubular silver wires
joined together for part of their length,
with a similar closing device; **c** (*centre*)
an open bangle, found on a woman's
wrist, composed of two gold wires
looped together into a reef knot.
D (**a**) 8cm
   a & **b**: From Deir el-Bahri (pit 3);
c: Mostagedda (grave 544)

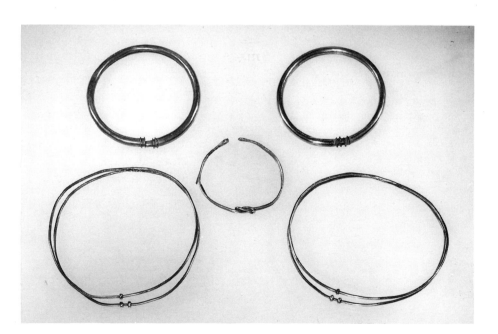

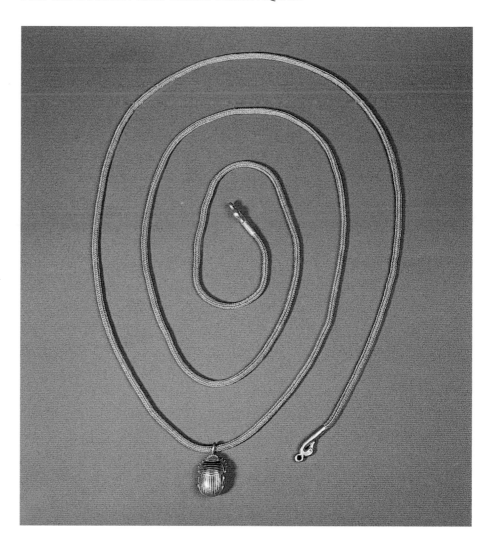

78 Amuletic necklace of Queen
Aahhotep. From a six-ply loop-in-loop
gold chain, ending in two ducks'
heads, hangs a gold scarab, made in
two halves from thick sheet gold, its
back inlaid with lapis lazuli strips in
cloisons. L (chain) 202cm, (scarab) 3cm
From the burial of Aahhotep, Dra
Abu Naga, W. Thebes. 18th Dynasty
(reign of Ahmose, c. 1540 BC)

Perhaps the most characteristic use of precious-metal wire in Egyptian
jewellery was in the production of chains of the loop-in-loop variety,
although some simple plain links were also employed. The links were
made initially by coiling wire around a rod and cutting it longitudinally.
For simple link chains the resultant open hoops were interlinked before
being soldered shut; for loop-in-loop, the pre-soldered oval hoops were
bent into the shape required, whether double straps or figure-of-eight,
before being linked one through the next. No further soldering was
required and the most elaborate effects could be achieved by interlocking
two, three, four or even six loops, so much so that the resultant chains
with their herringbone effect have often been mistakenly referred to as
plaited. Two-ply loop-in-loop gold chains were used in royal jewellery of
the 12th Dynasty; Queen Aahhotep's gold scarab was suspended by a   78
superb six-ply chain. An equally spectacular chain came from the tomb of
Tutankhamun, suspension for the small gold squatting royal figure.   109
Loop-in-loop chain continued to be used during the Ramesside Period; it   66
was found in the royal burials at Tanis and, to judge from Queen
Amanishakheto's treasure, it was still being produced by Meroitic goldsmiths in the first century BC.

CHAPTER FOUR

Diadem to choker: ornaments for the head and neck

A circlet for the head and rings for the ears

Every Egyptian, male and female, from the meanest peasant to pharaoh himself, could and did wear jewellery. Some forms of adornment, such as earrings, appeared surprisingly late; others, for example torques, never seem to have gained popularity and only sporadic examples occur before the Coptic Period. Some forms were popular at one time and not at another: openwork glazed composition 'wedding-band' finger-rings are characteristic of the Third Intermediate Period.

The most basic types of Egyptian jewellery were in general established in form by the end of the Old Kingdom, though they are often known only through representations when no actual examples have survived. Great care also needs to be exercised in drawing too many conclusions from the present appearance of Egyptian jewellery. When the earliest finds were made little care was taken to record exactly where each individual element

Left 79 Painted wooden anthropoid coffin lid of the Chantress of Amun Katebet, depicted wearing a choker, ear-studs, broad collar, pectoral and bracelets.
From Thebes, 18th–19th Dynasties (*c.* 1330–1250 BC)

Right 80 Copy of a New Kingdom wall-painting showing the tomb-owner Nakht and his family fowling in the marshes. The deceased wears a broad collar and matching bracelets, as do his wife and older daughter. In one half of the scene his younger daughter wears a collar and girdle, bracelets and anklets and heavy gold earrings, like those of her older sister. In the other his little son wears earrings and bracelets and a cloisonné lotus-shaped pectoral on beaded straps.
From W. Thebes (tomb no. 52). 18th Dynasty (reign of Tuthmosis IV, *c.* 1395 BC)

81 Detail of a painted limestone statue of Princess Nofret, wife of Rahotep, who wears over her thick wig a coloured diadem, clearly meant to represent a silver band studded with inlaid roundels and leaf patterns. Her broad collar represents rows of semi-precious stone beads, with an outermost row of drop-shaped pendants.

From the mastaba of Rahotep and Nofret, Meidum. Early 4th Dynasty (reign of Sneferu, *c.* 2610 BC)

lay, so restringing in correct original order has rarely been possible. Thus the amuletic collar of Queen Aahhotep can probably never be satisfactorily reconstructed. However, thanks to the brilliant work of Herbert Winlock using meticulously detailed notes made by Guy Brunton when he found the jewellery of Sithathoriunet at Lahun, it has been possible to rectify some of the worst errors of restringing in the Dahshur treasures. 163

The Egyptians wore jewellery on just about every part of their anatomy, with the notable exception, in contrast to some other ancient peoples, of the nose, though to judge from a number of Late Period bronzes of the cat-goddess Bastet in her animal form, nose-rings might be worn by sacred animals.

Diadems and circlets

In the Coffin Texts there are many specialised words for this type of head adornment but in everyday parlance the words were *nefer hat* (*nfr ḥȝt*), perhaps a closed circle diadem, and *seshed* (*sšd*) or *medjeh* (*mḏḥ*), meaning 'fillet' and thus referring to the open-ended type tied at the back. Diadems were worn by men as well as women; they made their first appearance even before the beginning of the 1st Dynasty, and could either be made of solid metal or have an openwork design.

The earliest surviving example is an openwork diadem, made from a single string of beads and roughly shaped chips of turquoise, garnet and malachite separated at intervals by sections of tiny gold ring beads; a string of gold beads forms a small loop at one end as a fastening. That this was a diadem is indisputable: it was found in place on the head of a woman whose body was excavated at Abydos, and it was still holding a piece of cloth like a veil over her face. It dates to the Predynastic Naqada II Period (*c.* 3200 BC) and already demonstrates the Egyptian jewellery-maker's delight in contrasting highly coloured semi-precious stones with precious-metal elements. 31

Well over a thousand years later the great lady Senebtisy, buried at Lisht beside the pyramid of Ammenemes I, founder of the 12th Dynasty, had set in place outside the bandages on her head an openwork circlet. It was formed from three gold wires, each intricately looped back on itself and joined together behind the head by an additional interwoven wire. Over the forehead the wires are straightened, reinforced with a further wire, and the lowest is looped into an inverted heart shape. 75

This, however, was only a plebeian version of the exquisite openwork diadem which Princess Khnumet, buried at Dahshur near the pyramid of her father Ammenemes II, took to her tomb among her personal jewellery. Based on a chaplet of wild flowers, it is formed from ten gold wires brought together at intervals by six gold elements in the shape of Maltese crosses, each formed from a cornelian boss between four open papyrus-heads inlaid with turquoise. The wires emerge from these elements in groups of three, four and three, and are united into pairs at frequent intervals by gold ring beads from which hang tiny lapis lazuli buds or five-petalled flowers of gold inlaid with turquoise around a cornelian boss. The effect is of flowers and buds sprinkled among wire stems. 82

The most basic type of head adornment, however, is a solid metal circlet; an early example survives from a 1st Dynasty burial at Nag ed-Deir, where the skull of a crushed female skeleton was still encircled by a plain band of sheet gold. Already by the opening years of the Old Kingdom the plain band circlet had acquired attachments, for on her painted limestone statue from Meidum (now in Cairo) Princess Nofret wears over her thick wig a white-coloured diadem clearly meant to represent a silver band studded with inlaid roundels and leaf patterns. 81

Khnumet owned a second gold diadem which is an elaborate openwork version of the same type. It comprises eight openwork gold units, each consisting of a gold rosette with lapis lazuli and turquoise inlaid petals around a cornelian disc, flanked and surmounted by an openwork gold 'lily of Upper Egypt', itself inlaid with cornelian, turquoise and lapis lazuli. Each unit is separated from the next by a single rosette, inlaid in exactly the same way. All the elements are chased on the inner surface with the same details that are worked in cloisonné on the other side. The front of the circlet is distinguished by a flying vulture of sheet gold with chased details of feathering and obsidian-inlaid eyes. A vertical gold tube attached to the inner face at the back of the circlet once held a tall gold tree, made from a central tube with attached gold leaves and fruits, possibly intended for dates, formed from lapis lazuli, turquoise and cornelian disc beads on silver rods. 38

Princess Sithathoriunet, buried at Lahun beside the pyramid of Sesostris II, also owned a diadem. This is composed of a broad band of sheet gold, ornamented at intervals with fifteen inlaid gold rosettes, attached by pegs; at the front is a central detachable gold ajouré uraeus with a lapis 83

82 Khnumet's second openwork diadem. It is based on a chaplet of wild flowers formed from gold wires linked by cross-shapes, formed from gold papyrus-heads inlaid with turquoise and cornelian. Sprinkled among the wire stems are lapis lazuli buds and gold flowers inlaid with turquoise around cornelian centres. D 18cm

From the tomb of Khnumet, Dahshur. 12th Dynasty (reign of Ammenemes II, c. 1895 BC)

83 Replica of the diadem of Sithathoriunet, composed of a sheet-gold band, with fifteen inlaid gold rosettes and a detachable inlaid gold ajouré uraeus. There are three sheet-gold streamers and a tall sheet-gold double plume mounted at the back. The hair ornaments are gold tubes for threading onto the tresses.
H (gold band) 2.7cm

The original (now in Cairo) from the tomb of Sithathoriunet, Lahun. 12th Dynasty (reign of Ammenemes III, c. 1830 BC)

lazuli head. Each rosette is formed from cloisons in the shape of a cross of flowering rushes with buds flanked by leaves at the interstices, all inlaid with cornelian and blue and green glazed composition (now decayed). To three of the rosettes, one at the back and one at each side, are attached double streamers of sheet gold, while a fourth, inverted to resemble a tall double plume, is carried by a gold open papyrus-head in the round, which is inserted into a tube soldered to the inner face at the back of the band.

A unique diadem which may actually be of Hyksos workmanship, or else of Egyptian manufacture under Asiatic inspiration, consists of a pennanular band of electrum, pierced at each end to take tie strings, with curiously prickly rosettes and animal-head attachments. The latter comprise four gazelles' heads on either side of a rather larger central stag's head with amazingly spiked horns. Its dating to the late Second Intermediate Period is by no means certain.

From the burial of the three wives of Tuthmosis III came a graceful diadem made by cutting sheet gold into a T-shape. One band encircled the head while the other passed over the top from front to back. The whole was fastened by a cord threaded through rings in the mouths of modelled leopards' heads, which are soldered one to each of the three ends. A row of gold pendants originally lay on the forehead. Four inlaid rosettes imitating marguerites set into circular frames decorate the band across the forehead, with a further two on the band passing over the crown of the head; these serve to frame two small but superbly modelled gold gazelles' heads attached side by side over the centre of the forehead by means of

84 A diadem composed of a penannular band of electrum with prickly rosettes and animal-head attachments – four gazelle heads flanking a central stag's head. The diadem was intended to be tied.
H (stag's head) 8.5cm

From the Eastern Delta. Hyksos Period? (c. 1650–1540 BC)

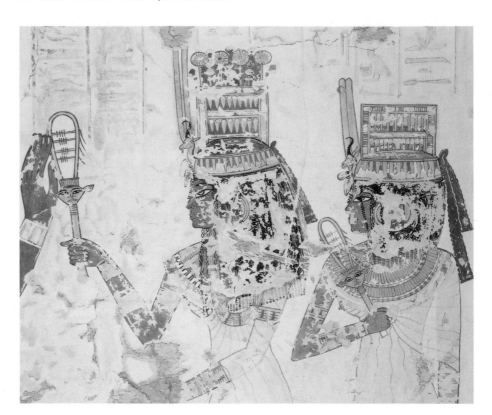

85 Copy of a New Kingdom
wall-painting, depicting the daughters
of the tomb-owner Menna as royal
concubines, wearing diadems with
gazelle heads and plumes (see 84).
They also wear earrings, broad collars,
bracelets and armlets and carry sistra.
The elaborate containers on their heads
were probably for cones of scented fat.
From W. Thebes (tomb no. 69). 18th
Dynasty (reign of Tuthmosis IV,
c. 1395 BC)

two up-curved pegs. They were each made in two halves, apparently over
a positive, and soldered down the centre, with the horns added separately. It has been plausibly suggested that this creature, synonymous with
grace and gentleness, was the badge of royal harim ladies of lesser rank
than the Great Royal Wife, who was entitled to wear the vulture on her
brow. Diadems with gazelle-head protomes are depicted being worn by
the daughters of the 18th Dynasty official Menna in his tomb at Thebes,
where the girls are termed 'royal concubines, beloved of their lord'.

A circlet from the so-called Gold Tomb in the Valley of the Kings was
probably once worn by Queen Tausret of the 19th Dynasty, one of only
three native queens to reign as pharaoh. It is formed from a narrow band
of sheet gold, pierced at irregular intervals by sixteen holes for the
attachment of gold flowers, of which some, at least, were made from red
gold. Each has ten petals formed by shaping foil into a mould and five bear
the cartouches of Tausret and Sety II. The centre of each flower is a domed
button backed by a ring; as the rings are too large to have passed through
the holes in the band, a wire attachment, now missing, must have been
employed.

It is possible that a set of similar gold repoussé rosettes, excavated by
George Reisner at Nuri in the Sudan, may have come from a circlet like
this. Graded in size, each has a horizontal suspension tube soldered at the
back. These rosettes date from the reign of the Kushite King Talakhamani
in the mid-fifth century BC, but the head-wear otherwise favoured by
Nubian royalty, depicted as early as Tutankhamun's reign in the tomb of
Huy at Thebes, was a simple gold band; later a double uraeus, for the
rulers of Kush, and two long attached ribbons were added.

Another type of circlet was clearly based on the fillet, a cloth band tied around the head, with a knot at the back and two long ends hanging down behind; such fillets are depicted early in the Old Kingdom. The first surviving example of such a circlet is a funerary diadem found at Giza in mastaba 294, dating from the late 5th or early 6th Dynasty. It takes the form of a gold band on which is mounted a flat central boss of gold with a chased floral design repeated four times in heraldic opposition around a tiny cornelian disc. On either side is a knot formed from two open papyrus-heads with chased decoration, also flanking a central cornelian disc. At the top of each knot are two crested ibises, their long curved beaks merging with the tops of the papyrus-heads. The ends of the bands were clearly meant to be pulled together by a ribbon passing through holes pierced for that purpose, and knotted to leave two long streamers. A second circlet of copper covered with very thin, brittle gold leaf and pierced by three copper nails was thought by the excavator to be a support for the gold example when not in use. It has been suggested, however, that both could be worn together, though none too securely, with the gold diadem resting on the nails of the copper one.

Painted cartonnage male mummy masks of the First Intermediate Period from Asyut often show the deceased is wearing a fillet with colourful block-decoration, a knot and hanging ends behind, with a large inlaid disc over the forehead; the whole circlet in these cases seems to have been made of inlaid metal. Just such a headband roundel of similar date is made of copper worked in repoussé, with alternating cornelian and green and black glazed composition inlays. Fifteen contemporary green glazed composition rosettes, certainly came from a headband of similar form. Each has a central black-coloured boss from which radiate slit-like perforations, a rope pattern around the outer rim and a suspension loop at the back.

The earliest metal fillet to survive was found around the head of the 13th

86 Cartonnage funerary mask of Khety, a provincial nobleman, depicting him wearing a fillet with block-decoration, knots and hanging ends, with a large inlaid roundel over the forehead. The original was probably made of inlaid metal.
From Asyut (tomb 7, pit 3) 1st Intermediate Period (c 2100 BC)

87 Headband ornaments: **a** eleven green glazed composition rosettes with a suspension loop on the back, intended for stitching onto a cloth headband. The remaining four rosettes are now in Cairo. In the centre is a contemporary copper roundel (**b**) worked in repoussé with cornelian and green and black glazed composition inlays. D (inlaid roundel) 4.8cm
From Matmar (graves 509 and 306). 1st Intermediate Period (c. 2100 BC)

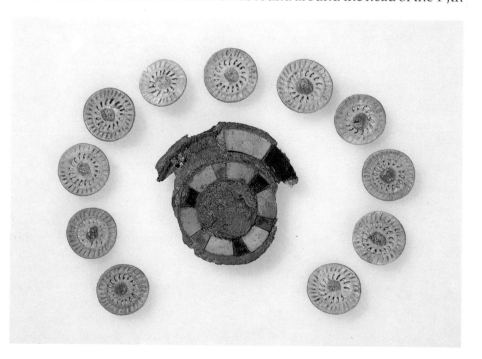

88 Detail of Tutankhamun's diadem, which was worn in life. It is composed of a sheet-gold band encircled by cloisons inlaid with cornelian. From the back hang two long streamers decorated in the same fashion as the headband. A hinged curved streamer at each side ends in an upreared cobra inlaid with red and blue glass. The inlaid uraeus and sheet-gold vulture head at the front are detachable.
w (band) 2cm

From the mummy of Tutankhamun, Valley of the Kings, W. Thebes. 18th Dynasty (c. 1336–1327 BC)

Dynasty Princess Nubhotepti, buried at Dahshur, but it is incomplete, for the hanging streamers had oxidised. However, it was identical in form and material with one dating to the late Second Intermediate Period over a hundred years later, which was discovered by modern robbers in the early part of the nineteenth century in the tomb at Thebes of a local 17th Dynasty ruler, Nubkheperre Inyotef; it is now in the Rijksmuseum, Leiden. Formed from a wafer-thin circle of gilded sheet silver with block-decoration, it has four streamers at the back, two long and two short, emerging from a knot which takes the form of a disc flanked by two inlaid lotus-heads. At the front is soldered a sheet-gold uraeus with chased details on its body, a solid gold modelled head, and a gilded wire tail. The whole piece is so flimsy it can only have been made for the burial, but Tutankhamun' mummy wore a metal fillet which he had obviously worn in life, for some of the inlaid roundels were missing. The sheet-gold band is encircled by round cloisons inlaid with cornelian. The spaces between the cloisons and the striped border are inlaid with coloured glass. At the back a large central disc inlaid with red chalcedony is flanked by two papyrus-umbels inlaid with malachite; from this hang two long, flaring streamers whose decoration matches that of the circlet itself. Attached by a hinge at either side of the papyrus-heads are two similarly decorated curved streamers, each of which ends in an up-reared cobra inlaid with red and blue glass. At the front of the circlet the gold uraeus, its hood similarly inlaid, and the solid gold vulture head are detachable. The cobra's tail winds over the crown of the wearer's head and is joined to the knot at the back by a hinge with pin. 88

Although fillet-diadems with block-decoration are depicted for another thousand years, worn especially by royalty over short wigs, only one 89 other metal example with roundel decoration like that of Tutankhamun has ever been found.

Hair ornaments

A range of ornaments were designed to be worn attached directly to the hair. With Senebtisy's wire circlet, for example, were found ninety-eight gold rosettes imitating marguerites; these must have been made by being 75 beaten into two different moulds, since they have different arrangements for fastening (either a bar soldered at the back or two holes pierced through to take a thread). The rosettes were intended to be attached to individual tresses, either by passing the hairs under the bars or tying the threads around them. A contemporary painted wooden head of a woman in a heavy wig (now in Cairo) has gilded squares scattered all over the hair, presumably representing similar ornaments. Khnumet owned twenty-four rather crudely formed gold birds with down-pointing wings. These were made by hammering into a mould, with an added back-plate pierced for the escape of air and to provide a means of attachment. They are almost certainly hair ornaments, worn on the wig by threading tresses through the airholes. A mass of short gold tubes found with Sithathoriunet's diadem undoubtedly served the same purpose, to be threaded onto the 83 royal tresses. Another type of ornament known to have been worn attached to the hair was a pendant in the form of a fish. It was worn during 157 the Old and Middle Kingdoms at the end of a plait of young women and 156 children, and it had an amuletic function.

A painted relief from the tomb of the 11th Dynasty Queen Nofret at Deir el-Bahri depicts dancing girls wearing what appear to be strings of silver ball beads alternating with silver cylinders down the centre of the head, at least as far as the shoulders. This is the sole representative of this form of head ornament and, curiously, it looks exactly like a silver bead string worn around the neck of the mummy of their male contemporary Wah. A gold example was also found on the mummy of a contemporary royal concubine at Deir el-Bahri, but no such strings have ever been found in position on the head in a burial.

From the 18th Dynasty burial of the wives of Tuthmosis III came a unique form of head-wear, a magnificent articulated inlaid gold head- 90 dress which, as currently strung, covers the hair like a hood beyond the level of the shoulders; a substantial part of a second was also recovered. The complete head-dress consists of a cascade of gold cloisonné rosettes suspended by rings from a roughly oval gold plate, which is decorated with alternately chased and inlaid palm-leaves. There were originally over 850 rosettes, each formed from a gold base-plate with rings at the edge to interlock with adjacent elements and inlaid with cornelian, turquoise, glass and glazed composition. Additional gold beads strung along with the interlocking rings gives the columns of rosettes the appearance of being separated by notched vertical ribs. A row of pendants must once have lain across the forehead.

Ornaments for the ears

Ear ornaments were introduced to the Egyptians during the Second Intermediate Period. The only word of Egyptian origin applied to them during the Dynastic Period, *shaqyu* (*šꜣḳyw*), actually means 'rings' and has to have the words 'for the ears' appended. At first they were worn by women, but later by men too, and by the reign of Tuthmosis IV even the

89 Upper part of a granite statue of Ramesses II wearing the double crown and carrying the insignia of royalty. Over his short wig he wears a diadem with block-decoration and hinged streamers ending in upreared cobras. A broad collar ending in teardrop shapes lies on his chest. On one wrist is a heavy bracelet incorporating an *udjat*-eye. H 1.43m

From the temple of Khnum, Elephantine. 19th Dynasty (*c.* 1279–1213 BC)

king had pierced ears. Pharaoh, however, is never depicted wearing ear ornaments, although queens are rarely shown without them. It is often suggested that the practice came from the east, since they had been worn in Mesopotamia a thousand years earlier and they first appear in Egypt during the Hyksos occupation. But there had been contact with people who wore earrings since the time of the Old Kingdom and it is not probable that the Egyptians would have aped a fashion of their unpopular overlords. It is rather more likely that the practice was adopted from the earring-wearing Nubian Pan-grave people, who served as mercenaries to the Theban princes and helped them to expel the Hyksos before settling in their adopted country. The earliest Egyptian and Pan-grave earrings, all intended to be worn in pierced ears, are of silver or copper wire either turned up into hoops with overlapping ends or else twisted into as many   49a,d
as five spirals.

Spiral earrings are, however, quite unlike the leech-shaped or open-ended forms favoured in the east, which were to become popular in Egypt during the New Kingdom. The earliest recorded earrings of the latter type   14b
from Egypt were found in the burial of a woman in western Thebes dating to the late 17th Dynasty. Each is formed from four tubes soldered together along their length into an open ring, the two inner tubes being extended to pass through the pierced ear-lobes. The tubes themselves are made up from rings of triangular-sectioned wire, soldered together side by side to give a ribbed effect.

New Kingdom versions of this form, always gold or electrum, can also be made from triangular-sectioned tubes formed by folding sheet metal over wire and pressing or hammering it to make the ribbed edge on the exterior. The extended section can be decorated at the point where it emerges with rope braid or by a patterned metal disc, often flower-   91e,f
shaped, soldered at right angles and intended to lie up against the front of the ear. The five pairs of gold earrings from the burial of Tuthmosis III's wives are all of this type, the floral elements inlaid.

Leech-shaped earrings were made by folding a piece of metal over a   91g
shaped core and masking the joins by rope braid; a wire extended from one end to pass through the lobe. From these developed a type particularly popular during the Ptolemaic Period with an animal-head protome,   91a,b
such as an antelope or bull, with wire and granulation details. Wire extended from the twisted shank to fit into a ring in the animal's mouth. Another earring form for pierced ears was hoop-shaped; it was made from   91c
two circles of metal raised by beating which were then soldered together, the join masked by rope braid; a central depression allowed room for the ear tip, and loops soldered at either side took a pin or wire which passed through the lobe. The shape was also reproduced in polychrome glass, a material used for earring pendants of a variety of shapes, such as looped   96
pomegranates and inverted leeches, palm and papyrus columns, the latter pierced through their length; all were suspended from the lobe by wire.

The most elaborate metal earrings for pierced ears consisted of a stud-capped tube screwed through the lobe into a second capped tube; from this hung an elaborate ornament attached to a stirrup-shaped fitting which accommodated the tip of the ear-lobe. Earrings of this type from the

90 Articulated inlaid gold head-dress, which covers the hair like a hood beyond shoulder level. From an oval plate hang gold cloisonné rosettes, graduated in size. They are strung in columns, which end in lunettes, and were originally inlaid with cornelian, turquoise, glass and glazed composition. A row of pendants once lay across the forehead. L 37cm

From the burial of the wives of Tuthmosis III. W. Thebes. 18th Dynasty (c. 1465 BC)

91 Selection of metal earrings, all of gold except **g**, which is electrum; **a** & **b** hollow with animal-head terminals. (**a**) a bull's head, (**b**) a gazelle's or antelope's head. The extended wire shank hooks into a loop at the animal's mouth. H (**a**, head) 2cm; **c** hollow, made in two halves, the outside join masked by rope braid; **d** hollow pennanular, barrel-shaped, with inlaid inset naming Queen Tausret. From the Gold Tomb (no. 56), Valley of the Kings, W. Thebes; **e** & **f** a single earring, and a pair, of the ribbed type, made respectively from six and five tubes soldered together; **e** has rope-braid decoration and **f** has flowers soldered at the point where the outer tubes end. D (**e**) 4.6cm; **g** leech-shaped, with rope braid masking the join around the outer face.

c, d, e, f & g: New Kingdom (*c*. 1475–1180 BC); **a** & **b**; Ptolemaic Period (*c*. 300–100 BC)

tomb of Tutankhamun were found not on the mummy but in a box. In one gold pair, inlaid mostly with coloured glass, each has a pendant in the form of a pair of cloisonné falcon wings, but with a blue glass duck's head attached to the bird's body. From the tail hangs a flexible appendage formed from openwork gold plaques decorated with gold and blue glass inlays in chevron patterns and terminating in five pendant uraei. The front stud bears a profile royal head visible under translucent quartz and flanked by a pair of attached uraei. A second pair is richly decorated with granulation; the studs are open flowers of red and yellow gold, and the large pendant is formed from alternating dark resin and hollow gold beads separated by blue glass. From a hinged gold bar attached to the lowest bead hang tassels of gold and blue glass beads ending in gold buds and seed-pods.

A later pair of royal earrings of similar type were found in the Gold Tomb in the Valley of the Kings. The front stud is a concave, eight-petalled flower of gold foil, the petals worked alternately in repoussé with cartouches of Sety II; the counterbalancing gold stud, incised with the king's nomen and prenomen cartouches, is decorated with applied tubes. Suspended from the interlocking tubes is a gold trapezoidal ornament, incised on both faces with Sety's cartouches; from its base hang seven cornflower pendants, each made in two ribbed hollow halves with an added plain flared rim, hanging from a striated tube stalk.

92

48a

93

92 Pair of Tutankhamun's gold earrings inlaid mostly with coloured glass. The front stud bears a profile royal head visible under translucent quartz and is flanked by attached uraei. The ducks' heads are of blue glass. In earrings of this type one capped tube screwed through the lobe into the second capped tube; the stirrup-shaped depression was to accommodate the ear-tip. D 5.2cm

From the tomb of Tutankhamun (Treasury), Valley of the Kings, W. Thebes. 18th Dynasty (c. 1336–1327 BC)

93 Gold earrings in which the front stud is an eight-petalled flower worked in repoussé with cartouches of Sety II; the counterbalancing stud is incised with the king's nomen and prenomen cartouches and the hanging trapezoidal ornament is incised with his cartouches on both faces. The pendants are cornflowers. L 13.5cm

From the Gold Tomb (no. 56), Valley of the Kings, W. Thebes. 19th Dynasty (Sety II, c. 1200–1194 BC)

Elaborately decorated studs on interfitting tubes, without pendant ornaments, could also be worn in pierced ears. Tutankhamun owned a pair in which the large circular gold front stud is inlaid in floral and striped patterns with blue and green glass around a central cornelian boss. Two inlaid gold uraei hang from the lower edge by the cornelian-inlaid sun-discs on their heads. On a smaller pair, probably a souvenir of his younger days, each of the domed inlaid gold front studs backs two small inlaid uraei. Three odd gold ear-studs of this type of Ramesside date, found at Tell Basta, have a large domed disc with applied wire and cloisonné or repoussé decoration as the cap. A magnificent gold Kushite specimen capped at the front with a repoussé ram's head wearing a sun-disc and double uraeus dates to the mid-sixth century BC and was excavated at Meroe in the Sudan.

48b

113

Plugs shaped rather like mushrooms and usually made of glazed composition were worn pushed through the pierced lobes in the same way. Since only the convex head was seen at the front of the ear, it alone was decorated, generally with a floral design, while the stem remained plain. Larger versions with short stems are usually made of plain calcite. Both forms are often seen in the ears of anthropoid coffin lids of women dating from the Late New Kingdom.

A particularly barbaric form of ear-plug was large and bobbin-shaped; indeed, when first found they were thought to be just that, or else furniture knobs. They have a domed decorated outer face and a groove around the circumference for the distended hole in the ear-lobe. They are usually made of gold, glazed composition or, as in the case of a particularly fine example in the British Museum, of translucent glass with impressed polychrome glass details. A unique royal pair of gold with hanging attachments dates to the end of the 20th Dynasty. Found on a female mummy buried below the sanctuary of the temple of Sety I at Abydos, each comprises a hollow red-gold disc with grooved outer circumference and cartouches of Ramesses XI on the underside. To the upper face, which has granulated decoration, are soldered five gold uraei in the round, each made in two hollow halves with wire and granulation details, the three central ones wearing sun-discs, the outer two *atef*-crowns. Soldered below is a plate with a repoussé winged sun-disc; at the

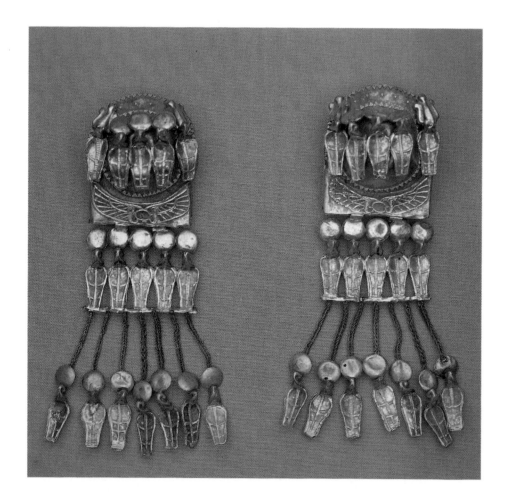

94 A pair of gold ear-plugs found on a female mummy, with cartouches of Ramesses XI on the underside of the red gold disc, to the upper face of which are attached five uraei in the round; the outer two wear the *atef*-crown. The sun-discs on the uraei below the repoussé winged sun-disc are hinged; loop-in-loop gold chains suspend the lowest uraei. L 16cm

From the temple of Sety I, Abydos (beneath the sanctuary). 20th Dynasty (reign of Ramesses XI, *c.* 1099–1070 BC)

95 Top part of a painted wooden anthropoid coffin of a woman who wears large floral decorated ear-studs, a pectoral with a scarab, a broad collar and bead choker.

From Thebes. 21st Dynasty (*c.* 1000 BC)

lower end of this are attached five further uraei crowned by hinged sun-discs and standing on a bar. From the bar hang seven loop-in-loop gold chains ending in seven more uraei wearing sun-discs.

There is some dispute over whether penannular earrings were worn by stretching the flesh of the lobe to pass through the open end or whether they were twisted through the pierced lobe. Fine metal pairs came from the Gold Tomb in the Valley of the Kings. One pair is barrel-shaped, made from two hollow halves of sheet electrum, triangular in section, soldered so the two points form the upper and lower rims; the end plates are pierced for the escape of air. Another similarly shaped pair of gold, one of which is now in the British Museum, has a rectangular plate sunk into the rounded outer surface into which are set gold cloisons forming the cartouche of Queen Tausret, surmounted by feathers. Much of the coloured glass inlay is now lost. Curiously, the placing of the cartouche is such that when the earrings were worn the hieroglyphs would be upside-down. Another pair from this tomb, of electrum, is circular in section with

91d

115

rope braid masking the joins between the two hollow shells, and each has six small rings attached at what would be the lowest point when worn. From them hang six short strings of cornelian and glazed composition cylinder and oblate beads, each originally ending in a pendant in the shape of a blue glazed composition flower-head or a cornelian bud, set in an electrum mount.

Plainer penannular earrings were made of glass canes bent round into an open circle or carved from red jasper or cornelian. Although the latter have sometimes been identified as hair-rings, jasper examples have been found at the ears of young females buried at Gurob and Matmar in the 19th Dynasty. Examples even exist in which the rope-braid decoration of metal earrings is imitated.

96k

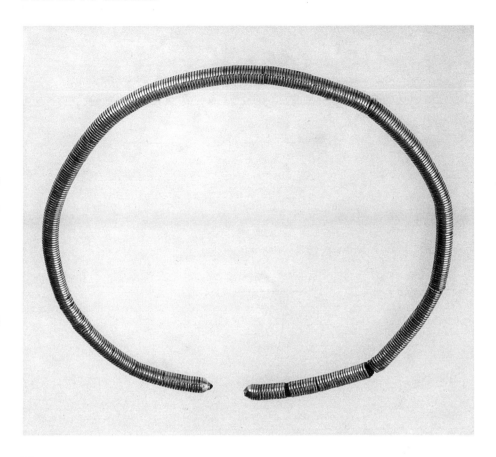

Left 96 Selection of non-metal ear ornaments: **a** is a glass palm column and **b**, **d** & **e** are glass papyrus column pendants, all worn on a wire. H 2.7–3.1cm; **c** is a domed ear-boss of calcite with inlaid glass petals. W (max) 2.5cm; **f** is a penannular glass earring with decoration imitating the rope braid of metal examples. The loops once held wire to pass through the pierced lobe; **g** & **i**, of glass, are bobbin-shaped plugs worn through the distended pierced lobe; **g** has impressed details. D (**g**) 3.5cm; **h** & **j** are glass pendants worn from wires through the ear-lobe: **h** has 'rope-braid' decoration; **k** red jasper penannular earring with carved rope-braid decoration imitating metal examples; **l** glazed composition stud with polychrome floral patterned dome. From el-Amarna; **m** penannular earring formed from two twisted rods of glass.
   All New Kingdom (*c.* 1375–1180 BC)

Right 97 Flexible torque formed from thin gold disc beads strung on a thick cord which passes through a holed gold cup at each end. D 15.1cm
   11th Dynasty (*c.* 2020 BC)

Torques

This form of neck adornment was extremely rare in Egypt before the Coptic Period. There are two examples in the British Museum (EA 37310 and 63211), both made from silver wire with the ends beaten out into a wide flange. One came from a Middle Kingdom burial at Abydos, the other from a Nubian Pan-grave burial. Another flexible torque, formed from thin gold discs strung tightly together on a thick cord which passes through a pierced gold cup at each end, is almost identical with one found around the neck of a royal concubine of Mentuhotep II, buried at Deir el-Bahri just before 2000 BC.

49b

97

Chokers

Women of all classes during the Old Kingdom, servant girls during the Middle Kingdom and well-to-do women on coffin lids during the New Kingdom are depicted wearing a tight choker formed, apparently, from rows of beads strung either horizontally between spacers or vertically between rims. Worn alone, they particularly complemented cropped hairstyles. However, chokers are often worn above a broad collar, especially when the hair is long. No identifiable examples of chokers have survived.

79,95

98

Left 98 Detail of a limestone relief stela from the tomb of the king's priest Iry; the deceased's wife wears a choker of vertically strung beads above a broad collar.
H (total) 71cm
   From Saqqara. 4th Dynasty (*c* 2550 BC)

Collars to girdles: adorning the body

Gold necklaces and collars worked with costly stones, jewellery for all the body

Left 99 Openwork gold pectoral inlaid with cornelian, turquoise and lapis lazuli, with an articulated floral frieze. A barque sails between papyrus and 'Upper Egyptian lily' supporters. The lapis lazuli sun-disc, protected by winged goddesses, shows Maat before Amen-Re-Horakhty in raised relief on both faces. The text names Sheshonq I, but the pectoral was found on Sheshonq II's mummy. w 7.8cm

From the burial of Sheshonq II, Tanis (tomb III). 22nd Dynasty (*c.* 890 BC)

Right 100 Blue glazed composition broad collar, the earliest to survive. The gold terminals are incised with the name of Impy; the pendants are stylised beetles. A funerary collar, it has no counterpoise. w 34.5cm

From the burial of Impy, Giza. Late 6th Dynasty (*c.* 2200 BC)

Collars

Perhaps the most characteristic form of Egyptian jewellery is the broad collar, *weskhet* (*wsḫt*), made from cylinders which are graded in size and strung vertically between semicircular terminals. The terminals are pierced along their flat side by as many holes as there are strings, which emerge united from a single exit hole in the centre of the curved side, to be tied together to fasten the collar. Usually, too, there is an outermost row of leaf-shaped pendants, sometimes strung between two rows of horizontal beads. Nofret on her statue in Cairo wears just such a collar at the beginning of the 4th Dynasty, and various forms of the same ornament are painted inside coffins of the First Intermediate Period and the Middle Kingdom among the frieze of the deceased's possessions.

A particularly fine example made from blue-green glazed composition and dating to the 11th Dynasty (*c.* 2000 BC) was found on the mummy of Wah at Thebes. The earliest to survive, however, came from the tomb of an official nicknamed Impy who was buried at Giza during the late 6th Dynasty, over 150 years earlier. The barrel-shaped beads are made of glazed composition, with some of gold, and the terminals, which are incised with his name, are also of gold; the pendants are in the form of

81

101

18

100

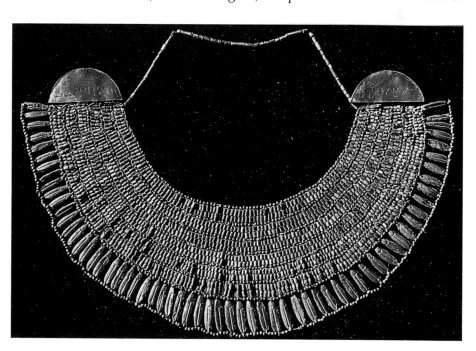

101 Detail of the inside decoration of the wooden outer coffin of the physician Seni, showing a painted frieze of broad collars with falcon-headed terminals and matching falcon-headed counterpoises.
H (frieze) 15cm
From el-Bersha. Middle Kingdom (c. 2000 BC)

stylised bettles. Both these collars were funerary and so lack a counter-poise, an essential feature of broad collars made from stone beads. This was joined to the terminals by bead strings and lay between the shoulder blades to counterbalance the weight of the collar and hold it in place on the chest.

The earliest surviving collar with a counterpoise was found in the burial of Princess Itaweret at Dahshur and dates to the 12th Dynasty (c. 1900 BC). Made from gold, turquoise and lapis lazuli beads, with an outermost row of gold drops and gold semicircular terminals, its *menkhet* counterpoise is of gold and cornelian cylinders and a miniature gold terminal. However, the finest collar of this period belonged to Princess Neferuptah, buried at Hawara about a hundred years later. It consists of six rows of alternating cornelian and feldspar cylinders, each separated by rows of small gold ring beads and all strung between two hollow gold falcon-headed termin-als; the outermost row is of gold drops inlaid with cornelian, feldspar and paste. The collar is matched exactly by a counterpoise which has a small gold falcon's head on top of rows of feldspar and cornelian cylinders separated by gold multiple bead spacers.

Broad collars could also be composed of individual elements to give an openwork effect: a fine example came from the burial of the wives of Tuthmosis III. Although it has been reconstructed, the gradation of the elements makes its order of stringing virtually certain; only the terminals and counterpoise may belong to another collar. It is composed of rows of gold *nefer*-signs, half originally inlaid, half plain. An outermost row of pendants, also originally inlaid, are shaped like palmettes. The gold terminals are semicircular in outline, each formed from two cloisonné lotus-heads, and once inlaid with cornelian, turquoise and blue glazed composition, flanking the incised prenomen cartouche of Tuthmosis III. A gold cloisonné lotus-head, once inlaid with the same materials, is strung as a counterpoise from a string of gold ring beads; the details of the lotus-head are also chased on the underside.

Another openwork collar from this burial has been reconstructed with less certainty. Details of the gold falcon-headed terminals are inlaid on the upper surface with cornelian and turquoise around an obsidian eye; on the underside they are chased and there is a text naming the king. The piercings around the lower edge show that originally there were eight rows of beads. Currently the innermost row is of vertically strung tur-quoise, the outermost of cornelian from which hang forty-nine gold pendants, inlaid variously with cornelian, turquoise and lapis lazuli, each with a pendant gold papyrus-head suspended from the tip. Two rows of teardrop-shaped gold pendants, divided in three zones for inlays of

26

102

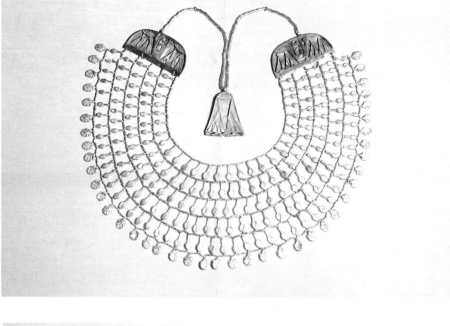

102 Openwork collar, composed of gold *nefer*-signs, graduated in size and half originally inlaid, with an outermost row of gold inlaid pendants. The lotus-heads of the terminals, once inlaid with cornelian, turquoise and blue glazed composition, flank the prenomen cartouche of Tuthmosis III. The gold cloisonné counterpoise was once inlaid with the same materials. w (terminals) 7.2cm
  From the burial of the wives of Tuthmosis III, W. Thebes. 18th Dynasty (c. 1465 BC)

103 Openwork collar reconstructed from elements found in the burial of the wives of Tuthmosis III. The gold falcon-headed terminals are inlaid with cornelian and turquoise around the obsidian eye; the underside names Tuthmosis III. The teardrop-shaped pendants are inlaid with cornelian, turquoise and decayed blue glass. H (terminals) 5.2cm
  From the burial of the wives of Tuthmosis III, W. Thebes. 18th Dynasty (c. 1465 BC)

cornelian, turquoise and decayed glass, alternate with two rows of spatulate gold pendants inlaid with bands of turquoise and lapis lazuli. One of the sections of teardrops is interspersed with tiny gold teardrops and all the rows are separated by one or more strings of tiny gold ring beads, some of them soldered to neighbouring elements. A third collar from this burial is now formed from identical inlaid teardrop-shaped pendants strung with rows of tiny gold discs between two identical inlaid gold falcon-headed terminals.

What must have been a superb openwork collar but now incapable of accurate reconstruction came from the burial at Qurna of Queen Aah-

103

hotep, ancestress of the 18th Dynasty. The falcon-headed terminals of gold foil have the characteristic eye and cheek markings and the chevron on the shoulder delineated in blue composition inlay. Although they are pierced by only eight holes, the collar is now strung with fourteen rows of stamped-out gold foil elements, some of which were certainly not originally part of it. These include bosses, leaf-shaped pendants, bells, crosses, flying birds, seated cats, scrolls and winged cobras, but also lions, ibexes and gazelles depicted with the wide-flung leg position known as the flying gallop; this posture is most un-Egyptian, and was adopted from contemporary Aegean work.

163

During the later 18th Dynasty collars of real flowers, which are often depicted in contemporary banqueting scenes being presented to guests, were imitated in collars composed of brightly coloured glazed composition floral elements. An example excavated at el-Amarna, Akhenaten's capital, has lotus-headed terminals inlaid with red, yellow, blue and green to indicate petals. The three rows of pendants, strung between tiny discs of red, blue, mauve and yellow, are yellow and blue mandrake fruit, green date-palm leaves, and yellow, white and mauve lotus-petals. Such collars were too light to require a counterpoise and although fragile were cheap to produce and easy to replace, for the glazed composition components were

105

104 Collar made from two unequal crescent-shaped hinged gold sheets, the larger with a repoussé kneeling goddess, the smaller with a scarab. It would have been worn by a Kushite queen high on the neck like a choker, to judge from the small diameter.
   From Kurru (tomb KU 72, burial chamber debris). 25th Dynasty (reign of Shebitku, c. 700 BC)

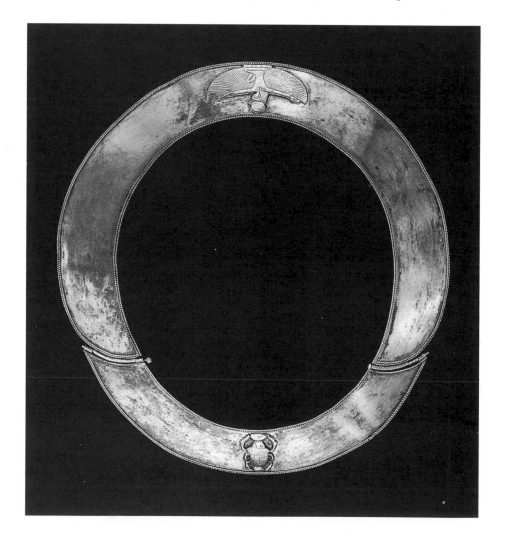

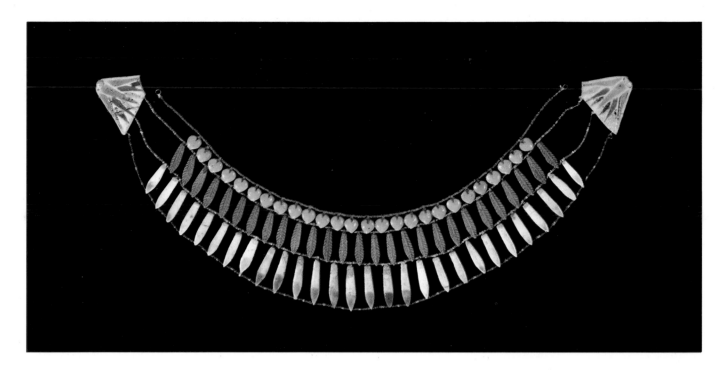

Above 105 Openwork broad collar of glazed composition beads and pendants with a floral motif. The rows are yellow mandrake fruit, green date palm leaves and zoned lotus-petals. The lotus-shaped terminals are inlaid with polychrome glazed composition. L (total) 52cm

From el-Amarna. 18th Dynasty (reign of Akhenaten, *c.* 1350 BC)

Below 106 Portion of a limestone relief from a temple, showing Ptolemy I making offerings; he wears a single string of beads. H (total) 33cm

Ptolemaic Period (*c.* 305–282 BC)

turned out in their thousands from open-backed moulds. Their forms, too, are many and varied, including red and mauve poppy-petals, red or blue bunches of grapes, blue or yellow and white daisies and variously coloured cornflowers, lotus-buds, thistles and multiple jasmine blossoms. The cornflower was the inspiration for a particularly popular stone pendant element in collars of the New Kingdom. A fine openwork example, restrung into nineteen rows from a mass of loose elements dug up at Tell Basta, consists of nearly four hundred gold and cornelian cornflowers and a great number of gold and cornelian disc beads and tiny gold spacers.

A unique collar worn by a Kushite queen in the time of the 25th Dynasty King Shebitku (early seventh century BC) was found in a ransacked burial chamber at Kurru in the Sudan. It is made of two unequal crescent-shaped hinged gold sheets, the larger with a repoussé kneeling winged goddess, the smaller with a scarab. It is without precedent in Egypt and, because of its small diameter, must have been worn almost like a choker. 104

Necklaces and bead strings

Long before the broad collar came into being the fashion was for single bead-string necklaces: ones made of shell, glazed steatite, horn, feldspar and alabaster beads have been found around the necks of men, women and children in burials of Badarian date. They continued to be worn throughout the Dynastic Period: on a block in the British Museum even Ptolemy I wears a single string of beads. Sometimes they were worn in conjunction with a broad collar: the royal concubine Ashayt, buried near her master, Mentuhotep, at Deir el-Bahri, is depicted on a painted relief wearing two single strings over a broad collar. The mummy of Wah was adorned with five single-string necklaces, all worn during his lifetime. 106 107

107 Painted limestone relief from the funerary shrine of the royal concubine Ashayt. She wears two single strings of beads over a broad collar, as well as matching anklets and bracelets. H 80cm
From the temple of Mentuhotep II, Deir el-Bahri, W. Thebes. 11th Dynasty (c. 2020 BC)

The most unusual comprises eleven hollow silver balls interspersed with smaller silver cylinders; another was made up of twenty-eight smaller hollow gold spheroids. A further two were of blue-green glazed composition balls and a fifth of barrels and cylinders of cornelian, moss agate, milky quartz, black and white porphyry and green glazed steatite. Two single-string necklaces, of gold and cornelian beads respectively, were found around the neck of the mummy of a contemporary royal concubine at Deir el-Bahri. The burial of the wives of Tuthmosis III contained a string of silver and green quartz spherical beads.

Almost invariably single-string necklaces are formed from large, highly coloured materials, sometimes metal-capped. The two magnificent lapis lazuli ball-bead necklaces adorning the mummy of the 21st Dynasty King Psusennes I, who was buried at Tanis, exemplify this well, although these are actually each strung in a double row. In both necklaces the beads are graded in size, with two gold spheres at the centre of each string. The gold two-part box-clasps are shaped on the top to resemble two beads and inscribed on the flat underside. That on the clasp of the larger necklace declares that Psusennes made the necklace of true lapis lazuli and no other king ever had its like. The other clasp gives only the royal name, but one of the stone beads bears a three-line cuneiform text in which an Assyrian dignitary offers prayers to the gods of Assur on behalf of his daughter. Its presence on this string has still not been satisfactorially explained. A third necklace with a semicircular clasp is composed of forty gold and lapis lazuli cylinders. A unique necklace from the burial of the wives of Tuthmosis III resembles a length of flexible gold rod, being made from a great number of interlocking beads, each formed from five gold balls soldered together around a stringing hole. 35

Necklaces with non-amuletic pendants occur just as early as the single bead-strings but they never had the popularity of those with amulets (see chapter 7). Princess Khnumet, however, owned a number of unusual pendants decorated with granulation; these are now strung onto gold chains to form necklaces. One has ten cockleshell-shaped pendants suspended by shorter links from a double loop-in-loop gold chain. The pendants are made in two halves from foil shaped in a mould and soldered around the outer edge over a light core. They flank two central elements, also on a loop-in-loop chain, in the shape of a five-pointed star, its outline and a central boss made from gold wire filled with granulation. Also suspended from a length of double loop-in-loop gold chain is a gold clasp in the shape of a butterfly, its upper surface detailed by gold wire cloisons soldered onto the shaped base-plate and inset with tiny granules rather than inlays. The typical sliding fastening is on the underside. The most unusual piece of all comprises three openwork gold stars, suspended by twisted gold wires from a central inlaid medallion, which is itself suspended by shorter links from a double loop-in-loop gold chain; this terminates in two large openwork rosettes. The latter have eight small rounded petals set about a large central element containing a lozenge shape; all are outlined with granules. The three smaller pendants are made in the same way except the petals have become points. The medallion is a circular plaque of blue frit held in a gold frame decorated with granules. At its centre, encircled by a halo of white, black and brown 64

108 Selection of Mereret's jewellery.

a Pair of bracelets with hollow gold lion amulets strung between beads of gold, turquoise, cornelian and lapis lazuli, ending in a gold knot clasp. L *c.* 16.5cm

b Necklace composed of unique pendants in the form of balls of turquoise, lapis lazuli and cornelian set in gold cages. The amuletic motto clasp, inlaid with the same materials, spells 'all life and protection'.

The other amuletic motto clasps (**c**) are inlaid with cornelian and decayed paste. Three of them read 'joy', and the fourth (upside down) states 'the gods are content'. The *shen*-sign (at the top) is not a clasp, but has five rings at its lower edge for pendants.

From the cache of Mereret, Dahshur. 12th Dynasty (reign of Ammenemes III, *c.* 1810 BC)

pieces, is painted a recumbent cow with a garland about its neck; a wafer-thin rock-crystal disc acts as a cover. Another loop-in-loop gold chain, which was repaired in antiquity, is hung with twelve sheet-gold pendants of elongated heart shape resembling prototype flies.

Both Sithathor and Mereret owned a number of hollow gold knots, once presumably strung into necklaces with clasps of a type which have a tongue-and-groove closing device on the undersides of its two halves. Another necklace strung from elements found in Mereret's tomb has eighteen pendants and an amuletic motto clasp. The pendants are unique in form, consisting of ball beads of turquoise, cornelian and lapis lazuli, each in a cage made from two encircling gold bands which are gathered together at the top into a tube; this, in turn, is pierced through the top end for suspension.

From the tomb of Tutankhamun, suspended from a gold loop-in-loop chain, came a superbly sculpted solid gold figure of a squatting king wearing a real necklace of gold and glass beads. Another royal figure, also hung as a pendant on a loop-in-loop gold chain, is slightly later, probably of Ramesside date. It was made in two halves by hammering sheet gold into a mould and adding a core before soldering around the edges. The profile figure wears a bead collar with drops and a counterpoise, the former made by cementing inlays into shaped sunken areas, the latter by cloisonné work. Nearly all the inlaid material is decayed, especially that of the sidelock, whose sunken shape alone remains. Like the new-born sun,

61

108b

109

66

109 A solid gold figure of a squatting king in the blue crown, carrying crook and flail in one hand and wearing a real necklace of gold and glass beads. Probably symbolic of the newly born sun, it is suspended by a loop-in-loop gold chain. H 5cm

From the tomb of Tutankhamun, Valley of the Kings, W. Thebes. 18th Dynasty (c. 1336–1327 BC)

the figure squats on a large cloisonné lotus and wears a sun-disc, behind which are the three rings for attachment. All the inlaid details of the upper face are repeated by chasing on the underside.

A particularly fine necklace was found in the Gold Tomb in the Valley of the Kings. It has now been reconstructed into two strings from loose gold elements, all of filigree work, comprising cornflowers and ball beads. Both the beads and the pods of the cornflowers are made from openwork shells, formed from wire rings of various diameters soldered together into a sphere. An additional openwork flared rim represents the flower-head and a striated tube the stalk.

110

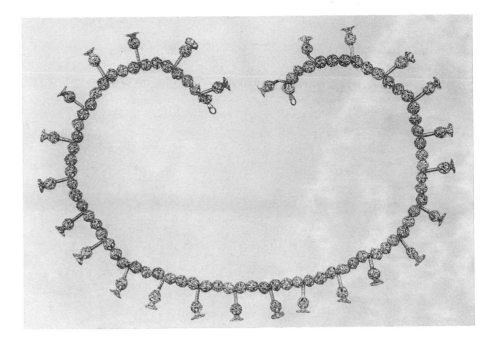

110 Necklace reconstructed from loose elements of gold filigree (the others now in Cairo), comprising cornflowers and ball beads. L 61cm

From the Gold Tomb (no. 56), Valley of the Kings, W. Thebes. 19th Dynasty (reign of Sety II, c. 1200–1194 BC)

Pectorals

There are a number of Old Kingdom representations of pectorals, later commonly known as *wedja (wd3)*, and jewellery-makers are depicted manufacturing them (for example, in the tomb of Mereruka). The pectorals shown most commonly are of key-hole design, with a trapezoidal pendant attached to broad bands of gold beads or a curved metal neckpiece. However, no actual pectorals of this date have survived. The first extant pectorals date to the 12th Dynasty, and are of openwork cloisonné with semi-precious stone inlays. These pectorals are among the finest ever made in Egypt. 51

The earliest was found at Lahun in the treasure of Princess Sithathor-iunet. Inlaid with cornelian, lapis lazuli and turquoise, it takes the form of two heraldically opposed falcons crowned with sun-discs and standing on a patterned bar representing primordial ocean. One claw of each falcon rests on a *shen*-sign, the other is raised to support the two palm ribs held by the kneeling god Heh, with a tadpole at his elbow, a rebus for 'hundreds of thousands and millions of years'. Above the god is the prenomen cartouche of Sesostris II flanked by two supporting uraei, each of whom wears an *ankh*. All these inlaid details are repeated by exquisite chasing on the metal of the underside. This pectoral is currently suspended from alternating gold balls and drop beads of gold, cornelian and turquoise. A second pectoral from this cache (now in Cairo) is almost identical in design except that the supported cartouche contains the prenomen of Ammenemes III. Unusually, its suspension tubes are set vertically, not horizontally. Moreover, a coloured paste has been used instead of turquoise. Although only fifty years or so separate the manufacture of these two pieces, the lowering of standards in jewellery-making as the dynasty drew to an end is clear, for the workmanship is far inferior. 15 111

A superb openwork gold pectoral made from cloisons inlaid with lapis

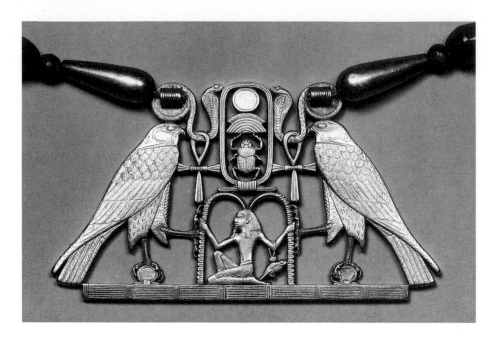

111 The reverse of Sithathoriunet's gold inlaid pectoral, showing the fine quality of the chased decoration, repeating the cloisonné scene on the upper face (see 15). H 4.5cm

lazuli, cornelian and turquoise was found at Dahshur, in the cache belonging to Princess Sithathor, who must have been in part a contemporary of Sithathoriunet. It takes the form of a pylon-shaped kiosk with cavetto cornice and block-decorated supports and base. At the centre the prenomen cartouche of Sesostris II, crowned by hieroglyphs meaning 'the gods are content' (the king's Horus-of-gold name), is appropriately flanked by two falcons wearing the double crown and standing on the sign for 'gold'. The area behind their backs is filled by a sun-disc from which hangs a uraeus wearing an *ankh*. All these details are repeated in chasing on the underside. This pectoral is currently strung with gold ball beads alternating with long drops of turquoise, lapis lazuli, cornelian and gold.

The cache of Queen Mereret, buried near Sithathor at Dahshur, contained two pectorals, the earlier dating to the reign of her father Sesostris III. Made of openwork gold with cloisons containing cornelian, lapis lazuli and turquoise, it takes the form of a kiosk with cavetto cornice supported by two slender-stemmed lotuses emerging from a block-decorated bar. At the top Nekhbet as a vulture stretches out her wings and holds a *shen* in each claw on either side of a central cartouche containing the prenomen of Sesostris III. This is flanked by two standing falcon-headed sphinxes wearing tall plumes and rams' horns. The curve of each sphinx's tail is echoed by the curved stem of a second lotus-flower, whose head unites the tip of the tail with the wing-tips of the vulture. Each sphinx tramples a prostrate negro while holding a pleading Libyan under an upraised front paw which also acts as a support for the cartouche. As usual, all these details are chased on the underside. Suspension is by a string of ball beads of gold and turquoise alternating with drop beads of gold, turquoise and lapis lazuli.

Mereret's second pectoral, like that of Sithathoriunet, was manufactured in the reign of Ammenemes III, so the inlays are not only cornelian

1a

112

43

and lapis lazuli but also glazed composition imitating turquoise, and the workmanship is similarly inferior. At the top of a kiosk, with cavetto cornice and block-decorated supporters and base, Nekhbet as a vulture stretches her wings from one side to the other, the gap between them and the cornice being filled by unhappily placed hieroglyphs for 'Lady of Heaven'. Below, in the centre, are prenomen cartouches of Ammenemes III flanking hieroglyphs reading 'the good god, lord of all lands and foreign countries'. On either side are two heraldically opposed figures of the king wearing a bag-wig and about to brain with an upraised mace a kneeling Asiatic holding a throw-stick. The space behind each royal figure is filled by an *ankh* holding an ostrich-feather fan and the hieroglyphs for Nekhbet's epithet 'Mistress of the Two Lands'. A combined *ankh* and *djed* in her claws is attached to the king's upraised arm; hieroglyphs between his legs and before the Asiatics label the scene as 'smiting the Bedouin of Asia'. All these details are repeated by chasing on the back, where there are two vertical suspension tubes for a string of gold ball beads alternating with drops of cornelian, lapis lazuli and gold. Mereret also owned a pendant in the shape of a small gold falcon with outstretched wings, holding a *shen* in each claw, its top surface inlaid with cornelian and glazed composition (now decayed). There are two rings for suspension on the underside, and two others under the tail for a further pendant which was never recovered.

112 Mereret's kiosk-shaped gold openwork pectoral, inlaid with cornelian, lapis lazuli and turquoise. Beneath the vulture Nekhbet and the prenomen cartouche of Sesostris II, two falcon-headed sphinxes trample Nubians. The same details are chased on the underside. Suspension is by balls and drops of gold, turquoise and lapis lazuli. H 6.1cm

From the cache of Mereret, Dahshur. 12th Dynasty (reign of Ammenemes III, *c.* 1810 BC)

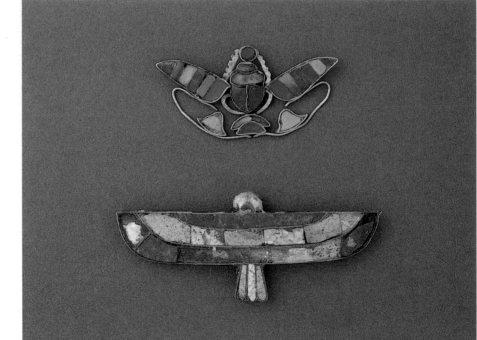

113 **a** (*top*) Electrum winged scarab, inlaid with cornelian, green feldspar and lapis lazuli. It clutches a sun-disc and stands on a *kha*-sign flanked by papyrus-heads, the whole spelling the prenomen of Sesostris II. There are tubes on the underside for suspension. H 1.8cm. 12th Dynasty (Sesostris II, *c*. 1897–1878 BC)

b (*bottom*) Gold human-headed *ba*-bird, representing the characteristics and personality of the deceased. Its back is inlaid with lapis lazuli and turquoise. The body is rounded on the underside and there are two suspension loops. W 5cm. 26th Dynasty or later (after 600 BC)

Two other pendant ornaments of this period rank with the best of the pectorals. One is an electrum winged scarab only 1.8cm high holding a sun-disc inlaid with cornelian in its forefeet and a *kha*-sign, inlaid with feldspar and cornelian, in its back feet. The *kha* is flanked by two feldspar-inlaid papyrus-heads whose wire stems surround and unite the lower elements. The scarab's head and wing-cases are inlaid with lapis lazuli, its back with feldspar, all in cloisons; the four legs are represented by flat gold wire soldered onto the underside of the body. The inlays in the wings are cornelian, feldspar (replaced at one side by green-painted inlay), lapis lazuli and dark-blue composition – all held in a bed of cement, not in cloisons. The design spells out the prenomen of Sesostris II. The lower half of a virtually identical cloisonné-work ornament was found on a corpse at el-Riqqa: it too spells out the royal name supported by inlaid lotus-heads.

From the same burial at el-Riqqa came an unusual cloisonné openwork gold pectoral, the only one of the period not from a royal burial. The framework has a block-decorated base-bar from which rise two long stems ending in drooping papyrus-heads; these are linked to the characteristic under-markings of two *udjat*-eyes flanking a central sun-disc. The main design is of two crows standing on gold signs facing each other over a central sceptre of the type called *nehbet*. All are formed from cloisons inlaid with lapis lazuli, cornelian and turquoise. The details are chased on the underside, where there are two horizontal tubes for suspension. The reason for the substitution of the crows for what would usually be a falcon representing Horus is not apparent.

Another gold openwork cloisonné pectoral, which probably came from Dahshur, comprises a central *Bat*-amulet, surmounted by a sun-disc and flanked by two uraei. The top of the frame is formed from heraldically

113a

114

69

opposed *udjat*-eyes flanking the sun-disc and supported on each side by the tall stem of a papyrus whose head droops under the weight. On one side of the *Bat* sits a falcon-headed sphinx, on the other a seated Set animal. Most of the inlays are lost. There are two horizontal suspension tubes on the back, where the details of the top are repeated in chasing. 71

Queen Aahhotep's burial contained a single gold openwork cloisonné pectoral which, although inlaid with turquoise, cornelian and lapis lazuli, 115 is crude by comparison with the best work of the 12th Dynasty. Within a kiosk with cavetto cornice and block-decorated surrounds Aahhotep's son Ahmose stands in a barque floating on the zigzag waves of the celestial ocean; he is purified by streams of water from vessels held by falcon-headed Re and the Theban god Amen-Re. The whole design is held together and linked to the frame by two protective flying falcons and by the hieroglyphs which name the king and the gods. All the details are chased on the reverse. The theme suggests this was part of the royal regalia made for Ahmose's coronation.

No less than twenty-six cloisonné pectorals came from the tomb of Tutankhamun: some were found on the mummy, others were inside the shrine beneath Anubis, inside a cartouche-shaped chest and inside an ivory and ebony casket with vaulted lid, all three housed in the chamber called the Treasury. Many are kiosk-shaped with block-decorated surrounds, but sometimes too a floral element, such as a frieze of pendant lotuses or buds, or poppies, is introduced, either beneath the cavetto cornice, or attached to the lower edge of the base-bar. What is new is the means of suspension, now rarely by tubes soldered to the back of the piece but by long, gently tapering fitments or boxes attached to the top of the frame which take a number of bead strings or plaque-formed straps. New, too, is the frameless three-dimensional pectoral in which many of the

114 Gold openwork pectoral, inlaid with lapis lazuli, cornelian and turquoise; two crows stand on gold signs flanking a *nehbet*-sceptre. The same details are chased on the underside. w 4.5cm

From el-Riqqa (tomb 124). Mid-12th Dynasty (*c.* 1878 BC)

115 Gold kiosk-shaped openwork cloisonné pectoral of Queen Aahhotep, inlaid with turquoise, cornelian and lapis lazuli. It depicts Ahmose in a barque purified by Re and Amen-Re. The same details are chased on the metal of the underside. W 9.2cm

From the burial of Aahhotep, Dra Abu Naga, W. Thebes. 18th Dynasty (reign of Ahmose, c. 1540 BC)

elements are modelled in the round. In addition, the inlays are almost without exception of coloured glass; cornelian is the only constantly occurring semi-precious stone set into cloisons and even it is sometimes imitated by translucent quartz in a bed of coloured cement. Only in a few of the finest pieces were lapis lazuli and turquoise employed.

Much of Tutankhamun's jewellery was worn in life: many pieces show signs of wear. One pectoral still attached by magnificent articulated straps to its counterpoise was almost certainly part of the coronation regalia. The kiosk-shaped frame has a frieze of gold hieroglyphs spelling and respelling the word for 'eternity' as the base-bar and is surmounted by a cavetto cornice over a star-studded bar of lapis lazuli representing heaven. Within the frame stands Tutankhamun in a short jubilee cloak before the god Ptah enthroned. Behind the king sits Ptah's consort Sekhmet, who holds the sign for 'years' and raises her hand in blessing. The frame behind her is formed by a falcon-crowned *serekh* containing the royal *ka* or spirit double; behind Ptah is a rebus for 'millions of years' surmounted by a uraeus. The two straps are each made from fifteen inlaid gold plaques with four different designs comprising the royal names and titles, and emblems of good wishes and protection, flanked by a double string of small beads. From the other end of the straps hangs the matching counterpoise: inside a square kiosk Tutankhamun is enthroned. Before him stands the goddess Maat, her wings spread in protection and proffering the sign of life. Papyrus columns form the edges of the frame, supporting a block-decorated bar and cavetto cornice. From the lower edge, below the inlaid base-bar, hang tassels of gold and glass beads, the outer three at each side ending in bell shapes, the central eight in gold fish. The materials used are quartz in coloured cement, green, red, dark-blue and light-blue glass, gold, electrum and silver.

47

116 One of Tutankhamun's pectorals, formed from an electrum crescent and full moon in a gold barque floating on an inlaid gold openwork floral base. Four strings of lapis lazuli, gold, turquoise and cornelian beads attach it to a large inlaid floral counterpoise with bead tassels. The inlays are lapis lazuli, feldspar, cornelian, quartz in coloured cement and polychrome glass. w (pectoral) 10.8cm

From the tomb of Tutankhamun (Treasury), Valley of the Kings, W. Thebes. 18th Dynasty (*c.* 1336–1327 BC)

117 Tutankhamun's rigid gold
cloisonné falcon pectoral. It wears a
sun-disc and holds *shen*-signs
surmounted by *ankhs*. The inlays are
lapis lazuli, cornelian and blue glass.
W 12.6cm

From the tomb of Tutankhamun
(Treasury), Valley of the Kings,
W. Thebes. 18th Dynasty
(*c*. 1336–1327 BC)

Other pectorals have also retained their means of suspension and
counterpoise. One of these has a gold openwork inlaid base in the form of
lotus-buds and flowers, their tall stalks growing from a solid bar inlaid
with pendant drops below the sign for 'heaven'. Above the base floats an
archaic gold barque containing a combined crescent and full moon in
electrum. On either side, from box fitments incised with the royal name,
are attached four strings of alternating oblate and long barrel beads of
gold, lapis lazuli, turquoise and cornelian, some of the metal beads being
soldered together to form spacers. The counterpoise is a gold trapezoid
inlaid with a large lotus-bloom flanked by two buds over rosettes. From its

116

134

118 Tutankhamun's openwork gold inlaid pectoral, spelling out the royal prenomen. The plain gold back has chased details and a suspension tube behind the sun-disc. The inlays are lapis lazuli, cornelian turquoise, green feldspar and cement. W 10.5cm

From the tomb of Tutankhamun (Treasury), Valley of the Kings, W. Thebes. 18th Dynasty (*c.* 1336–1327 BC)

lower edge hang tassels of composition and gold beads ending in tiny bells. The inlays are lapis lazuli, feldspar, cornelian, quartz in coloured cement and white, green, light-blue and dark-blue glass.

Probably also part of the coronation regalia is a great openwork gold inlaid pectoral whose central feature is a scarab of translucent green stone. 20 Its inlaid up-curved wings and front legs support an archaic barque of gold inlaid with turquoise in which two uraei flank an inlaid lunar *udjat*-eye; this is surmounted by a gold crescent and silver moon-disc with applied gold figures of the king blessed by Thoth and Horus. Uniquely, the king also wears a crescent and full moon on his head. The scarab holds, in its bird's claws, not only *shen*-signs but an 'Upper Egyptian lily' and three lotus-heads which are joined to a solar uraeus at each side. From the solid gold base-bar, inlaid with roundels, hang large inlaid lotus-heads, buds and stylised circular flower-heads, with a large cornflower of gold and cornelian at each end. The other materials employed in this piece are chalcedony, calcite in coloured cement, lapis lazuli, obsidian and white, red, green and blue glass.

Another element of the coronation regalia may have been a rigid gold cloisonné falcon pectoral. The gold back legs hold the usual inlaid *shen*- 117 signs, which are linked to the base of the wings by inlaid *ankhs*. The materials used are lapis lazuli, cornelian and blue glass, with obsidian for the bird's eye.

A magnificent rigid gold vulture pectoral was worn in life, for it shows signs of wear. It has cloisons which are so closely fitted with blue and red glass that it has been suggested they represent the first example of true enamelling from Egypt. The chased feathering on the underside is just as detailed and there is even a pectoral formed from the royal cartouche on a loop-in-loop chain, depicted in repoussé around the bird's neck. From two rectangular fitments on the wings an articulated strap of alternating plaques of gold and lapis lazuli, flanked by a string of gold and blue glass beads, ends in a clasp. This is formed from two resting falcons modelled in the round; the top surface is inlaid with glass in cloisons to imitate feathering, the underside with the same details chased.

Other pectorals represent the royal throne name. One is composed of a lapis lazuli scarab encircled by cloisonné wings, inlaid with lapis lazuli, cornelian and feldspar. In its front legs the scarab holds a cornelian-inlaid sun-disc, and it stands on a feldspar-inlaid basket, the gap between being filled by the three cornelian plural strokes of the name. The innermost curves of the wings are of sheet gold with chased feathering; the same technique is used for the details on the underside.

Another pectoral pendant incorporating the royal throne name has two interesting variants to its normal form, presumably pure artistic licence.

119 Gold pylon-shaped pectoral of Tutankhamun, containing a lapis lazuli scarab in a barque flanked by baboons wearing a crescent and full moon. The articulated straps, formed from inlaid openwork gold plaques, attach it to a kiosk-shaped counterpoise containing the god Heh. W 10.8cm

From the tomb of Tutankhamun (Treasury), Valley of the Kings, W. Thebes. 18th Dynasty (c. 1336–1327 BC)

The basket on which the central lapis lazuli-inlaid scarab stands has been turned into an inlaid festival basin and the sun-disc supported by its inlaid front legs into a gold crescent with electrum full moon. From the up-curved cloisonné wings, inlaid with lapis lazuli, cornelian and green glass hang two loop-in-loop gold chains, though there are also attachments for two other strings. The chains end with two inlaid gold lotus-flowers and a large heart-shaped pendant inlaid with Tutankhamun's prenomen cartouche flanked by uraei.

Yet another pectoral representing the throne name depicts three lapis lazuli scarabs set side by side in a gold frame. Each scarab sits on a feldspar-inlaid basket; the two outer ones hold in their front legs the gold disc of the sun, but the central scarab holds a crescent and a full moon in electrum. The substitution of the moon for the sun is probably only artistic licence. The craftsman who made this piece certainly had an eye for the unusual, since instead of providing the three vertical strokes necessary for the writing of the name the three scarabs alone serve legitimately as a version of the plural. The splendid openwork counterpoise, which is still attached by strings of gold and glass beads, is inlaid with glass and shows the god Heh kneeling on a block-decorated base and raising a horizontal royal cartouche.

One of the other pectorals also has some puzzling features. It shows, within a pylon-shaped frame, a gold inlaid archaic barque sailing on a lapis lazuli base whose zigzag pattern represents primordial ocean. Within the barque is a central lapis lazuli scarab standing on a *shen* and pushing an inlaid sun-disc. At either side on a gold shrine squats an inlaid baboon, its lapis lazuli front paw raised in adoration. On its head is a silver crescent and gold disc which would make sense if the baboons represented the moon-god Thoth, but here they clearly have solar connotations. Two *was*-sceptres provide the side supporters to the top of the frame, which takes the form of the sign for 'heaven', inlaid with lapis lazuli and studded with gold stars. Two articulated straps are still attached, each formed from twenty-two openwork inlaid plaques, flanked by a string of gold and lapis lazuli beads. The design of the two plaques nearest the pectoral is a kneeling Heh holding palm ribs below the sign for 'heaven'; then come two with a rebus for 'jubilee'; all the remainder have a *sa*, *ankh* or *djed* over a festival basin. The kiosk-shaped counterpoise contains a kneeling Heh holding a *shen*, flanked by two cobras on baskets, one in a white crown, the other in a red one, representing Nekhbet and Wadjet respectively.

A number of Tutankhamun's pectorals appear to have had a purely funerary function, and these will be discussed later (chapter 7). Of his remaining examples two are gold cloisonné vultures, both with solid gold heads and suspended by tasselled cords from loops on the undersides of the wings. Two other pectorals have the *udjat*-eye as a theme, and another is a rigid falcon with a green stone body, inlaid wings and a heart-shaped counterpoise. All the remaining pectorals are based on scarab motifs; nearly all incorporate the royal prenomen, some are winged and some still attached to a counterpoise.

Although during the three hundred years between the death of Tutankhamun and the founding of the 21st Dynasty there are representations

119

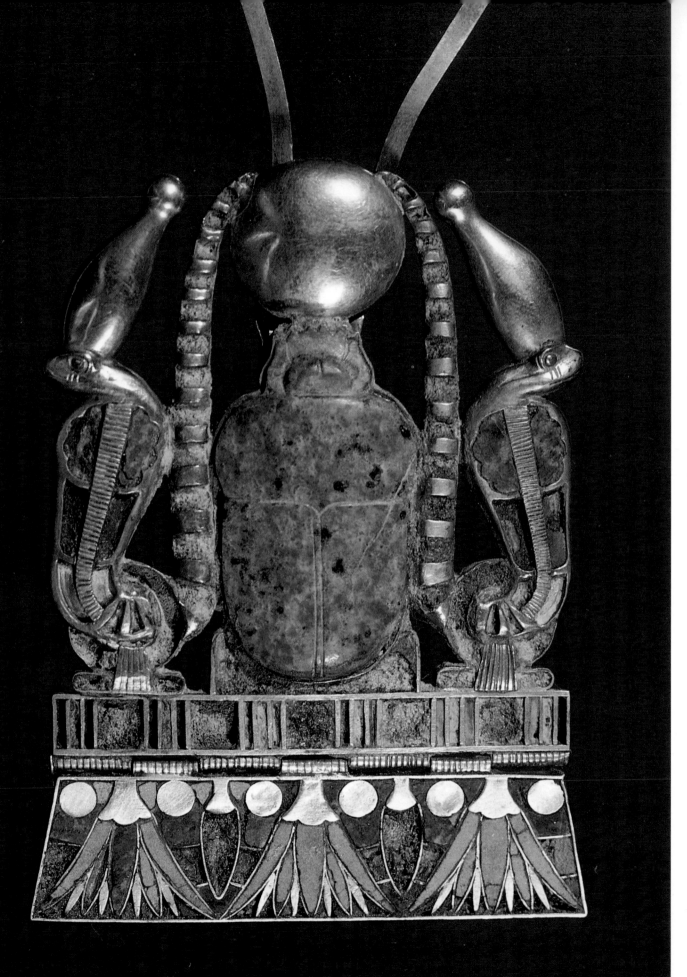

120 Gold pectoral of Sheshonq II, comprising a lapis lazuli scarab emerging from the horizon over an articulated cloisonné frieze and flanked by two uraei wearing white crowns. All inlaid details – the materials are lapis lazuli and coloured faience – are repeated by chasing on the underside. Suspension is by a gold ribbon. w 5cm

From the burial of Sheshonq II, Tanis (tomb III). 22nd Dynasty (*c.* 890 BC)

121 Lapis lazuli bull's head, probably Mesopotamian in origin, set into a gold mount of Egyptian workmanship with floral decoration. H (total) 2.3cm

21st–23rd Dynasties (*c.* 1070–715 BC)

of inlaid metalwork pectorals being worn or presented, hardly any actual pieces of this type have survived. However, from the four intact burials at Tanis, three of them royal, have come examples which not only echo those of the earlier ruler in form but in one way surpass them, for in the finest the inlays are generally of semi-precious stones rather than glass or glazed composition. The only two pectorals without funerary connotations, however, were both found on the mummy of Sheshonq II.

One, of openwork gold, a family heirloom to judge from the inscription, depicts an archaic barque sailing on the primordial ocean, represented by a bar with a zigzag water pattern. Above, the sign for 'heaven' in lapis lazuli dotted with stars is upheld at one side by the stalk of a pendant papyrus and at the other by that of a pendant 'Upper Egyptian lily'. In the barque is a large lapis lazuli sun-disc set in a gold cloison, bearing on both faces in raised relief a scene of Maat before a seated Amen-Re-Horakhty. The disc is protected between the wings of two goddesses, one wearing a disc and ostrich feather, the other horns and disc; both hold an ostrich feather. The space between each set of wings is filled by an *udjat* on a basket surmounted by a *nefer*-sign, the gap in the lower corners by horizontal plaques with a text asking for protection on behalf of Sheshonq I, founder of the 22nd Dynasty. Along the pectoral's lower edge is an articulated frieze of individual inlaid lotus-heads and buds; at the top edge two falcons wearing the double crown mask the suspension rings. The falcons, supporting plants, barque and goddesses are all of hollow gold, made in two halves in a mould; the inlays are lapis lazuli, turquoise and cornelian. Suspension is by means of a flat gold ribbon. 99

The other pectoral takes the form of a large lapis lazuli scarab in a gold cloison, whose underside imitates a beetle's contours, emerging from the symbol for the horizon and pushing ahead the gold disc of the sun. Flanking the scarabs are two gold uraei wearing the white crown, their bodies hung with a *shen*-sign and inlaid with lapis lazuli and red composition. From the base-bar hangs an articulated cloisonné frieze of inlaid lotus-heads and buds with gold discs, all on an inlaid undulating background. All the details of the top surface of the pectoral, which is suspended by a gold ribbon from rings behind the sun-disc, are repeated by chasing on the gold of the underside. 120

From the burial of Queen Kama, mother of the 23rd Dynasty pharaoh Osorkon III, at Tell Moqdam in the Delta has survived a pectoral depicting the ram-headed Amen-Re, squatting with an *ankh* on his knee and flanked by two standing goddesses. On the front of the pectoral the figure of Amen-Re is carved on a lapis lazuli plaque inset into a gold cloison, and the same details are chased on the reverse; above is a sun-disc with uraeus. The goddesses are of gilded silver worked in repoussé; one wears horns and a disc, and proffers a sceptre with a tadpole symbolising '100,000'. The other is Maat, wearing an ostrich feather with disc and holding up an attachment (now lost). Suspension rings are behind their heads. 72

The Tanite delight in placing lapis lazuli beads and cylinders of Mesopotamian workmanship in Egyptian settings allows a superb bull's head set into a gold mount to be dated with all probability to the 21st to 23rd Dynasties. The lapis lazuli carving has a most un-Egyptian spiral on the 121 bull's forehead but the gold setting, with its modelled papyrus-head flanked by a lotus-bud over a basket and solar uraeus at each side, it typical of Egyptian work.

Although metalwork pectorals continued to be depicted until the Late Dynastic Period, no examples have been found.

122 Schist torso of a high official wearing a pectoral depicting the goddess Neith and King Psammetichus II, named by the cartouches. The original pectoral, presumably naming an earlier pharaoh, has been erased. H 36cm
26th Dynasty (*c.* 595–589 BC)

Girdles and belts

The earliest girdles, which date to the Predynastic Badarian Period, are characterised by long multiple strings of bright-green glazed steatite short and standard cylinders, strung closely together and separated by spacer-beads. They are also unique to male burials. Bead belts, though in a rather different form, continued to be worn by men during the Old Kingdom. Ptahshepses, a prince of the 6th Dynasty, owned a belt made from a penannular band of gold, covered by a solid network of disc beads of coloured composition threaded tightly into diamond patterns; they are held in place top and bottom by horizontally strung gold cylinders. The belt is closed by a sheet-gold trapezoidal clasp inset with inlays of cornelian, obsidian and turquoise, depicting the owner seated twice in mirror image, protected by a flying vulture and named in hieroglyphs. Behind the clasp two semicircular gold pieces cover the ends of the belt and draw together the threads of the bead belt. There is provision at the back of the belt for the addition of a tail (now lost), a standard part of royal regalia known as *besa* (*bs3*).

The first belt to survive complete, probably made purely for the burial, was on the body of Senebtisy, a high-born lady of the early 12th Dynasty buried at Lisht. The narrow beadwork belt is fastened by a wooden buckle covered with gold foil bearing its owner's name. Pendant strings hang from it at intervals to the knees and there is a tail at the back. The belt is composed of two outer strings of black glazed composition discs between which others of light and dark green and black are strung vertically into a pattern of lozenges and chevrons. To the wearer's left the pendant strings are composed of long truncated bicones of alternating green and dark-blue glazed composition, separated by black quadrifoil beads, the topmost in each string forming the stem to a single papyrus-head of green glazed composition immediately below the belt. On the other side the beads are long thin, glazed composition cylinders, the topmost in each string acting as stalk for a bead shaped like the 'Upper Egyptian lily'. The badly damaged tail appears to have had a wooden core tipped with gold, its broadest section covered by patterned beadwork.

Princess Neferuptah of the later 12th Dynasty, buried at Hawara, also wore a bead belt with pendant strings, just like that of Senebtisy. It even had the same papyrus- and lotus-headed beads where the strings joined the belt, presumably strung to the left and right of the clasp respectively.

It was at this time that girdles became the prerogative of women. Particularly characteristic are those formed from bead strings interspersed with larger, often precious-metal elements in the shape of leopards' heads, cowries, acacia-seed beads and, by the New Kingdom, wallet and nasturtium-seed beads. Cowries and, presumably, the wallet beads based on them are known to have had amuletic significance, but whether any attached to the other forms is not apparent.

122
37
123

The earliest girdle of this type, almost certainly worn by Senebtisy in her lifetime, is formed entirely from acacia seeds of gold, cornelian, feldspar, lapis lazuli and glazed composition strung between tiny discs of the same materials in six strands. In a number of places the gold acacia seeds are double, formed by soldering two together one above the other. In the centre of the girdle, however, a double bead from each row is joined together in the same way to form a spacer. Khnumet's burial contained gold, turquoise, lapis lazuli and cornelian acacia-seed beads in sufficient numbers to form a double-stringed girdle. Sithathoriunet at Lahun owned two girdles. One comprises eight large hollow gold cowries, one of them a clasp with the usual tongue-and-groove closing device on the undersides, each made in two halves with a loose piece of metal inside to rattle as the wearer walked. They have been strung to alternate with acacia-seed beads of gold, cornelian, lapis lazuli and feldspar in two rows. The other girdle is formed from seven large, hollow gold double leopards' heads set back to back (one of them a clasp with tongue and groove), strung between rows of amethyst ball beads; each section of beads is pulled together at midpoint by a pair of small hollow gold double leopards' heads, one on each string, soldered together. Sithathor had a cowrie-shell girdle like that of Sithathoriunet, but composed of six gold cowries instead of eight and strung between acacia-seed beads. Mereret, like Sithathoriunet, had two girdles, one composed of large and small hollow gold cowrie-shells (one of them a clasp), which would have rattled when she walked; the twelve small cowries currently strung between the large ones may well have come from another girdle entirely. Mereret's other girdle had large hollow gold double leopards' heads, though without the smaller examples. This time, however, the leopards' heads also contained metal pellets to make a tinkling sound. Contemporary cosmetic containers with female figures as

124

16

1b

123 Senebtisy's glazed composition beadwork belt, with pendant strings to the knees and a tail at the back. The gold-foil covered buckle bears her name. w 58.5cm

From the burial of Senebtisy, Lisht. 12th Dynasty (reign of Ammenemes I, c. 1991–1962 BC)

124 A detail from a girdle of Sithathoriunet, composed of amethyst beads strung between large double and smaller quadruple gold leopard heads. One of the larger leopard heads acts as a clasp. L (total) 82cm

From the tomb of Sithathoriunet, Lahun. 12th Dynasty (reign of Ammenemes III, c. 1830 BC)

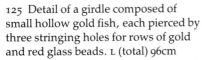

125 Detail of a girdle composed of small hollow gold fish, each pierced by three stringing holes for rows of gold and red glass beads. L (total) 96cm

From the burial of the three wives of Tuthmosis III, W. Thebes. 18th Dynasty (c. 1465 BC)

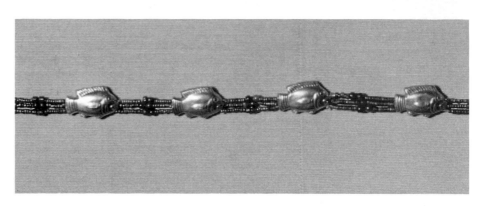

supporters and concubine figurines, the latter at least intended to stimulate sexual activity in the Afterlife, are frequently depicted wearing cowrie girdles. 156

A female burial of late 17th Dynasty date found by Petrie at Qurna contained a girdle in the form of a double string of small electrum barrels 14c passing at intervals through the double piercing of twenty-six electrum wallet beads. This is the first appearance of this form of bead, which was to have great popularity as a girdle component during the New Kingdom. It is not surprising that, just like their 12th Dynasty counterparts, the three minor wives of Tuthmosis III, buried in an inaccessible cave on the Theban West Bank, should also have owned a number of girdles. Two now comprise seven rows of acacia-seed beads made from cornelian, turquoise, and gold, the latter soldered together to form vertical spacers, which Winlock was able to reconstruct with a fair degree of accuracy, even though a great many of the elements were lost. They are closed by slipping a pin through the interlocking rings soldered to the two gold end-plates. An unusual buckle is all that survives with certainty from what must once have been a girdle with two rows of elements, since soldered to one side of its outer edge are two rings; the other side has a single ring to take a loop of the stringing thread. The buckle takes the form of the two hieroglyphs *hotep neb* (*ḥtp nb*), which mean 'all contentment'. The *hotep*-sign was once inlaid with glass or composition which is now completely decayed; the *neb* is a piece of shaped agate in a gold rim. The signs for 'life' and 'stability' are incised on its base. It is currently strung with various loose beads of gold,

126 Detail of a New Kingdom wall-painting from the tomb of Nebamun depicting dancing girls at a banquet. They wear girdles, earrings, bracelets and armlets. They are accompanied by female musicians wearing earrings, broad collars, bracelets, armlets and finger-rings.

From W. Thebes. 18th Dynasty (reign of Amenophis III, c. 1370 BC)

lapis lazuli and feldspar, including some shaped like conus shells and others ribbed like nasturtium seeds. Of the remaining girdles, one is composed of gold and lapis lazuli wallet beads, each pierced by three holes to take the short strings of tiny gold discs threaded between each element. Another has small gold fish, each made in two halves hammered into a mould and soldered around the outer edge and, like the wallet beads, pierced by three stringing holes for intervening rows of gold and red glass beads. 125

From the New Kingdom there are a number of representations of girdles, especially those formed from wallet beads, all worn by women. Usually it is servants or dancing girls who are shown dressed in little more than this scanty article, whether serving banqueters in wall-paintings, as part of the decoration of ointment spoons, as shapely supporters to cosmetic containers, or as small wooden figurines serving the same function as concubine figures of Middle Kingdom date. But the girdle seems also to have been the uniform of prepubescent girls who appear wearing it at their parents' side with no apparent sexual connotation. 126 80

Encircling the hips of Tutankhamun's mummy was a ceremonial girdle with a chased gold band and name buckle from which once hung long beaded strings and a tail. A magnificent electrum belt with incised chequered pattern, which tied at the back and had the metal frame for a patterned beadwork apron still attached at the front, was found on the mummy of Sheshonq II at Tanis. However, no other examples of girdles have survived after this period, nor are they depicted being worn.

127 One of Aahhotep's hinged gold armlets, formed from the encircling wings of a cloisonné vulture inlaid with cornelian, lapis lazuli and turquoise. It is closed by a retractable pin. D 6.6cm

From the burial of Queen Aahhotep, Dra Abu Naga, W. Thebes. 18th Dynasty (reign of Ahmose, *c.* 1540 BC)

CHAPTER SIX

Bracelets, finger-rings and anklets: jewellery for the arms and legs

Bands of gold for the arms and legs

Bracelets and bangles

The Egyptians used the same term, *menefret* (*mnfrt*), for bracelets and anklets but by adding the words 'for the arms' – *net awy* (*nt'wy*) – they were able to distinguish quite clearly the functions of these ornaments, which often came in matching sets. Another even less informative term, 'appurtenance of the arms' – *iryt awy* (*iryt 'wy*) – was employed in the same dual way.

The earliest bracelets are in some ways little more than shorter versions of the strings worn around the neck. The finest examples – four in all – were found on a wrapped arm in the tomb of Djer at Abydos. The one nearest the wrist consists of lapis lazuli and hollow gold balls, flanking irregularly shaped turquoise beads and gold triple ring-bead spacers, with a single hollow gold rosette at the centre; these are strung on gold wires and animal hair plaited together and were originally closed by a loop-and-ball fastening. The best-known bracelet is composed of twenty-seven alternating turquoise and gold plaques, the latter apparently cast in an open mould in the form of an archaic crouched falcon atop a rectangular *serekh*, with its characteristic palace façade panelling. The *serekh* usually contained the Horus name of the king, associating him with the ancient falcon-form sky-god, and a series of dots on each bead may be a crude rendering of the serpent hieroglyph with which Djer's name was written. The beads are graduated in size, with markings on the back of each to indicate its position; a single pyramid-shaped bead of gold at each end acts as a terminal. A series of gold plaques embossed with the cartouches of Sety II surmounted by feathers, with suspension rings at each corner, came from the Gold Tomb in the Valley of Kings; although eighteen centuries later than Djer's *serekhs*, these plaques presumably formed a similar royal bracelet.

The third bracelet comprises four groups of three gold and amethyst toggles held vertically by wire and hair wound around a central groove. Between each group small turquoise balls flank larger gold-capped turquoise lozenges. The fourth is formed from three strings of gold balls, turquoise discs and long bicone beads, some of spiral gold wire, the others of lapis lazuli grooved in imitation, all gathered into three sections by two

128 Gold bangle, its surface inlaid with cornelian, feldspar and lapis lazuli hieroglyphs naming the owner, Psusennes I, flanking a central baboon carrying an *udjat*. He is also named in the texts incised on the inner face. Worn by the mummy. D (ext.) 12.2cm

From the burial chamber of Psusennes, Tanis (tomb III). 21st Dynasty (*c.* 1039–991 BC)

groups of turquoise and hollow gold ball beads. It is closed by a double loop-and-ball fastening.

Bangles without any fastening and merely slipped onto the wrist over the hand were made from the Badarian Period onwards; the earliest examples are simple circles of bone, shell, ivory, horn or tortoiseshell, later also of slate, chert, flint, marble and schist. Indeed, this form of bangle remained fashionable throughout the Dynastic Period, although it came to be made of precious metal and was often elaborately decorated. The twenty silver bangles of Queen Hetepheres are fine early examples, though now badly decayed. They were made from thin sheet metal, with a strongly curved outer face, and each was impressed with four schematic butterfly designs which had been filled with inlays of cornelian, lapis lazuli and turquoise, the lapis occasionally supplemented by coloured plaster, all set in cement.

Sixteen centuries later, at Tanis, the mummy of King Psusennes wore on his right arm a narrow strip of sheet gold encircled on the outside by an inscription with sunk inlays of cornelian, feldspar and lapis lazuli naming the owner. The central element is a large *udjat*-eye, fronted by a uraeus and held by a baboon, all of which forms a cryptic writing of the word for 'king'. Two heraldically opposed texts, again naming Psusennes with epithets, run around the inner face of the band. His contemporary, general Wendjebauendjed, wore an even more unusual bangle consisting of two thin bands of sheet gold separated by a wafer-thin layer of resin and capped top and bottom by gold strips. The repoussé decoration of the outer face consists of a large inlaid *udjat*-eye adored by two baboons, who are flanked by smaller *udjats*; elsewhere smaller baboons and *udjats* are turned to flank an *ankh*. Around the inner face runs an incised line of text, asking protection for an unknown woman.

These, of course, are the most decorated bangles, but twenty-one plain bands of gold, graduated in size and with turned-in rims, came from the

128

hoard beneath the pyramid of the 3rd Dynasty pharaoh Sekhemkhet. At Dahshur Khnumet owned a single bangle cut from plain sheet gold, and a woman buried at Qurna during the 17th Dynasty wore four bangles made from plain gold rods of semicircular section bent into a circle and soldered. A number of identical solid silver examples of the Ramesside Period were found at Tell Basta. Queen Tausret probably owned a pair found in the Gold Tomb in the Valley of the Kings, each formed from a length of square-sectioned gold rod, tapering into wires which are coiled back on themselves. The two ends are united by an additional gold wire curled into a spiral. A second pair from the same source, made from hollow electrum and sharply triangular in profile, have applied rope braid at the upper and lower rims. At Tanis the mummy of Psusennes wore on his left arm a solid gold bangle with a triangular profile, weighing almost 1.8 kilogrammes and inscribed around the inner face with a martial blessing by Amen-Re. The companion bangle on the right arm is also of solid gold but is circular in section, and the corresponding martial blessing is delivered by the goddess Mut.

The Tanis burials also contained a new type of bracelet without fastening which looks exactly like a large finger-ring, complete with shank, collars and bezel. A fine example, found in the ransacked burial of Hornakht, is a penannular gold band ending at each side in an inlaid papyrus-head between which is attached, by means of a wire, a gold-mounted scarab with a cryptic inscription on the underside. The incised inner face of the band names the prince and depicts Decan deities; another has a cylinder as a bezel. Two bangles found on the mummy of Sheshonq II are identical to Hornakht's, except that the lapis lazuli scarab, attached by pins, is set in a gold mount decorated with rope braid. Curiously, although the undersides of both scarabs bear names, neither names Sheshonq. Some hundred and fifty years later bracelets also identical to Hornakht's but made entirely of glazed composition were found in non-royal Kushite burials in the Sudan.

A third bracelet in this form found in the tomb of Sheshonq II is a penannular gold tube made in two sections which are pinned together and bridged by a Mesopotamian lapis lazuli cylinder-seal; this is carved with symmetrically arranged heroes and animals in a style thirteen centuries earlier than the setting. Another two tubular gold bracelets have an *udjat* and a long barrel as the bezels. General Wendjebauendjed wore a tubular gold example with scrolls and discs raised on the surface at the shanks' ends; a gold-capped agate bead forms the swivelling bezel. Amenemope also had a pair of tubular gold bangles, each set with a stone ball bead as bezel but with differently shaped collars.

Less elaborate forms were found on the mummy of Psusennes, consisting of collarless penannular gold tubes or twisted wires bridged by a semi-precious stone or gold bead. These echo ones found on the body of Tutankhamun, who owned two tubular gold bangles, one with a gold-capped lapis lazuli barrel bead as the bezel, the other with an identically shaped capped inscribed cornelian bead. The origins of such bangles lie in the Old Kingdom some thousand years earlier: a single cornelian bead on a gold wire was found at the left hand of a woman buried at Giza during the later Old Kingdom. Twisted wire bangles date back to the Early

14d

131

130

Left 129 One of a pair of hollow gold bracelets belonging to Psusennes I. The outer face is decorated with two heraldically opposed texts naming the owner in gold on a lapis lazuli background. D (ext.) 7.6cm

From the sarcophagus of Psusennes, Tanis (tomb III). 21st Dynasty (*c.* 1039–991 BC).

Right 130 Gold bracelet of Sheshonq II, imitating a scarab finger-ring in form, with papyrus-head collars and swivelling lapis lazuli bezel set in a gold funda with braid decoration. D (ext.) 6.7cm; L (scarab) 2.5cm

From the burial chamber of Sheshonq II, Tanis (tomb III). 22nd Dynasty (*c.* 890 BC)

Left 131 Solid gold bangle, one of a pair worn by Psusennes' mummy, each weighing almost 1.8 kg. It is inscribed around the inner face with a blessing for its owner. D (int.) 6.5cm

From the burial chamber of Psusennes, Tanis (tomb III). 21st Dynasty (*c.* 1039–991 BC)

Dynastic Period in Nubia, where A-group burials contained ones made from copper; they were still being produced in massive form in gold in the Graeco-Roman Period three thousand years later. *76*

Penannular metal bangles appear as early as the First Intermediate Period: either gold wire looped into a knot opposite the open ends, or sheet gold pierced by holes at the ends to allow a tie cord. At Dahshur Ita, Sithathor and Mereret all owned pairs made from sheet gold; the latter two pairs have, in addition, an incised central groove as decoration. Their greatest popularity, however, was in the Graeco-Roman Period, when they often had animal-head protomes attached to the ends of precious-metal shanks made of rods, plain or twisted tubes or coiled wire. *77c*

The earliest bangles to have a closing device are two pairs, of silver and silver gilt, dating to the 11th Dynasty. The latter are tubular with rings slipped over each end to form a 'push-fit' closing device: the closed end of the tube is pushed into the open end opposite. The second pair are closed in a similar way. Each is made from two tubular wires joined for part of their length, with a ring slipped over each end of one wire and over a single end of the other. In this tradition is a gold pair from the burial of the three wives of Tuthmosis III. These bangles, which have a concave profile, are closed by a hinge with interlocking pins, one of them retractable, at each side of a box-clasp; around the outer face is incised the prenomen cartouche of the king's co-ruler, Hatshepsut. There were also three pairs of plain sheet gold, each made in two hinged halves with a retractable pin, with the king's two names incised down their inner faces. *77a* *77b*

Psusennes at Tanis wore a pair of hollow gold bracelets, semicircular in section, each made in two uneven interlocking segments which are closed by pins, one of them retractable. Each segment is formed in two halves soldered along the rims, the joins masked by a gold spiral pattern on an inlaid lapis lazuli background. The inner faces are completely plain except for the markings 'left' and 'right'; the outer face, however, is decorated with two heraldically opposed texts giving the royal nomen and pre-nomen in gold on a background of lapis lazuli. A pair of tubular bracelets, found in the cache at Deir el-Bahri on the mummy of the High Priest of Amun, Pinedjem II (*c.* 970 BC), are made in two halves, the wire hinge at one side hidden by a large lapis lazuli oblate bead. From the opposite side, beside the tenon-and-pin closing device, hung five tassels (one bracelet now has only four); two of the tassels are of gold chains ending in lapis lazuli flower-heads, the other three of alternating gold, lapis lazuli and cornelian beads ending in gold flower-heads. The almost flat inner surface of each bracelet is plain gold, but the whole of the outer surface is inlaid with cornelian and lapis lazuli in a stylised feather pattern. *129* *132*

A bracelet from the hoard beneath the pyramid of Sekhemkhet at Saqqara is one of the earliest examples of a type which was to be extremely popular throughout the Dynastic Period, formed from ten rows of nearly four hundred gold ball beads strung between spacers. A woman buried at Giza during the later Old Kingdom wore bracelets of gold and glazed composition cylinders and discs, separated by gold spacer-bars and ending in gilded semicircular terminals; the cords had to be tied and untied whenever the bracelet was worn. Bracelets of this type under the name *hadret* (*h3drt*) are depicted inside Middle Kingdom coffins. *25*

132 Pair of tubular gold hinged bracelets, the wire hinge hidden by the lapis lazuli bead. The outer surface is inlaid with cornelian and lapis lazuli in a feathered pattern. There were originally five tassels, two of gold chains ending in lapis lazuli pendants, and three of gold, lapis lazuli and cornelian beads ending in gold flower-heads. D (ext.) 6.8cm

From the mummy of the High Priest Pinedjem II, Deir el-Bahri cache, W. Thebes. 21st Dynasty (c. 970 BC)

In most instances only the presence of gold multiple bead spacers and magnificent clasps served to show that all the royal ladies of the 12th Dynasty originally wore bracelets of this kind. The position of the masses of loose beads which once formed the strings went unrecorded, and so it was not until the discovery and patient reconstruction of Sithathoriunet's jewellery at Lahun that it became possible to reconstitute them. In the tomb of Ita were openwork gold clasps from two bracelets; they took the form of djed-pillars inlaid with cornelian, turquoise and lapis lazuli, and between them must have been strung some of the large numbers of loose cornelian and glazed composition beads that were also found. From Khnumet's burial came ten bracelet clasps, the two finest taking the form of an openwork gold sa-amulet, the top surface inlaid with lapis lazuli, except for the ties, which are of cornelian and turquoise; the same details are incised into the gold of the underside. At the top of the amulet is a tiny gold leopard's head, and the whole is set into a gold frame, each side of which slides into a three-sided gold box. This is pierced by sixteen holes to take sixteen strings of beads, which are undoubtedly to be found among the hundreds of lapis lazuli, turquoise and cornelian examples from this treasure. As in the burial of Ita, there were a number of gold spacers made from tubular beads soldered to a back-plate.

Sithathoriunet owned a pair of bracelets made from thirty-seven rows of alternating sections of cornelian and turquoise discs strung between six such gold spacers. Its two plain gold end-plates are grooved to take a sliding clasp which is cut into a T-shape at each side; it bears on each face a cloisonné inscription inlaid with decayed blue material on a cornelian ground naming Ammenemes III. Two of Sithathor's bracelet clasps are identical in every way with those of Ita: the inlaid djed is between two vertical gold bars, one of which is a three-sided box over which a second box, pierced by holes for stringing threads, can be slid. Another pair of Sithathor's bracelets, also with sliding box-clasps, was once formed from rows of cornelian beads strung between ribbed rectangular gold spacers. Queen Mereret owned an identical pair of cornelian bracelets and a pair of inlaid gold bracelet clasps naming Ammenemes III, just like those of Sithathoriunet. Neferuptah's bracelets were made from cornelian and feldspar cylinders strung horizontally between rigid columns of gold beads; they ended in two gold bars, from which the stringing threads would have emerged as one cord to be tied and untied each time the piece was worn. The turquoise bracelets with ribbed gold spacers worn by Princess Nubhotepti exhibit for the first time a different type of closing device, which was to be the most common during the New Kingdom and later: soldered to the gold end-pieces are interlocking tubes which are held in place by a retractable locking pin.

Queen Aahhotep's jewellery continued the traditions of the Middle Kingdom, for there were two pairs of bracelets made from beads and spacers between locking end-pieces. One has gold, turquoise, cornelian and lapis lazuli cylinders threaded on gold wires in thirty rows between thin gold spacers to form triangular patterns. The spacers are unusual, being formed from a rectangular sheet of gold with the two long sides turned up at right angles and pierced by thirty holes for the stringing wires. The two gold end-pieces, closed by aligning loops and passing a pin

16

133

133 Bracelets of Aahhotep, made from beads of gold, turquoise, lapis lazuli and cornelian strung between gold spacers and locking end-pieces. Both bear the name of Ahmose. H 4.3, 3.6cm

From the burial of Queen Aahhotep, Dra Abu Naga, W. Thebes. 18th Dynasty (reign of Ahmose, c. 1540 BC)

through them, are chased with the nomen and prenomen cartouches of Ahmose, one of each bracelet, one half of the inscription on each end-piece. A second pair has eighteen rows of cornelian, lapis lazuli and turquoise beads strung in individual single-coloured sections between seven gold spacers formed from beads soldered together. The eighth spacer-bar is an open gold box containing a lapis lazuli ground into which are inset gold hieroglyphs spelling the prenomen of Ahmose. This piece was originally closed by a pin interlocking two gold end-plates but at some time, in order to enlarge the bracelet, an extra plate with hinge and second pin was inserted between them which now splits the text chased on them in two.

Both Sithathoriunet and Mereret owned bracelets made from bead strings and recumbent lion amulets. Sithathoriunet had four matched pairs of hollow gold lions, each made in two halves in a mould and soldered along the spine before being attached to a base. They are in two sizes; the smaller have a single threading hole pierced through the length of the base, the four larger have two threading holes. They are currently strung with large amethyst ball beads and are closed by hollow gold knot-clasps with the usual tongue-and-groove closing device. Mereret had only one pair of bracelets with matched pairs of hollow gold lions, which are pierced by two holes, not through the base but between the front legs. They are now strung with tiny gold, turquoise, cornelian and lapis lazuli beads and a gold knot-clasp.

These feline-form elements are probably the origin of the bracelet

29

108a

spacers with cats which are a feature of female royal burials from the time of the Second Intermediate Period onwards. In the British Museum are two such pieces, each formed from a gold rectangular box enclosed at the short ends but open at the sides; on top recline three gold cats, one group with bodies to the left, the other to the right, heads erect and facing forward. Their solid bodies are hand made, the ears and the wire legs and tails added separately. Through the width of the box run twelve tubes for threading. On each base are two lines of roughly incised text, one naming Queen Sobkemsaf, the other her husband, the 17th Dynasty ruler Nub-kheperre Inyotef.

Each of the wives of Tuthmosis III originally wore a pair of bracelets made from rows of cornelian, feldspar, lapis lazuli and gold long bicones, the metal beads in each row soldered together to form spacers which flank a central hollow gold box. To its top were once attached five reclining cats, each with alert, raised head and elegantly crossed front paws, their bodies to the left on one box and to the right on the other. The central cat, carved from cornelian, is set in a cloison, as were the two outer ones; these were probably made from composition which has decayed away. The two inner gold cats, however, made in two halves over a core and soldered down the spine, are for the most part soldered directly to the plate, which is pierced by fifteen stringing holes. At each end of the bead strings is a hollow gold bar with interlocking rings and retractable pin. The remains of five such bracelets have survived.

Possibly based on the form of these bracelets are a number of examples from Tutankhamun's burial. They comprise bead strings, sometimes with gold spacers, and a large ornamental centre-piece, such as a lapis scarab in a gold mount, a cornelian *udjat*-eye or an inlaid gold plaque smothered with granulation and applied wire. Long bicones, barrels, discs, some of them fancy, are the commonest forms for the strings but occasionally small scarabs and other amulets serve as beads. Gold proliferates but lapis lazuli, cornelian, red jasper, turquoise and, in particular, glass and glazed composition in imitation of them are also used.

Aahhotep's jewellery, although it was essentially traditional, also contained the earliest example of a new, rigid type of hinged bracelet. It is made from two interlocking semicircular gold bands, which are closed by two pins, one retractable so the bracelet can be opened. The outer surface

134 Bracelet belonging to one of the three wives of Tuthmosis III, composed of rows of feldspar, cornelian, lapis lazuli and gold beads with a central gold spacer-bar surmounted by reclining cats of gold, cornelian and probably composition. It was closed by a retractable pin. The remains of five such bracelets were found in the burial. L 24cm
From the tomb of the three wives of Tuthmosis III, W. Thebes. 18th Dynasty (*c.* 1465 BC)

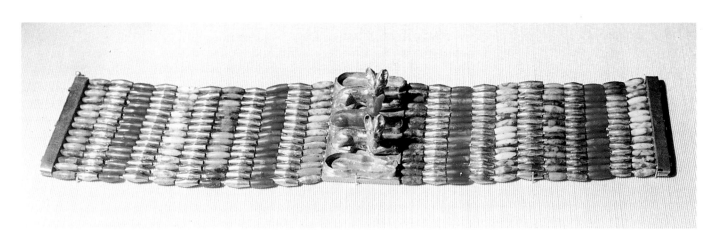

135 Rigid hinged conical gold bracelets, the outer surface inlaid with strips of cornelian, turquoise and blue glass imitating sections of beads, the inner incised with the names of Tuthmosis III. D (max) 5.6cm

From the burial of the three wives of Tuthmosis III, W. Thebes. 18th Dynasty (*c.* 1465 BC)

has gold figures and text in chased raised relief, with a background of inset lapis lazuli pieces. At one side of the hinge the royal ancestors, in the shape of two falcon-headed Souls of Pe, counterbalanced by two jackal-headed Souls of Nekhen, are shown in the posture of jubilation. In two separate scenes the kneeling Ahmose is protected by Geb enthroned; in one the god wears the red crown of Lower Egypt, in the other the double crown.

From the burial of the wives of Tuthmosis III came three pairs of rigid hinged conical bracelets. In form and decoration these represent those most commonly depicted being worn. The outer surface is inlaid with vertical strips of cornelian, turquoise and blue glass, ribbed to give the effect of bead strings between gold spacers; the smooth inner face is incised with the nomen and prenomen cartouches of Tuthmosis III. Each is made in two halves with two hinges, one with a retractable pin to allow opening.

In this tradition are the superb gold bracelets from Tanis which incorporate inlaid panels, some of them openwork. Although Tutankhamun's mummy wore openwork bracelets, the independent elements, often scarabs, are framed by bead straps rather than rigid supports. A pair of openwork bracelets found on the mummy of Psusennes is each formed from four articulated sections of three gold and two lapis lazuli lunettes, separated by four rectangular gold plaques incised with the royal nomen and prenomen and name of the donor, the High Priest of Amun, Smendes. The mummy of Amenemope wore a conical pair of openwork inlaid gold bracelets, each made in two equal hinged halves with an inlaid border, containing a lapis lazuli scarab with inlaid vertical wings. Flanking each panel are the nomen and prenomen cartouches not of Amenemope but of Psusennes, surmounted by a sun-disc. From Hornakht's burial came a rigid hinged bracelet formed from two semicircular segments with inlaid rims; the outer surface of one segment is inlaid with a scene of two baboons wearing a moon-disc and crescent, flanked by cartouches of Osorkon II and adoring an *udjat* on a sign for 'gold'. Unusually, the remainder of the outer surface is not inlaid, but has an incised interlocking floral design. On the inner face the adoration scene is repeated by chasing, and the rest of the surface is incised with a row of Decan deities and two lines of text.

Of the seven bracelets worn by Sheshonq II, one rigid pair takes the form of two unequal segments of sheet gold, hinged and closed by a retractable pin. Two raised relief cartouches on the plain inner face show that these pieces were family heirlooms, for the names are those of Sheshonq I. The central feature of the outer face is a cloisonné panel inlaid with lapis lazuli, cornelian and white material to form an *udjat*-eye (the left eye on one bracelet, the right on the other) over a chequered basket. The remainder of the band is decorated with alternating vertical strips of gold and lapis lazuli. A similar pair belonged to Prince Nemareth (Nimlot), son of Sheshonq I. Again, the gold segments are unequal; in the smaller central panel flanked by hinges is the figure of Harpocrates seated on a lotus wearing a moon-disc and crescent and flanked by two large uraei. God and uraei are of raised chased gold; the lotus, background, block border and rim decoration were once inlaid with red and blue glass or glazed composition. The owner is named on the plain inner face.

An unusual pair of rigid hinged bracelets found on Psusennes is made of seven gold tubes, alternately striated, soldered together along their length; they are closed by interlocking tubes and retractable pin. On the inside, along the third and fifth tubes, are inscriptions, one naming the king, the other his wife Mutnedjmet, the bracelets' donor. The only similar example, which is amuletic, came from Hornakht's burial and takes the form of two unequal gold segments, each resembling three gold tubes soldered together along their length, the outer surface striped with

24

136

137

136 Pair of rigid hinged gold conical bracelets, the smaller segment of each depicting the figure of Harpocrates flanked by uraei. The inlays are lapis lazuli and decayed polychrome glass. The inner faces are incised with the name of the owner, prince Nemareth (Nimlot), son of Sheshonq I. H 4.2cm
From Sais(?). 22nd Dynasty (reign of Sheshonq I, *c.* 940 BC)

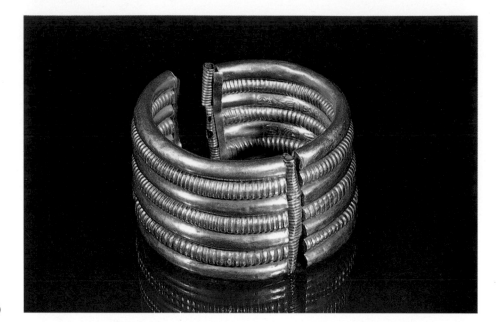

137 Rigid hinged gold bracelet, worn by the mummy of Psusennes, made from gold tubes soldered together and closed by a retractable pin. The inscription on the inner face names Psusennes and his wife. H 4.5cm

From the burial of Psusennes, Tanis (tomb III). 21st Dynasty (c 1039–991 BC)

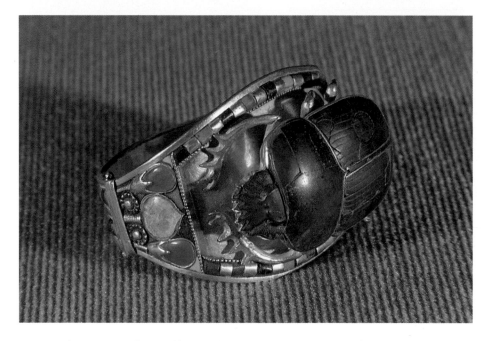

138 Massive hinged gold hoop-shaped bracelet found on the mummy of Tutankhamun. Its central plaque bears a large gold scarab inlaid with lapis lazuli. All the floral and block-decoration is inlaid with lapis lazuli, turquoise, cornelian and quarz in coloured cement. D (max, int.) 5.4cm

From the tomb of Tutankhamun, Valley of the Kings, W. Thebes. 18th Dynasty (c. 1336–1327 BC)

insets of, apparently, niello. At the centre are three gold wires carrying six scarabs and a frog.

A form of rigid hinged bracelet which is first encountered among Tutankhamun's jewellery is hoop-shaped with an enlarged plaque as its central feature, which is often inlaid or inset with ornaments in the round; hinges at either side join the plaque to a curved broad gold band. In the finest example from the boy-king's burial a massive gold scarab in the round, its back inlaid with lapis lazuli, squats on an oval plaque which is decorated with inlaid lapis lazuli, turquoise and cornelian and a line of gold granules. At each end of the scarab is a trapezoidal panel with cloisonné decoration depicting a mandrake fruit and poppy-buds, with gold rosettes filling the interstices. The buds are inlaid with cornelian and

138

the background with lapis lazuli and turquoise, but the green of the mandrakes comes from coloured cement covered by translucent quartz. The remainder of the band's outer surface, plain gold on the inside, carries two strips of inlaid block decoration. Others of Tutankhamun's bracelets of this type have front plaques based on the *udjat* eye – examples are worn by royal statues – or are inlaid with flying vultures.

Since this form of bracelet was particularly popular during the Ramesside Period it is not surprising that one of the most spectacular examples is a pair bearing the name of Ramesses II, found at Tell Basta. The roughly oval upper section, hinged at one end and closed by a pin at the other, is dominated by a large convex-topped lapis lazuli inset which forms the body of a duck whose two heads of hollow gold, with applied wire details and inlaid eyes, turn back towards the ribbed gold tail. The surface round about, and the gold bands over the duck's shoulders and lower back which hold the inlay in place, are a mass of granulation and applied wire, mostly rope-braid decoration. The cartouche containing the prenomen of Ramesses II worked in repoussé lies between one hinge and the duck's heads; corresponding to it at the other end are lozenge and boss patterns

139 Two of the bracelets found on Tutankhamun's arms (see 19). The massive rigid hinged gold example (**a**) has a cylinder of turquoise inset into a plaque smothered with applied wire and granulation. The other (**b**) has a flexible strap of gold and glass beads attached to a circular gold plaque, also highly decorated, with a central lapis lazuli inset. L (**b**, total) 17.4cm

From the tomb of Tutankhamun, Valley of the Kings, W. Thebes. 18th Dynasty (*c.* 1336–1327 BC)

in granulation. The other half of the bracelet is formed from alternating plain and ribbed half-cylinders, and the whole of the inner face is backed onto plain sheet metal.

A rather poorly made pair of silver bracelets of this type came from the Gold Tomb in the Valley of the Kings. They have a central oval plaque of sheet metal with hinges at each end; the remainder of each bracelet has embossed chevron and stylised flower-head patterns. The scene on the plaque, worked by embossing and chasing, shows a seated King Sety II holding out a stemmed cup into which his wife Tausret pours a libation from a vase. Because the king also holds a fan-shaped emblem in his hand, composed of the kneeling figure of Heh, god of millions, grasping palm-ribs which symbolise 'years', it has been suggested that this jewellery was connected with the royal jubilee.

Armlets

Since the armlets worn by both men and women are usually depicted as matched sets with bracelets, it is almost impossible, with a handful of exceptions, to distinguish between actual examples of the two forms. Queen Aahhotep, however, owned two pieces of jewellery which were clearly intended to be worn on the upper arm. One consists of a gold hoop with a hinge at each end, one fixed, the other with a retractable pin. Half of   127 the hoop is formed by the embracing outstretched wings of a vulture, its top surface inlaid with cornelian, lapis lazuli and turquoise. The tail and outspread back legs, holding *shen*-signs, would have helped to hold the piece in place on the upper arm. The other side of the hoop is composed of two broad gold bands, their outer surface inlaid with vertical strips of blue and green material. Between them is a central boss inlaid with cornelian from each side of which runs a gold wire, ending at the hinge end in a lotus-bud inlaid with turquoise.

The other gold armlet has a tall plume, whose outer surface is inlaid in a chevron pattern with cornelian, lapis lazuli and feldspar; this would have   140 lain along the inside of the upper arm to hold the piece in place. On the outer surface of the gold loop, on the half below the plume, cloisonné *djed*- and *tit*-amulets are inlaid with the same semi-precious stones as the plume. The inner face on this part of the hoop is flat, but on the other half of the armlet it is raised by repoussé to imitate thick plaited cord. Attached to the top surface of the armlet, opposite the plume, is a hollow gold box shaped like a cartouche, its sides decorated by cloisonné triangles inlaid with lapis lazuli, cornelian and turquoise. The inscription on the top, formed from hieroglyphs cut out of sheet gold and set into lapis lazuli, names Ahmose. It is flanked by two gold foil, recumbent sphinxes, each made in two halves by hammering into a mould and soldered down the spine. Their *nemes* wig-covers are formed from cloisons, but most of the inlays have been lost.

Five pairs of magnificent hinged gold armlets came from the cache discovered in the pyramid of the Meroitic Queen Amanishakheto at Meroe. Each is made in two halves and decorated with true polychrome cloisonné enamelling. In all but one the edges are framed by rope braid. The most spectacular pair also has strips of wire and granulation framing a   6 row of concentric circles between rows of lozenges. The central band on

Far right 140 Sphinx armlet of Aahhotep, made from gold inlaid with lapis lazuli, cornelian and turquoise. The cartouche names Ahmose. The spike would have lain inside the upper arm to hold the piece in place. D (max) 11cm

From the burial of Queen Aahhotep, Dra Abu Naga, W. Thebes. Early 18th Dynasty (reign of Ahmose, *c.* 1540 BC)

141 Gold hinged armlet with fused polychrome glass inlays, belonging to Queen Amanishakheto. There is a double winged Mut at the hinge, and on each half of the armlet are two other winged goddesses holding *ankhs*. L (open) 17.5cm

From the pyramid of Amanishakheto, Meroe. Meroitic Period (late 1st century BC)

142 A conical hinged gold anklet inlaid with lapis lazuli and cornelian, found on the mummy of Psusennes. The central panel depicts a winged scarab and the remainder of the band is decorated with gold and lapis lazuli lunettes. The inner face names the donor, the High Priest Smendes.

From the burial chamber of Psusennes, Tanis (tomb III). 21st Dynasty (*c.* 1039–991 BC)

each half is divided into seven panels separated by a horizontal feathering pattern. The central panel has a raised relief frontal bust of a crowned god; the others have a crowned goddess. Attached at the hinge of one of the pairs is the figure of Mut wearing the vulture head-dress and double crown, her two pairs of inlaid wings spread out in the fashion of a St Andrew's cross; she stands on an inlaid lotus-head. In the companion armlet, otherwise identical in every way, the goddess wears a Nubian wig with a circlet and uraeus, and a falcon with sun-disc perched on her head.

Another pair has a similar double-winged Mut at the hinge, and a frieze of cobras around the top edge. On each half of the armlets are the raised relief figures of two goddesses holding *ankhs*. The third pair has at the top a frieze of cobras above an openwork lozenge pattern; at the lower edge a band of openwork drops is surmounted by openwork lozenges. The central strip has five panels on each half of the armlet with raised relief cobras separated by horizontal feathering. The fourth pair has a central band with four panels in each half of the armlet containing two male and two female crowned frontal busts in raised relief separated by horizontal feathering. From wire threaded from suspension loops attached to the lower rim hang a number of hollow gold pendants representing a tied bundle. The whole field of the fifth pair is covered by bands of decoration. Over the hinge is a plaque in the shape of a naos from which emerges an aegis collar crowned by a ram's head.

141

59

Anklets

Not only armlets, but also anklets were often made to match bracelets, and therefore are usually difficult to identify if not found *in situ* on the legs. Indeed, the Egyptians knew bracelets and anklets by the same word – *menefret*. They merely distinguished them by the term 'for the legs', *net redwy* (nt rdwy). In the same way, anklets could be called 'appurtenances of the legs' – *iryt redwy* (ìryt rdwy). There is, however, a single instance in a Middle Kingdom coffin of a word which can mean nothing but 'anklets', *seru n(u) redwy* (srw n(w) rdwy). At all events, formed from beads or shells, anklets were certainly worn by women at least as early as the Badarian Period, and they remained a popular female fashion during the Old and Middle Kingdoms, to judge from representations. It is worth noting that the estate manager Wah, buried at Deir el-Bahri during the 11th Dynasty, wore matched anklets and bracelets made from blue-green glazed composition. King Hor, buried at Dahshur, also owned matching sets.

A pair of anklets of gold and glazed composition discs, separated by gold spacer-bars and ending in gilded semicircular terminals, were found around the ankles of a woman buried at Giza during the later Old Kingdom. They matched exactly a pair of bracelets from the same burial. Sithathoriunet at Lahun had a matching pair of bracelets and anklets of alternating sections of cornelian and turquoise discs between gold multiple spacers; the anklets' gold sliding bar-clasps, however, lack the hieroglyphic text of the bracelets. Princess Neferuptah at Hawara also owned matched bracelets and anklets, the latter of cornelian cylinders strung horizontally between rigid columns of gold beads and ending in two gold bars. As with the pair from Giza, the stringing threads would have emerged as a single cord to be tied and untied every time they were worn. Those of Nubhotepti, who was buried at Dahshur, though also of cornelian with ribbed gold spacers and a matching pair of bracelets, were, in contrast, closed by interlocking tubes and a pin.

143

143 A pair of Sithathoriunet's anklets, formed from cornelian, turquoise and gold beads between gold spacers, closed by a plain sliding clasp. A matching pair of bracelets was also found (see 16). H 4.6cm

From the tomb of Sithathoriunet, Lahun. 12th Dynasty (reign of Ammenemes III, *c.* 1830 BC)

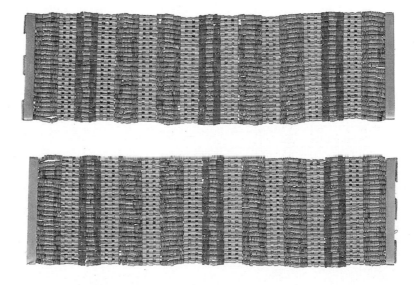

144 A pair of Sithathoriunet's anklets, formed from amethyst and gold beads strung with matched hollow gold claw amulets and closed by a knot clasp. L 17.5cm, (claw) 3.1cm

From the tomb of Sithathoriunet, Lahun. 12th Dynasty (reign of Ammenemes III, *c.* 1830 BC)

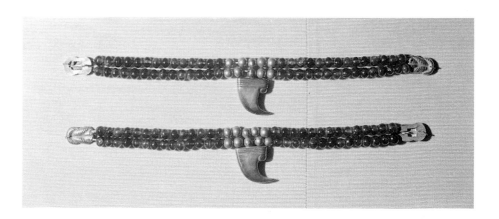

However, the most characteristic feature of anklets from Middle Kingdom royal burials is a pair of matched claw-amulets, one facing right, the other left, usually strung with double rows of amethyst ball beads and closed by a gold knot-clasp. The claws from the burial of Khnumet are of gold, the section at the top of the upper surface incised to look like granulation, the area below inlaid with turquoise, cornelian and lapis lazuli in cloisons to look like feathering. All these details are chased on the underside. A single suspension loop shows they were, unusually, intended to be strung with a single row of beads, some of which at least must have been gold discs. The claws from the burial of Sithathoriunet are only hollow gold, but the attachment is two gold ball beads set one on top of the other, flanked at each side by another four, so the stringing must have been double. Those of Sithathor and Mereret are solid gold with chased details, again with double suspension. 144

The wearing of anklets was far more restricted during the New Kingdom; there are a few representations of them, usually worn with archaic-style costume, but the only identifiable ones to survive — and their function has been disputed — came rather surprisingly from the burials of Tutankhamun and Psusennes. Tucked into the hollow of the former's groin was a rigid gold conical form with two hinges, one with retractable pin, its outer surface inlaid with ribbed vertical strips of coloured glass. However, scattered over his abdomen and legs were four pairs of narrow gold bands, the outer faces of three inlaid with polychrome glass, the fourth with blue glass alone. The mummy of Psusennes apparently wore a pair around the ankles. They are hinged, in the shape of truncated cones of gold with inlays of lapis lazuli and cornelian. Each is made in two unequal parts closed by slipping a pin through interlocking tubes. The smaller segment in each is a gold plaque inlaid with a winged scarab and sun-disc over the sign for 'great', flanked by two uraei, the whole spelling out the royal prenomen. On the inner face a vertical text names the donor, the High Priest of Amun, Smendes. The remainder of each anklet is formed from three articulated sections, each with five horizontal lunettes of alternating gold and lapis lazuli. The upper and lower rims are inlaid with blocks of lapis lazuli between gold. 142

Finger-rings

In the Badarian Period simple rings of horn or stone were probably worn on the finger. That was certainly the function later of small strings of beads, gold-foil bands and wires of copper or silver closed by twisting the ends together. By hanging a scarab on the wire before twisting it shut the most popular form of Egyptian finger-ring came into being, although sometimes, as in the case of a 17th Dynasty woman buried at Qurna, it was merely held in place on the finger by a fibre cord. Two fine early examples of scarab finger-rings were owned by Sithathoriunet. In each the gold wire shank is twisted together opposite the gold scarab bezel; the scarab's wings are inlaid with strips of turquoise and lapis lazuli, its thorax with cornelian, its head with green stone and its legs with cornelian and blue and white composition. There were a number of finger-rings in Mereret's cache, of which two gold examples have an elongated oval rigid bezel, one patterned with tiny granulation lozenges, the other chased with four

145 Painted and gilded cartonnage mummy mask of a high-born lady, wearing calcite ear-studs, an elaborate broad collar, bracelets and armlets decorated with *udjats*, a pectoral and real finger-rings, including one of cornelian. H 58cm
Thebes, 18th–19th Dynasties (*c.* 1370–1250 BC)

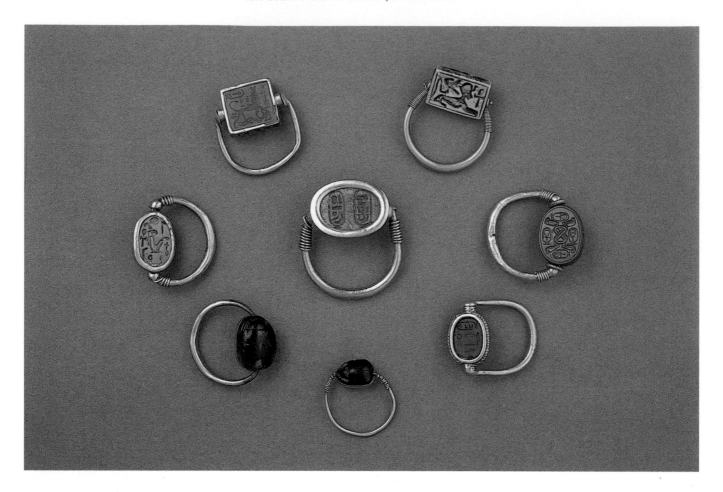

146 Gold finger-rings with swivelling bezels: **a** rectangular blue glass bezel, depicting Tuthmosis III as a sphinx; the verso has the royal Golden Horus name. w (bezel) 1.6cm; **b** rectangular green glazed steatite bezel depicting a royal sphinx; on the verso is 'son of Amun'; w (bezel) 1.8cm; **c** green glazed composition scarab naming Hatshepsut. L (scarab) 1.8cm; **d** green glazed steatite scarab naming Sheshonq I. L (scarab) 2.3cm. **e** green jasper scarab inscribed with good luck symbols. L (scarab) 1.8cm; **f** plain amethyst scarab – an early example of this form of finger-ring. L (scarab) 1.6cm; **g** plain obsidian scarab, another early example. From Abydos. L (scarab) 1.1cm; **h** lapis lazuli scarab naming Hatshepsut. L (scarab) 1.5cm

   f, **g**: 12th Dynasty (*c.* 1820 BC); **a**, **c**, **e**, **h**: 18th Dynasty (*c.* 1470–1425 BC); **b** New Kingdom (*c.* 1250 BC); **d**: 22nd Dynasty (*c.* 945–924 BC)

spirals. Her remaining gold rings have scarab bezels, one of them inlaid exactly like that of Sithathoriunet, the others made of lapis lazuli, turquoise, amethyst and glazed composition, some with texts, the others plain.

Scarab finger-rings from contemporary non-royal burials now in the British Museum have shanks of tubular gold with decoration formed by beating out their ends; the resultant wire is passed through the bezel and wound around the shank on both sides. The scarabs, of obsidian, amethyst and lapis lazuli, are set in a gold funda or else rimmed, so that the underside can be seen. The latter is the method which was to become the most popular for the swivelling bezel. Throughout the New Kingdom the decoration of the mount becomes more and more elaborate, with applied wire and granulation, and the bezels themselves can take the form of a plaque or cylinder or fancier shape made from semi-precious stone, glazed composition or glass. Sometimes the shank and bezel mounting have collars, and the wire encircling the shank ends is added, not an extension of the shank. From the rigid bezel forms of the Middle Kingdom developed the massive stirrup-shaped signet, sometimes with double or triple shank, like those of Tausret and Tutankhamun; a later version had a chunky bezel and cut-away back. A less substantial metal signet is represented by nearly a score of finger-rings of Ramesside date dug up at Tell Basta, in which a mere flattening of one side of the shank provides a

146

148

Right 147 Gold cloisonné finger-ring with a three-dimensional bezel showing two prancing horses, probably the royal chariot team. The floral decoration was once inlaid with red and blue material, now decayed.
  From Saqqara. 19th Dynasty (reign of Ramesses II, *c.* 1279–1213 BC)

Below 148 Precious-metal signet rings: all of gold except **a**, which is silver.
  a names and titles of a priest of Sheshonq I and Psammetichus I. H (bezel) 2.6cm; **b** name and title of Seshonq, a priestly official. L (bezel) 3.4cm; **c** rectangular bezel bearing the name of Amenophis II flanked by Nile gods. L (bezel) 1.4cm; **d** swivelling rectangular bezel bearing the *nebti*-name of Tuthmosis III; the verso has the prenomen and epithets. L (bezel) 1.9cm; **e** the name of the priest Padipep. L (bezel) 1.6cm; **f** stirrup-shaped, with a royal figure, probably Akhenaten. W (bezel) 1.4cm; **g** stirrup-shaped, with the prenomen of Akhenaten. L (bezel) 2.2cm; **h** stirrup-shaped, with the name of a Ptolemy, probably the third. H (bezel) 2.9cm
  c, **d**, **f**, **g**: 18th Dynasty (*c.* 1450–1336 BC); **a** & **b**: 26th Dynasty (*c.* 600–575 BC); **h**: Ptolemaic Period (*c.* 250–200 BC)

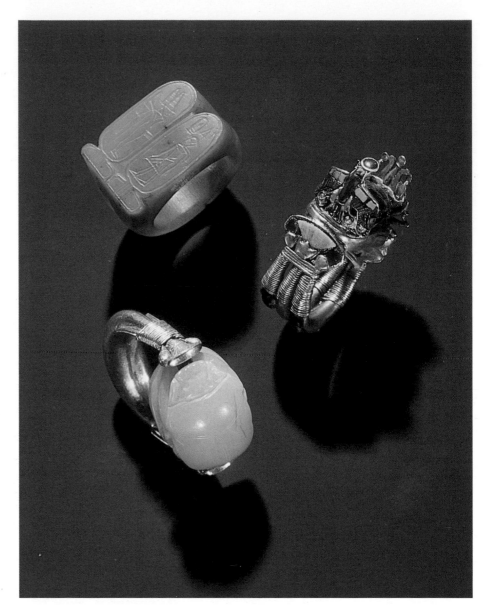

149 Three of Tutankhamun's rings. The green nephrite signet (**a**) shows the king and Min. One of gold with a three-dimensional bezel (**b**) is formed from a lapis lazuli scarab flanked by an inlaid falcon and moon barque on a cartouche-shaped base. The inlays are green jasper and glass. The scarab bezel of the gold ring (**c**) is of chalcedony; the underside shows Thoth and the *udjat*. H (**a**, bezel) 2.6cm; L (**b**, bezel) 2.2cm

From the mummy of Tutankhamun, Valley of the Kings, W. Thebes. 18th Dynasty (*c*. 1336–1327 BC)

surface for chased decoration. The metal stirrup-shaped signet was also imitated in glazed composition, which was itself the medium for new openwork forms.

From Tutankhamun's burial came fancy metal finger-rings which for the first time have a fixed, cast, three-dimensional bezel. The finest has an 149b enthroned falcon-headed god, adored by the kneeling king who is flanked at either side by a worshipping baboon. The Gold Tomb in the Valley of the Kings contained some rings of unusual form, a few of which were precursors of a distinctive type found at Tanis. One unique example, possibly a family heirloom, has a filigree-work shank, made from gold wire in the form of hieroglyphs, repeated four times and arranged heraldically, meaning 'all life and dominion'. The bezel, of individual sheet gold hieroglyphs which project far above the level of the shank, spell out a variant of the prenomen of Ramesses II. Another gold ring has a bezel formed from eight small oval inlaid cloisons arranged in two rows, while the shank is four horizontal wire spirals separated from the cloisons by vertical twisted and striated wires. The third, also of gold, is an openwork deep 'wedding-ring' shape, formed from the encircling wings of a falcon wearing a sun-disc and holding horizontal flabella in its claws; at each wing tip is the cartouche of Sety II. The design is chased on the inside of the band but formed from cloisons inlaid with coloured glass on the outer face.

Of the thirty-six rings worn by Psusennes' mummy the finest is undoubtedly one of gold which looks like a miniature bracelet, its inlaid outer surface divided into sections of lapis lazuli cartouches and cloisonné lozenges inlaid with lapis lazuli and cornelian, all separated by strips of inlaid rectangles between gold. Psusennes and Amenemope both wore plain gold 'wedding-band' rings; that of Wendjebauendjed, however, is not only massive, but its outer face is incised with tiny well-formed hieroglyphs asking his royal master to intercede for his servant's well-being. Bezels in the shape of the *udjat*-eye, or plaques incised with it, were

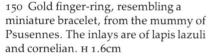

150 Gold finger-ring, resembling a miniature bracelet, from the mummy of Psusennes. The inlays are of lapis lazuli and cornelian. H 1.6cm
From the burial chamber of Psusennes, Tanis (tomb III). 21st Dynasty (c 1039–991 BC)

151 Solid gold 'wedding-band' finger-ring, the outer surface incised with hieroglyphs asking King Psusennes to intercede for the ring's owner, Wendjebauendjed. H 0.9cm
From the burial chamber of Wendjebauendjed, Tanis (tomb III). 21st Dynasty (reign of Psusennes, c. 1030 BC)

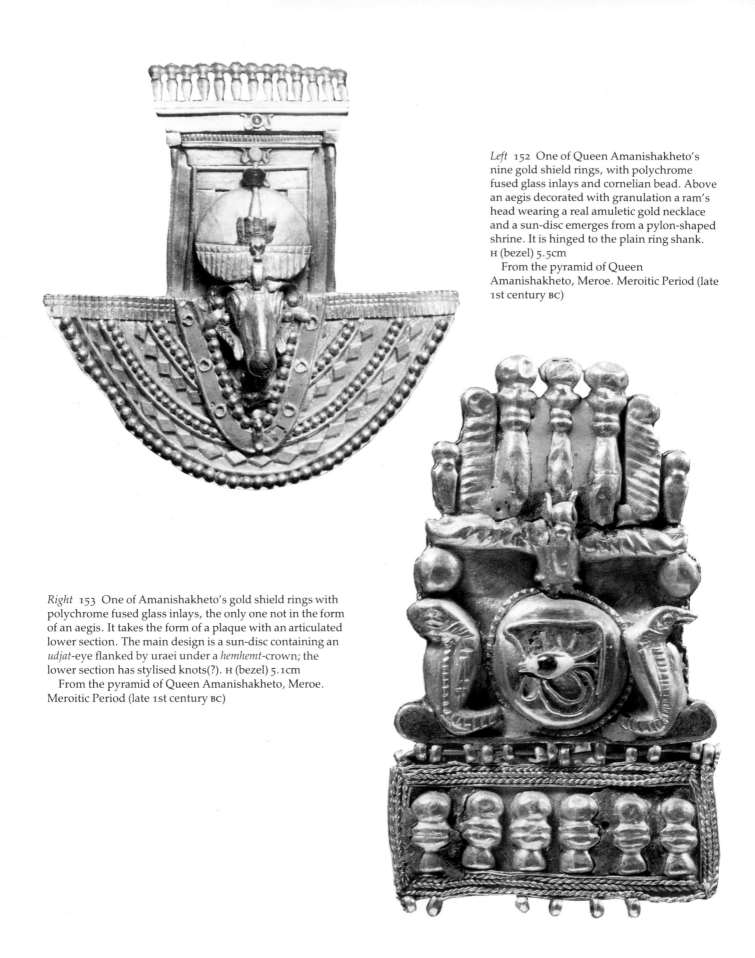

Left 152 One of Queen Amanishakheto's nine gold shield rings, with polychrome fused glass inlays and cornelian bead. Above an aegis decorated with granulation a ram's head wearing a real amuletic gold necklace and a sun-disc emerges from a pylon-shaped shrine. It is hinged to the plain ring shank. H (bezel) 5.5cm

From the pyramid of Queen Amanishakheto, Meroe. Meroitic Period (late 1st century BC)

Right 153 One of Amanishakheto's gold shield rings with polychrome fused glass inlays, the only one not in the form of an aegis. It takes the form of a plaque with an articulated lower section. The main design is a sun-disc containing an *udjat*-eye flanked by uraei under a *hemhemt*-crown; the lower section has stylised knots(?). H (bezel) 5.1cm

From the pyramid of Queen Amanishakheto, Meroe. Meroitic Period (late 1st century BC)

particularly popular in finger-rings at Tanis. Wendjebauendjed owned four, one an heirloom with the name of Ramesses IX.

Unique to the Meroitic culture of the Sudan are so-called shield rings, with massive gold-shaped and inlaid bezels, hinged and set at right angles to circular shanks. Queen Amanishakheto owned nine, of which eight take the form of an aegis, a broad collar crowned by a head; in four the head is a ram's. The finest is one in which the broad collar is decorated with alternating bands of large granules and solid lozenges, all separated by wire strips and originally inlaid with glass; gold shells once hung from the lower edge. The horizontal top edge, formed by a frieze of uraei, is surmounted by a ram's head in the round wearing a crowned uraeus topped by a cornelian bead and a large sun-disc. Beneath the ram's head hangs a bead necklace represented by large granules and a strap necklace inlaid with green glass, with a divine figure as pendant. The head itself is backed by a rectangular plaque shaped like a pylon-form naos with cavetto cornice, torus moulding and frieze of uraei. A gold wire passing through eyelets at the back of the naos attaches it to the shank. In another of the ram-headed rings some of the outermost row of shell pendants are still attached by wire, the ram wears an *atef*-crown, and the shank has spiral decoration. A third ram-headed example is almost identical, but the shank has a granulated lozenge pattern. In the fourth the ram's head wears a sun-disc and two tall inlaid feathers, flanked on each side by a winged goddess, probably Mut; the shank was once inlaid. One shield ring still has an outermost row of hollow shells attached by wire. Above the aegis, flanked by two *udjat*-eyes, is a bearded male bust in the round, wearing the double crown with uraeus, a broad collar and two pectorals on granulation chains; he has been identified as the Meroitic god Sebiumeker.

152

185

In another shield ring a lion's head in the round wears a *hemhemt*-crown and two necklaces; the shank is decorated by a band of granules. The last aegis-form ring is surmounted by a lion's head wearing the *hemhemt*-crown and flanked by two rams' heads wearing sun-discs; all wear jewellery. The ring shank was once inlaid with glass. The only shield ring not in aegis form comprises a plaque in two parts, connected by wire threaded through loops. The larger upper section depicts a sun-disc containing an applied wire *udjat*-eye flanked by uraei and surmounted by a *hemhemt*-crown. The smaller lower section, edged by rope braid and hung with suspension loops for missing shell pendants contains six raised relief stylised knots (?). The last hinged ring has as bezel a hollow bust of Mut in the round decorated with rope braid and granules and wearing a double crown.

153

However, Amanishakheto's jewellery-makers also continued pharaonic traditions, for she owned no fewer than sixty-four signet-rings, mostly of gold, a few of silver, with shanks and bezels cast in one and all worked in intaglio; there were also three with stone inlays and one completely of stone. A set of four gold rings show episodes from the Meroitic king's divine birth; others show Meroitic deities and themes, pharaonic symbols, some Hellenistic elements and a few subjects, such as lion-headed bees, whose significance is not apparent.

CHAPTER SEVEN

Amuletic jewellery, awards and insignia

One of the most basic uses of Egyptian jewellery was to add colour to costumes, which were essentially of plain white linen, but since, as has been seen, colours had a symbolism for the Egyptians, a further magical element was always present. Funerary jewellery, made expressly for the burial, often without means of fastening or of flimsy or cheap materials, was purely amuletic; this is discussed in the following chapter. However, because everyday jewellery was often taken to the tomb it is not always possible to make a distinction between the ornamental and the amuletic. 12

Purely amuletic jewellery was worn by the living as well as the dead. The pendant known as *nekhau* (*nkȝw*), in the shape of a fish, was attached to the end of the plait of a child or young female as a charm against drowning. Its first mention is in a literary text preserved in the Westcar Papyrus, which recounts feats of magic at the court of Old Kingdom pharaohs and the miraculous birth of the founding kings of the 5th Dynasty. This copy of the text dates appropriately to the Middle Kingdom, which was the time of the amulet's greatest popularity. Examples of this date, modelled in the round, are of hollow gold, silver or electrum, sometimes with inlays, representing the batensoda fish. Another type was flat, with a green stone inlaid cloison for its body and added metal tail 157a and fins; this represented the Nile perch. It was an amulet of this type which was lost by one of King Sneferu's harim ladies as she rowed him on

His majesty gave to me of gold: 2 pairs of bangles, 4 collars, 1 armlet and 6 flies . . .

Left 154 Mereret's gold oyster-shell pendant with a design inlaid with cornelian, turquoise and lapis lazuli in the shape of a lotus-head with floral elements. H 4.6cm

From the cache of Mereret, Dahshur. 12th Dynasty (reign of Ammenemes III, *c.* 1810 BC)

Right 155 Middle Kingdom cylinder amulets (*c.* 1850–1800 BC); **a**, hollow gold with a removable cap, has granulation on the shaft. H 7.3cm; **b** & **c** are solid cylinders, made from alternating amethyst beads and gold foil over a core, with gold caps. H 5.4cm, 4.6cm

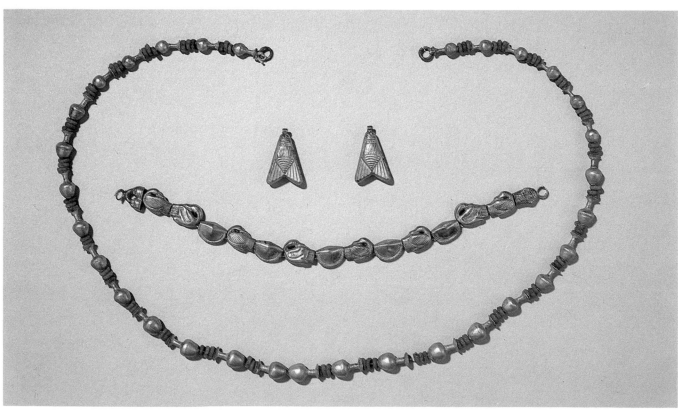

Above 156 Steatite cosmetic container in the form of a kneeling girl supporting a footed jar. She wears a fish pendant at the end of her plait and a cowrie girdle. H 8.3cm
    12th Dynasty (*c.* 1800 BC)

Above left 157 Amuletic jewellery: **a & d** four gold fish pendants (*nekhau*) with cloisons containing inlays; in the top pair (**a**) the inlay is green feldspar, in the lower (**d**) quartz and chalcedony. H (**a**) 1.9cm, L (**d**) 3.6cm; **b** two hollow gold sphinx beads intended to be threaded with beads, possibly to form bracelets. L 2.6cm; **c** an uninscribed electrum oyster-shell amulet. W 3.4cm
    Middle Kingdom (*c.* 1900–1800 BC)

Left 158 Amuletic jewellery: **a** pair of gold foil flies, made over a core – part of an honorific award. L 2cm. New Kingdom (*c.* 1500–1250 BC); **b** gold trussed ducks, wallet beads, snake's head and lotus-flower. L (ducks) 1.1cm. 18th Dynasty (*c.* 1470–1330 BC); **c** amulets shaped as gold *hes*-vases strung with blue glass beads. L (41.8cm). Middle Kingdom (*c.* 1800 BC)

the lake, according to the Westcar text, for she speaks of her '*nekau* of fresh turquoise'. Contemporary representations show it worn by the tomb-owner's daughter in a wall-painting at Meir and by a girl carved from stone who kneels to provide the support to a cosmetic container.

Cylindrical pendants, which also make their first appearance during the Middle Kingdom, though they continued in use until after the New Kingdom, are also exclusively associated with women. They exist in two forms. A solid type has a shaft usually of gold or silver bands alternating with those of amethyst, feldspar, turquoise, cornelian, lapis lazuli or even rock-crystal, all on a rod. Mereret at Dahshur owned one with bands of turquoise and amethyst separated by thin strips of gold. Occasionally the shaft is a solid stone cylinder, like that of Sithathor, which was made from lapis lazuli. Both ladies owned a cylinder amulet of solid gold with granulation patterns; Sithathor's is covered by tight chevrons, while Mereret's has granulation chevrons alternating with the plain gold of the shaft. Each end is always closed by a metal cap, slightly conical in shape, one of them surmounted by a suspension tube.

The second type of cylindrical pendant is of hollow metal with a removable upper cap and granulated decoration on the shaft. The patterning on a splendid gold example in the British Museum resembles that on Mereret's. In contrast, three gold cylinders and one of silver, which came from the burial of the wives of Tuthmosis III, have attached droplets which give the effect of studs rather than granulation. To judge from later examples, which still contain amulets or spells written on papyrus to protect women and children, the hollow cylinders were amulet-cases and the solid ones dummies in the same shape.

Amuletic claw pendants, worn exclusively by women on the ankles, are usually of gold or silver, occasionally with cloisonné inlays like those of Khnumet; Sithathor, Sithathoriunet and Mereret all owned pairs. Although a dancing girl is depicted wearing anklets with attached claws in the 12th Dynasty tomb of Wahka II at Qaw el-Kebir, and real claws have been found in burials of Predynastic date, their significance is not clear.

The cowrie was held to have amuletic significance because of its resemblance to the female genitalia, and so girdles made from beads in this form would protect their female wearers from malevolent forces, especially if they were pregnant. Girdles were also made of semicircular wallet-beads, so-called because the markeings around their curved edges look rather like stitching; these beads are clearly based on the cowrie and would have served a similar function. Girdles with hollow gold cowries were owned by the 12th Dynasty great ladies Sithathoriunet and Mereret, and the metal pellets inside would have made a tinkling sound as they walked. Wallet-bead girdles, however, were more popular in the New Kingdom, and examples have survived from the burial of a 17th Dynasty woman at Qurna and from that of the wives of Tuthmosis III.

Amulets of deities were commonly worn by the dead, but they could also be worn by the living, especially when they might extend their particular protection, as did the hippopotamus-goddess Thoeris; instantly recognisable with her pendent breasts and swollen stomach, she aided women at childbirth. From the burial of the wives of Tuthmosis III came a string of gold beads with twenty-seven hollow gold Thoeris pendants

156

155b,c

155a

144

1b

14c

159

160

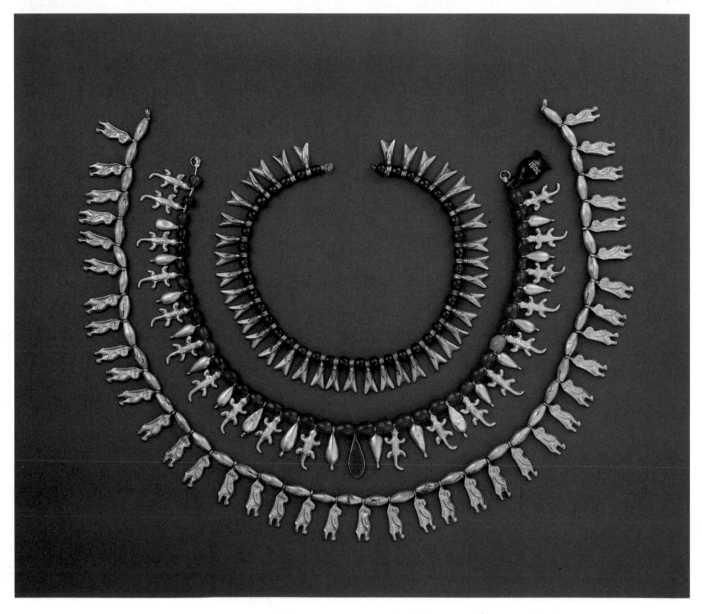

Top left 159 Gold amuletic figures of deities, all solid cast in the round except **a**, which has a flat back.

a squatting Amun, king of the gods. After 600 BC; **b** Ptah, creator god at Memphis. After 600 BC; **c** Mut, wife of Amun at Thebes. H 2.9cm. c. 1200–1100 BC; **d** jackal, probably Anubis, patron of embalming. 21st–22nd Dynasties (c. 1000–900 BC); **e** ibis-headed Thoth (c. 1000–900 BC); **f** kneeling ram-headed archer, pierced for suspension. Meroitic, after 300 BC

Bottom left 160 Amuletic strings: **a** solid cast gold fly amulets and garnet beads. L 24cm; **b** gold date-shaped pendants, gold drop inlaid with lapis lazuli and gold lizards, symbolic of regeneration, with cornelian beads. L 26.8cm; **c** hollow gold Thoeris amulets strung with long gold beads. L 41.8cm

18th Dynasty (c. 1470–1350 BC)

Right 161 Gold amuletic finger-rings; **a** upreared cobra. H (bezel) 2cm; **b** 'wedding-ring' shape, inset with *ankh*, *djed* and *was*-sceptres. D 2.2cm; **c** looped wire ending in a falcon-headed cobra hood and sun-disc at one end, cobra head at the other. From Alexandria. W (max) 2cm; **d** three human-headed uraei attached to wire shank: (*left to right*) Serapis, Harpocrates and Isis. H (bezel) 2.2cm; **e** bezel in the shape of the emblem of Neith, who is also incised into it. H (bezel) 2.3cm; **f** oval bezel with scene of Mut, lady of heaven, seated in a barque. D (max, ext.) 2.3cm; **g** bezel bearing a text naming Mut. H (bezel) 2.8cm; **h** heavy wire in double uraeus form. W (max) 1.5cm; **i** swivelling bezel with granulation, surmounted by a frog in the round. D (shank, ext.) 2.4cm; **j** massive solid cast shank and lapis lazuli cylinder as bezel. D (shank, ext.) 3.1cm; **k** swivelling bezel of cornelian cat on a plinth. D (ext.) 2cm

i, **j** & **k**; 18th Dynasty (c. 1370 BC); **f** & **g**: New Kingdom (c. 1370–1190 BC); **e**: 26th Dynasty (c. 600 BC); **a**: Ptolemaic (c. 300 BC); **b**: possibly Meroitic (after 300 BC); **c**, **d** & **h**: Graeco–Roman Period (c. 300 BC–AD 100)

(made by beating into a mould and soldering on a back-plate), and a bracelet formed from gold beads strung with small hollow gold amulets of Thoeris and her dwarfish helper Bes, suspended through rings on the heads, sides and below the feet. Seven hollow gold Thoeris amulets, each with a ring on top of the head, came from the Gold Tomb in the Valley of the Kings.

Amulets could also endow their wearers with the particular powers or attributes of the deities concerned. The cat, the animal manifestation of Bastet, goddess of fertility and festivity, makes its most spectacular appearance on the spacer-boxes of bracelets once worn by a 17th Dynasty queen and by the wives of Tuthmosis III. For non-royal ladies small semi-precious stone cats formed amuletic bezels to gold finger-rings. A splendid gold frog on the granulated bezel of a gold finger-ring now in the British Museum again suggests a female owner, for Heqat the frog was a goddess associated with childbirth and fertility. The openwork glazed composition 'wedding band', so typical of the Third Intermediate Period, invariably depicts deities, whether the seated sun-god, the aegis of Bastet, or a continuous frieze of dwarfish Bes figures, each standing on the shoulders of another.

An amuletic necklace found around the neck of an Old Kingdom woman buried at Giza is composed of fifty hollow gold pendants, threaded on a gold wire through suspension loops attached at the top and also through horizontal holes in the bodies of the pendants to give a radiating effect when worn. The pendants, shaped by working sheet metal into a mould, are in the form of the coleoptera beetle, emblem of the goddess Neith, and would presumably have placed the wearer under the protection of that deity. This was probably also the purpose of one of the three gold amulets found in the Early Dynastic burial of a woman at Nag ed-Deir. This comprises a foil capsule made in two parts in the shape of a beetle, its top surface incised and inlaid with the emblems of the goddess

65b
134
161k
161i

45a–c

162

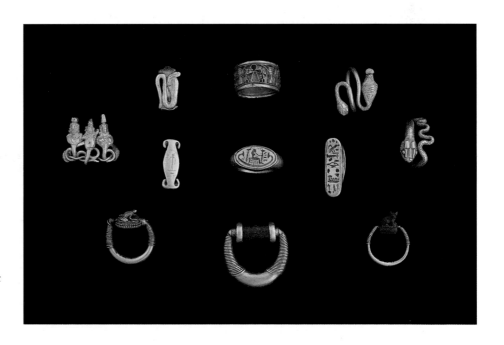

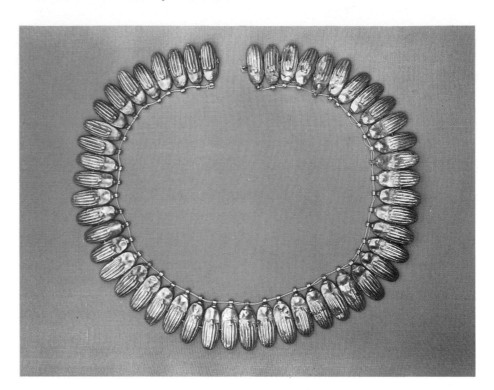

162 Amuletic necklace of hollow gold pendants in the form of the coleoptera beetle, emblem of the goddess Neith. L (each beetle) 2.7cm

Found around the neck of a woman at Giza (mastaba 294). Late 5th–early 6th Dynasties (*c*. 2355–2335 BC)

Neith. The second, an oryx with a Girdle Tie of Isis about its neck, and the 11b,c
third, a bull lacking horns and wearing the *Bat*-amulet, fetish of the goddess Hathor, were probably also protective. They were shaped by hammering into a mould, with the addition of a flat back-plate bearing two small suspension tubes.

Senebtisy wore twenty-one *sa*-amulets – signifying protection – of electrum, cornelian, silver, feldspar and ivory, strung between two rows of tiny feldspar beads. Around her neck was a row of beads shaped like *hes*-vases – the hieroglyph for 'praise' or 'favour' – strung through their length and made from cornelian, feldspar, glazed composition and gold leaf on plaster, with a central gold element in the shape of a *shen*-sign inlaid with cornelian and glazed composition.

Khnumet wore an amuletic collar which is currently strung into four rows between solid gold inlaid falcon-headed terminals; these are pierced by seven holes for what must have been originally seven rows of elements. The gold amulets are in the shape of *djed*-pillars, *ankhs* and *was*-sceptres – symbolising stability, life and dominion – inlaid with turquoise and cornelian; they are graduated in size and have suspension rings top and bottom. An openwork effect has been achieved by stringing gold discs alongside the rings to form intervening rows of beads. The lowest row of the collar is formed from drop-shaped gold pendants and the third of long gold bicones strung vertically. Another necklace is composed of small *ankhs* carved from cornelian, turquoise and lapis lazuli. They are made in two parts – the loop with crossbar, and the shaft – and are held together by threads which pass up the shaft and along the crossbar; two further threads secure the amulets from rings soldered at top and bottom. The centre-piece is an openwork element of gold, comprising a solid *ankh* in a trapezoid frame over which, on each side, slides a three-sided box pierced by three holes to take the threads. Another of Khnumet's collars has been arbitrarily restrung from a number of pairs of matched gold amulets, with a right and left aspect, which are inlaid with turquoise, lapis lazuli and cornelian. There are two hornets, two *sma*-amulets, two *ankhs*, two *djeds*, two vases in the shape of the hieroglyph *khenem*, two *udjat*-eyes, two *Bat*-amulets, two upreared cobras on a basket, each with a *shen*-sign at the breast, two vultures on baskets with a flail over the shoulder, two elaborate *was*-sceptres and a central element composed of an *ankh* on a *hotep*-sign, all signifying power, protection or good wishes. These are strung with two rows of gold ring beads, between two small falcon-headed terminals inlaid with turquoise and lapis lazuli. An outermost row comprises gold tear-drops inlaid with three zones of turquoise, cornelian and lapis lazuli.

The royal burials of the 12th Dynasty are rich in gold amuletic clasps, usually inlaid with lapis lazuli, cornelian and turquoise but also with glazed composition, which probably hung on the chest as a pendant; most are currently strung with a single row of gold disc beads. In all but one the suspension tube which lies across the back divides into two, one half remaining attached to a fixed T-shaped rod over which slips a sleeve attached to the other half of the suspension tube. In the other type the fixed element, with half the suspension tube, is an open-sided box of T-shaped section into which slides a T-shaped rod with the remainder of the tube attached to its top.

Khnumet owned two groups of amuletic clasps which spell out the message 'all life and protection are behind [her]'; another wishes the wearer joy. A fourth appears to claim she is 'beloved of every mother'. Others comprise symbolic signs such as the *shen*, one of them flanked by inlaid lotus-heads with knotted stems, and the *mes*-apron. Sithathoriunet had two *shen*-signs, and three other clasps spelling out the phrases 'all life and protection', 'the heart of the two gods is content' – a reference to the reconciliation of Horus and Set – and 'joy'. One of Sithathor's clasps also spells out 'the heart of the two gods is content'; the other is composed of two pendant inlaid lotus-heads whose stalks emerge from an inlaid knot above an inlaid *Bat*-amulet. Mereret owned three clasps formed from the hieroglyphs for 'joy', another reading 'the heart of the two gods is content', and a fifth with the message 'all life and protection'. An inlaid gold *shen*-sign, however, is not a clasp, but has five rings soldered to its lower edge for the suspension of further pendants.

The scarab, symbol of new life and regeneration, was a particularly powerful amulet but, like all representations of living creatures, capable of doing harm to the dead if taken to the tomb. Wah's mummy wore two spectacular large solid silver scarabs, each made up from individual elements soldered together, with a gold tube running through the base-plate for a suspension cord. The back of the larger was inlaid with pale gold hieroglyphs giving the title and name of its owner and that of his master, Meketre. The underside of each was chased with a scroll design and heraldically arranged hieroglyphs with amuletic significance. Although both scarabs would have been worn in life, when they were placed in the burial they were ritually 'killed' by having their eyes and mouths hammered and chipped. Then, together with an uninscribed lapis

9c

9a

108c

177

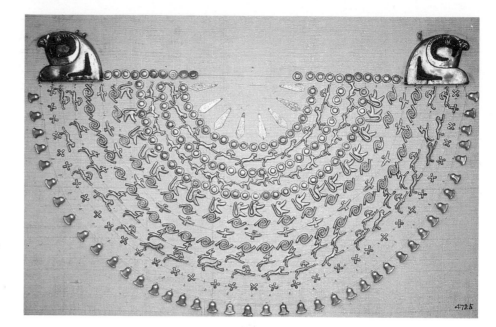

163 Openwork collar, now composed of gold foil elements strung between inlaid gold foil falcon-headed terminals. They include lions, ibexes and gazelles depicted in a wide-flung leg position, the so-called flying gallop, better known in contemporary Aegean work. w (terminal) 5.5cm

From the burial of Queen Aahhotep, Dra Abu Naga, W. Thebes. 18th Dynasty (reign of Ahmose, *c.* 1540 BC)

lazuli scarab, they were strung between a barrel and a cylinder bead on a flax cord to form an amuletic string. A fourth plain blue glazed composition scarab was strung alone.

Most of the royal 12th Dynasty burials contained unmounted scarabs of various materials which must have been worn on cords. Sithathoriunet owned two of lapis lazuli, one inscribed with the name of Ammenemes III; Sithathor had five, three of amethyst, one of turquoise and one of composition, two with heraldic designs on the underside, two with gold-rimmed stringing perforations. Mereret's were of lapis lazuli, turquoise and composition, most bearing her name and titles. Even the burial of the wives of Tuthmosis III contained an unmounted gold inlaid scarab which must have been worn in the same way. There were also three large uninscribed scarabs of gold and one of lapis lazuli with an unusual side-to-side piercing; these were obviously intended to be worn together on one cord.

The only amuletic necklace from the burial of Queen Aahhotep comprises a gold scarab made in two halves from thick sheet gold; its back is set with cloisons inlaid with lapis lazuli strips; the legs, added separately and folded into the underbelly, hold two rings, one at the front, the other at the back and these are connected by a double gold thread to form a buckle. Suspension is from the front ring by a six-ply loop-in-loop gold chain whose ends terminate in gracefully recurved ducks' heads. The two rings at the back of their heads were meant to be tied together by a cord. A gold-mounted alabaster scarab on a long loop-in-loop chain from the burial of Hornakht at Tanis must have been an heirloom, for it bears the name of the 18th Dynasty King Amenophis III. Another uninscribed scarab from the same source, similarly mounted and suspended, is of lapis lazuli.

From the burial of the wives of Tuthmosis III came a number of loose beads and amuletic elements now strung into necklaces. There are two strings of gold falcon amulets wearing the double crown and another of

78

flat gold plaques incised with the seated figure of the goddess Maat. Originally worn on a cord around the neck were five crudely embossed gold plaques, three with Hathor cows, one with an enthroned Sekhmet, and a fifth with Maat seated. There are also gold *udjat*-eyes and a seven-petalled gold flower, all with suspension loops. The Gold Tomb in the Valley of the Kings also contained a number of embossed gold and electrum amulets, all with suspension loops, including *udjat*-eyes, a heart, Hathor heads and shells.

General Wendjebauendjed, buried at Tanis, owned a set of superbly carved three-dimensional lapis lazuli amulets in gold housings which were intended to be worn as pendants. One of the finest is a recumbent 164 ram just over 2.5 centimetres long wearing a gold disc and uraeus; its flank clasped by the wings of a sheet-gold vulture, it is set in a tall oval plinth decorated with rope braid and granules. The whole figure fits into a rectangular gold shrine with sliding door raised by a knob, its sides adorned with a repoussé recumbent ram-headed sphinx wearing a sun-disc, a frieze of uraei over its shoulder and two suspension loops on the roof. Another of the set consists of a reused lapis lazuli amulet of Ptah set inside a double gold naos, the sides of which are adorned with multiple friezes of heraldically opposed seated deities; the entrance is flanked by two papyrus columns, each surmounted by a pair of falcons wearing sun-discs. Again, the suspension tube is on the roof. There was also a collection of solid gold figurines of deities. One of the finest in a group of six on a single cord over the mummy's chest depicts the goddess Bastet, 23 modelled in the round with a lion's head, wearing the sun-disc and uraeus. Two smaller identical gold amulets with a text make it clear that Bastet not Sekhmet is intended. An even larger, superbly modelled female figure in the round, wearing cow's horns and disc but named on the base as Isis is suspended from a long loop-in-loop gold chain of its own.

164 Pendant of Wendjebauendjed in the form of a three-dimensional lapis lazuli recumbent ram, its flanks clasped by a gold vulture, set in a plinth decorated with granulation. The whole is housed in a gold shrine, its sliding door raised by a knob. L (ram) 2.5cm, (shrine) 3.8cm

From the burial chamber of Wendjebauendjed, Tanis (tomb III). 21st Dynasty (reign of Psusennes, *c.* 1030 BC)

165 Cast gold, long-eared, long-tailed animal identified as a canine but with hooves. The suspension loops are on the left side, two on the body and two on the base. H 3.1cm

From the pyramid of Queen Amanishakheto, Meroe. Meroitic Period (late 1st century BC)

Presumably these were all family or Dynastic patron deities. Hornakht, too, possessed a number of pendants in lapis lazuli, including a recumbent ram in a gold mount, a standing falcon-headed god, a gold-mounted *udjat*-eye, and a seated Maat inset into a gold cloison, with chased details on the underside. Nine tiny gold or electrum pendant amulets represent some of the major Egyptian deities; larger coarser examples are of bronze, silver and composition.

A number of amuletic collar elements from the cache of Queen Amanishakheto at Meroe have been reconstructed into complete pieces on the basis of pictorial representations. One, an openwork string without terminals, now in Berlin, comprises variously shaped beads, pendants and *udjats*, *djeds*, *ankhs*, fish, uraei and scarabs made from semi-precious stones, glazed composition and glass. Of three other necklaces, one is made from eleven hollow gold Hathor heads with a clay core, inlaid on the top surface with blue glass; the second has seventeen hollow gold scarabs, and the third eight gold shells each bearing a royal head in raised relief. The queen also owned two pairs of superb small cast elements in the form of gold long-eared long-tailed animals identified as canines but with hooves. Two of these animals are supported by a uraeus and stand on a base with stringing tubes soldered below, though how they were worn is far from clear. The two others, however, and a fifth now in the British Museum, lack the uraeus, and suspension is by means of four rings on one side, two at each end of the body, the other two on the far side of the base plate. 165

The oyster-shell amulet, called by the Egyptians *wedja* (*wḏ3*), meaning 'sound, whole, healthy', naturally enough was thought to endow its wearer, usually a woman to judge from representations and finds, with these attributes. It was particularly popular during the Middle Kingdom, although one of silver and another of gold came from the later burial of Tuthmosis III's wives. Senebtisy's burial contained twenty-five sheet-gold oyster-shells, which hung from the lowest of three rows of tiny ball beads of cornelian, feldspar and dark-blue glazed composition, all strung between gold multiple bead spacers. Thirty-one small gold oyster-shells from Sithathor's cache were formed into an amuletic necklace, and another large example was worn as a single amulet, suspended by a tube soldered to the underside. Mereret owned three large gold oyster-shell pendants, two of them inlaid on the upper surface. Only one has the inlays of cornelian, turquoise and lapis lazuli surviving intact in the design, with a lotus-head at the top, a rim pattern of lotus-petals and a chevron pattern at their centre. Another twenty-six small plain gold oyster-shells are soldered at intervals to gold multiple bead spacers to form a necklace. 157c

154

Real oyster-shells, inscribed with the name of the reigning pharaoh, appear to have been worn during the 12th Dynasty as a military badge, perhaps by members of the royal bodyguard. It is possibly from this practice that some gold oyster-shells also came to bear the names of 12th Dynasty rulers and so are an example of jewellery functioning as insignia. One found on the corpse of a royal courtier at el-Riqqa is of gold, with the prenomen cartouche of Sesostris III, flanked by uraei, worked in applied wire.

166 Sheet-gold oyster-shell pendant with repoussé emblem of Hathor holding *menat*-collars. The butterfly and flanking lotus-heads and buds are inlaid with polychrome glass. H 2.9cm 12th Dynasty (*c.* 1800 BC)

During the early New Kingdom a system of honorific awards was instituted which at first rewarded military valour but soon became a decoration for which any civil servant was eligible. The most unusual element is the gold fly, awarded, perhaps because of the Egyptian variety's typical behaviour, for persistence in attacking the enemy. A single loop-in-loop gold chain with hook-and-eye fastener is the means of suspension for three large gold flies from Aahhotep's burial. Each is made from a sheet-gold plate cut into the outline of the fly's wings to which has been soldered a second piece of metal representing the head and protuberant eyes, made by hammering into a mould and chasing the details. The characteristic striated markings of a fly's back have been imitated by cutting slots to give an openwork effect; a ring soldered between the eyes provides the means of suspension. A pair now in the British Museum are of gold foil moulded over a core which remains inside, with details of the eyes, ridging around the neck, curved markings over the rump and striations on the folded wings. From the burial of Tuthmosis III's wives came thirty-three, each made in two parts, the top stamped into a mould with a back-plate soldered on; these are currently strung with gold barrels and discs. Solid cast gold examples with a decorated upper side and flat underside were sometimes strung with garnet beads; Aahhotep also owned two small flat sheet-electrum examples, and five of gold came from the Gold Tomb in the Valley of the Kings.

The most spectacular elements of the award, however, were the *shebyu*-collar, pair of *awaw*-bangles and single *mesketu*-bangle, all of gold. So proud were the recipients that they had themselves depicted wearing the regalia on their tomb statues or, like the Mayor Sennefer, sporting them in virtually every scene on their tomb walls. General Horemheb had the award ceremony shown in his tomb. The earliest existing example of a *shebyu*-collar was found in the burial of a 17th Dynasty woman at Qurna. It is composed of four rows of small gold disc beads; the fastening, as always in such collars, is made by soldering a number of beads at each end of a

167

158a

160a

169

171

168

14a

167 Aahhotep's gold flies on a loop-in-loop gold chain, with hook-and-eye fastening. Part of an honorific award for valour, perhaps a reminder of this queen's part in the war of independence against the Hyksos rulers of Egypt. L (fly) 9cm
From the burial of Queen Aahhotep, Dra Abu Naga, W. Thebes. 18th Dynasty (reign of Ahmose, *c.* 1540 BC)

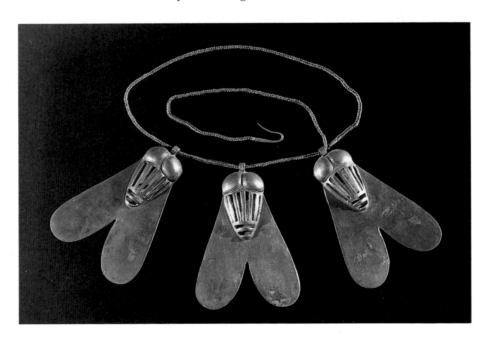

string into a tube fitted with a cup into which a ring is soldered at right angles. The rings on one side interlock with the rings on the other so that a locking pin can be inserted vertically through them. A miniature *shebyu*, to adorn a statue, now in the British Museum, is composed of three rows of gold discs strung tightly together; the closing system is identical but attached to each terminal are two loop-in-loop gold chains, each ending in a lapis lazuli bell-shaped bead.

169

At Tanis the mummy of Psusennes wore three magnificent *shebyu*-collars. Two are almost identical, composed of five and six rows respectively of solid gold rings strung on cords, the knots hidden by the sheet gold clasp. The clasp of the first collar is rectangular, decorated on both faces by the nomen and prenomen cartouches of the king flanking a papyrus sceptre; above and below is a frieze of uraei with sun-discs and at the very top a winged scarab. The inscription on the outer surface is inlaid with lapis lazuli, that on the underside merely incised. The clasp on the second collar is square and the inlaid inscription on the upper face is different from the one incised on the underside. On the front, beneath a winged scarab, are Psusennes' nomen and prenomen cartouches; the first faces out to a seated Mut named as Lady of Isheru, the prenomen faces the other way to a seated Amen-Re, king of the gods. On the reverse, from either side of a tall cartouche surmounted by pendant wings, containing the two names combined, Wadjet and Nekhbet as cobras rear up; they are named with epithets in the text. From the clasps hang respectively fourteen and ten loop-in-loop gold chains which divide and subdivide

5

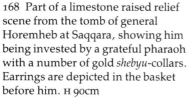

168 Part of a limestone raised relief scene from the tomb of general Horemheb at Saqqara, showing him being invested by a grateful pharaoh with a number of gold *shebyu*-collars. Earrings are depicted in the basket before him. H 90cm

18th Dynasty (*c.* 1330 BC)

169 Miniature gold *shebyu*-collar for a
statue and two hollow gold
awaw-bangles, all part of an honorific
award. A contemporary granite torso
of an official depicts them being worn.
D (armlets, ext.) 11.9cm
    18th Dynasty (*c.* 1500–1300 BC)

into four as they pass through hollow gold striated bell-shaped flower-
heads; further flowers hang at the ends of the chains. The third *shebyu* has
five rows of hollow gold truncated bicones made in two halves; the clasp is
of sheet gold over wood, the upper face shaped in imitation of rows of
beads, the lower bearing seven lines of text giving the full five-name
titulary of Psusennes.

Amenemope wore two *shebyu*-collars. One comprised only three rows
of gold discs and a trapezoidal clasp of gold-plated wood incised on both
faces with the royal nomen and prenomen cartouches flanked by uraei.
The second collar was more unusual, being composed originally of eleven
rows of large gold beads, inlaid in a zigzag fashion with blue composition
imitating lapis lazuli; gold spacers divide the beads into sections. The top
surface of the trapezoidal clasp imitates the pattern on the beads; all that
remains of the five loop-in-loop gold chains which once hung from its
lower edge are the hollow gold lotus-heads through which they once
passed as they divided and subdivided.

Gold *awaw*-bangles, characterised by their square section, have rarely
survived. Interestingly enough, from the burial of the wives of Tuthmosis
III came a string of large, thin, blue glazed composition discs looking for all
the world like a poor man's *shebyu*, and with them were two sets of large
blue glazed composition, square-sectioned bangles, to serve as the matching *awaw*. Aahhotep, however, owned eight hollow sheet-gold *awaws*,
four with a strip of rope-braid wire at one edge of the outer face and a

170 A rare example of a gold *mesketu*-bangle, part of an honorific award, with a characteristic convex profile and incised with the prenomen cartouche of Tuthmosis III. D 7.1cm
18th Dynasty (*c.* 1450 BC)

double rope braid at the other; the remaining four are identical but lack the added wire decoration. Another pair are each made from a band of sheet gold; these were beaten into shape on a wooden ring, and the two ends soldered together in a step-shaped join so as to form a three-sided hoop with an open internal face, which was subsequently closed by soldering on a further strip.   169

Just as rare are examples of the award's third element, the *mesketu*-bangle, with its characteristic convex profile between projecting rims. Although there are a number of representations of it, only four actual examples have survived, one from Aahhotep's burial and three others, one naming Tuthmosis III, all now in Leiden.   171   170

Certain articles of jewellery served as badges of office or rank. The *Bat*-emblem is in part identical with the fetish of the goddess Hathor – a frontal woman's face with cow's ears and curved cow's horns. It has, however, in addition long pendant ribbons which in their folds resemble the ties of the Girdle Tie of Isis or *tit*-amulet. It first occurs around the neck of the gold amulet of a bull from Nag ed-Deir, dating to the 1st Dynasty, and it continued to be represented, although extremely rarely, worn at the belt or around the neck of the highest-ranking officials until the Late Period. No actual examples have survived, and its function is far from clear. The most plausible explanation is that it was part of the original insignia of the vizier, the Egyptian Prime Minister; it has also been suggested, however, that it marked the wearer as a judge, before being replaced by the pendant figure of the goddess Maat, or was perhaps worn during the celebration of the royal jubilee festival.   11c

At less infrequent royal appearances flimsy glazed composition finger-rings were dispensed from the Window of Appearances. Made in two parts in a mould, they had a circular shank and flat, oval bezel bearing an imprint of the royal name and they survive, usually damaged, in their thousands. Rather less common are solid stirrup-shaped signet-rings, still of glazed composition; these were presumably given to more favoured courtiers. Solid gold or silver signet-rings, whether of stirrup shape (most common during the New Kingdom), or with chunky square bezel and cut-away back (more popular during the Late Period), often bore the titles and name of the owner and could be used as a seal by impressing them into the mud which sealed the ties of papyrus documents. Other exam-   45   148

Right 171 The mayor of Thebes, Sennefer, and his wife Meryt in their tomb. He wears a *shebyu*-collar, *awaw*-bangles, a *mesketu*-bangle, a broad collar and earrings. She wears earrings, broad collar and matching bracelets and armlets. In one hand she carries a sistrum and Cos lettuce, in the other a *menyet*-collar and counterpoise.

From W. Thebes (tomb no. 96). 18th Dynasty (reign of Amenophis II, *c.* 1415 BC)

Below 172 Vignette from the *Book of the Dead* papyrus of the Royal Scribe Hunefer. The deceased raises his arms in adoration of the solar falcon perched on an animated *djed* representing Osiris (not visible in this detail), to whom Hunefer will present the pectoral with counterpoise which he carries over his arm. H (vignette) 18cm

19th Dynasty (reign of Sety I, *c.* 1285 BC)

ples, including a rare form with a swivelling bezel in the form of a solid metal square plaque, bear pharaoh's name, and although some at least must have been worn by the king himself, others are known to have come from the burial of favourite courtiers.

A special form of collar originally worn by priestesses of Hathor and shaken to provide a musical sound like the rattling of the sistrum was later carried by all high-ranking women as a symbol of their non-secular duties, which were part and parcel of their rank. Known as a *menyet*, it is formed from a mass of loosely strung rows of beads attached by a single bead string strap to a large counterpoise in the shape of a pendulum. The finest of these counterpoises are made of bronze, often openwork and adorned with images of the goddess, usually including her manifestation as a cow sailing through marshland. A type of pectoral attached by straps to a smaller kiosk-shaped counterpoise appears to have played a part in the Raising of the *Djed* ceremony, once connected with the rites of Sokaris, the funerary god of Saqqara, but soon absorbed into the festivities connected with Ptah and especially Osiris. The ritual involved the adornment of the fetish with this piece of jewellery and this explains a vignette on the first sheet of the funerary papyrus of Hunefer. He is shown adoring an animated *djed* – personifying Osiris – and carries over his arm an example of just this type of ornament.

171

40

172

CHAPTER EIGHT

Funerary jewellery

Placed on the neck of the glorious dead on the day of interment . . .

173 Wendjebauendjed's openwork gold pylon-shaped pectoral, inlaid mostly with green glazed composition and a little of red and white. The central scarab is of lapis lazuli, the double suspension strings of feldspar and gold. H 9.2cm

From the mummy of Wendjebauendjed, Tanis (tomb III). 21st Dynasty (reign of Psusennes, c. 1030 BC)

Although jewellery worn in life could be taken to the tomb, far more was made expressly for the day of burial. Indeed, certain pieces were prescribed by the *Book of the Dead*; even their materials were stipulated. Chapter 157 is a 'spell for a vulture of gold placed at the throat of the deceased' and the vignette illustrates a vulture with outstretched wings clutching a *shen* in each claw. Just such a superb gold example was found on the mummy of Tutankhamun. It is flexible, with huge up-curved wings, its head turned to the left. Its top surface is composed of over three hundred cloisons inlaid with dark-blue, red and green glass, and its underside is chased with identical details; there is a small matching *menkhet* counterpoise. Two other gold inlaid flexible collars in the series represent the golden falcon and 'Two Ladies', Wadjet the cobra set side-by-side with Nekhbet the vulture, both collars having matching counterpoises.

However, Tutankhamun also owned identical collars cut out from thin sheet gold with incised details and, except for the vulture example, attached by a gold wire to a cut-out sheet-gold *menkhet* counterpoise: there is a Horus collar of a falcon with up-curved wings holding *shen*-signs, and another of the vulture and cobra combined. In addition, there is Wadjet alone as a winged cobra. Another is a sheet-gold broad collar with small falcon-headed terminals on a bar which duplicates exactly the falcon collar depicted in vignettes of Chapter 158 of the *Book of the Dead*: 'spell for a golden collar'. Each of the wives of Tuthmosis III owned sheet-gold vulture- and falcon-headed collars, the latter with incised details of rows of beads and pendants, the former with incised details of feathering but no means of suspension: they must have just lain on the mummified breasts.

At Tanis, over the chest of Amenemope, lay an inlaid rigid gold collar in the form of a falcon with outspread wings, the feathering represented by a mass of cloisons; in its claws it holds *shen*-signs, to which are attached two horizontal plaques incised with the royal nomen and prenomen with funerary epithets. On Sheshonq's mummy was a gold collar in the form of a vulture holding *shens*; its wings were made in two parts, with hinges closed by pins at the shoulders, and curved around the back of the neck to meet in a *menkhet* counterpoise with horizontal strip cloisons. The numerous cloisons on the body and wings indicating feathering were once filled with a polychrome composition, now mostly decayed or destroyed. Although Psusennes wore no funerary collars he owned small sheet-gold amulets in the shape of miniature collars all-in-one with the *menkhet* counterpoise: there is a vulture, two falcons, a winged cobra, two 'Two Ladies' and a winged human *ba*, all with chased details. Hornakht, too, owned small sheet-gold amulets in the form of non-human deities, some winged, and of ritual equipment, as well as larger ones of gold inlaid with coloured paste, including a *ba* with outstretched wings, a vulture, Osiris and an archaic crouched falcon. Similar pieces also came from the burial of Wendjebauendjed.

Although not among prescribed pieces, some fine pectorals have survived which have purely funerary function. Eight of Tutankhamun's inlaid gold pectorals were found in compartments within the pylon-shaped shrine in the Treasury, beneath a jackal. They appear to have been made for the burial, for their themes are all funerary. Six have kiosk-shaped frames with cavetto cornice; the inlays are cornelian, rock-crystal, quartz on a red cement ground imitating cornelian, and variously coloured glasses. The frame of one is almost completely filled by the huge down-hanging wings of a vulture named as Nut, the sky-goddess depicted on the inside of coffin lids so that she could spread her protective wings over the mummy. Nut also appears as a woman standing with cloisonné up-curved wings, her flesh and hair inlaid, her highly patterned shift dress chased into a solid sheet of gold with inlaid block-decorated surrounds. The incised text is purely funerary, and, most interestingly, the cartouches have been changed, apparently from those of Akhenaten.

A large green stone scarab is the central feature in two pectorals. In one the scarab has large inlaid vertical wings which almost fill the frame, and the base-bar is a frieze of inlaid poppy-heads and buds. In the second the scarab is wingless, but supported at each side beneath a sun-disc by a kneeling goddess named as Isis and Nephthys. In another Isis and Nephthys stand to spread their wings above and below a central *djed* crowned by a sun-disc. In a similar composition the vulture Nekhbet

176

Above 174 Vignettes from a funerary papyrus (Ptolemaic Period, *c.* 300–100 BC), illustrating funerary jewellery prescribed by Chapters 156–9 of the *Book of the Dead*: a Girdle Tie of Isis, a vulture, a collar and a papyrus column. H 31cm

175 *Right* Damaged silver cloisonné falcon, once inlaid with polychrome glass and holding *shens*. W 16.1cm
Probably from Thebes. New Kingdom (*c.* 1370 BC)

Far right 176 Tutankhamun's sheet-gold pectoral with a winged Mut, inlaid with cornelian and polychrome glass. The cartouches in the inscription have been altered to the king's. H 12.6cm
From the tomb of Tutankhamun (Treasury), Valley of the Kings. 18th Dynasty (*c.* 1336–1327 BC)

wearing the *atef*-crown and the cobra Wadjet in the red crown, both resting on inlaid baskets, open their wings around a standing mummiform Osiris, who is crowned with the *atef* and carrying a flail and a crook with an abnormally long stock. A gold plaque with inlaid hieroglyphs set behind the god lists his epithets; horizontal *shen*-signs link it and Osiris to the goddesses, behind whom are plaques which mention only Isis and Nephthys, showing how they had become assimilated with the protectresses of Egypt.

From the Ramesside burials of the Apis bulls in the Serapeum at Saqqara came a gilded silver inlaid pectoral of traditional pylon shape with cavetto cornice, its top, base and supports with block decoration. The vulture Nekhbet with outspread, upwardly curving wings, her co-goddess the cobra Wadjet upreared at her side, fills most of the frame; the space below each wing is clumsily bridged by a *djed*. At the top a horizontal cartouche naming Ramesses II surmounts a small winged deity with a ram's head. That all the inlays are glass and the details of the underside badly chased illustrates well the decline in workmanship characteristic of the period. Much finer is a flat, rigid ram-headed vulture pectoral with outspread wings, holding inlaid *shens*; it is made from gold with a cloisonné-work back. The ram's head is set at right angles to the plate and the area under it extended in a fan-shaped decorated collar. Except for the solid gold head and the gold outstretched legs, all the details are inlaid with lapis lazuli, turquoise and cornelian, a return to the standards of Middle Kingdom jewellery-making.

At Tanis the mummy of Psusennes wore two openwork gold cloisonné pectorals with a funerary theme. The inlays are of lapis lazuli, feldspar, red jasper and cornelian, exemplifying the return to the use of semi-precious stones rather than glass and composition. Both take the shape of a kiosk with cavetto cornice and block-decorated surrounds and have a scarab flanked by Isis and Nephthys as the central feature; both also have a

178

7

177 Psusennes' miniature sheet gold collars, with all-in-one counterpoises, representing the royal *ba*, a falcon, Two Ladies, and a vulture, all with chased details. W (Two Ladies collar) 4cm

From the tomb of Psusennes, Tanis (tomb III). 21st Dynasty (*c.* 1039–991 BC)

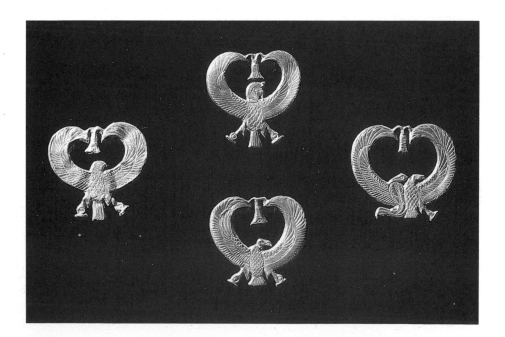

178 Tutankhamun's openwork gold pectoral inlaid with cornelian and polychrome glass, in which Osiris is protected by a winged cobra and vulture who are named as Nephthys and Isis, rather than Wadjet and Nekhbet. H 15.5cm

From the tomb of Tutankhamun, Valley of the Kings. W. Thebes. 18th Dynasty (*c.* 1336–1327 BC)

hinged openwork lower section. The inlaid design of the top surface is repeated on the underside by chasing, and the means of suspension is a double string of long drop-shaped beads of lapis lazuli, feldspar, red jasper and gold; a gold *menkhet* counterpoise is inlaid with strips of the same materials as the beads. In the finer example the scarab, set to show its back, is of lapis lazuli flanked by vertical wings inlaid in bands of colour, striated to imitate beads. Below is a horizontal inlaid cartouche of Psusennes and above a vertical cartouche containing his prenomen flanked by uraei and surmounted by a pendant-winged sun-disc; the space in both top corners is filled by a many-coiled cobra, while over all is the blue bar of heaven. Before the faces of Isis and Nephthys, who kneel to support the scarab's wings, are two texts: 'Isis the great, divine mother, mistress of the west' and 'I have come to be your protection'. The articulated frieze below comprises alternating *djeds* and *tit*-amulets surmounted by sun-discs. In the second pectoral Isis and Nephthys stand, and their wings, one held up, the other held down, frame the central ivory(?) scarab, which is supported by a *djed* and flanked by two vertical cartouches containing the nomen and prenomen of Psusennes. The small space between the goddesses' wings is filled by horizontal *shen*-signs; an

34

191

udjat fronted by a uraeus fills the gap above the wings. The articulated lower section shows two scenes on either side of two cobras framing a stylised pendant lotus. On the left, edged by a *djed*, the king paddles Osiris in an archaic boat; on the right, edged by the emblem of the east, he paddles the phoenix.

Amenemope's gold ajouré pectoral is a conventional kiosk shape, with a winged sun-disc covering most of the cavetto cornice and a block-decorated border on all four sides. A central scarab, standing on a horizontal prenomen cartouche, is supported by a kneeling Isis and Nephthys as he pushes a sun-disc. Two pendant gold plaques name the goddesses and an incised horizontal text beneath the scene names the king. All these details are chased on the metal of the underside. Far more unusual is the other pylon-shaped pectoral with a loop-in-loop gold chain, for it is made from two sheets of gold with a thin filling between, one with a scene in repoussé, the other with the same scene incised. At the top is a 68 cavetto cornice almost hidden by a winged sun-disc; all four sides have block-decorated borders and at the bottom is a frieze of alternating *djeds* and *tit*-amulets. Beneath a sun-disc flanked by cobras Amenemope, named in two cartouches, raises an incense-burner before an enthroned Osiris, who wears the *atef*-crown and carries the crook and flail. A column of hieroglyphs before the king describes his action as 'censing and libating for his father, Osiris'.

On the mummy of Wendjebauendjed was a fine gold openwork pylon-shaped pectoral inlaid almost exclusively with green glazed composition, 173 with only a little red and white, the colour echoed by the feldspar beads in

179 The reverse of Psusennes' pylon-shaped cloisonné pectoral (see 34), showing the chased details of the scene inlaid on the front surface. The underside of the scarab bears the name of the king. L 13.8cm

From the mummy of Psusennes, Tanis (tomb III). 21st Dynasty (*c.* 1039–991 BC)

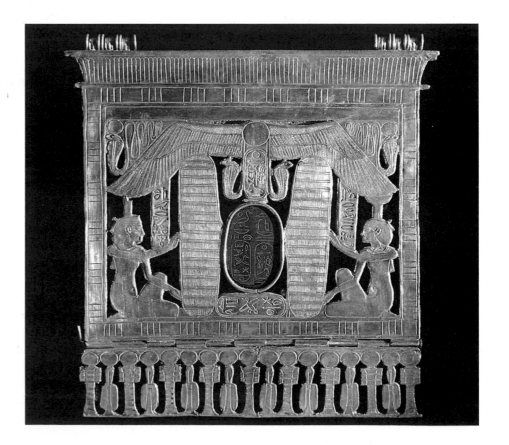

180 Solid gold and lapis lazuli pendant of the Osirian sacred family (Horus and Isis flanking Osiris, squatting on a tall block). The underside bears a text blessing Osorkon II. H 9cm
Probably from Tanis. 22nd Dynasty (c. 874–850 BC)

the double suspension string. Beneath a cavetto cornice all four sides are block-decorated; at the lower edge is a frieze of pendent *menkhet* counterpoises, with small papyrus sceptres between. Within the frame set in a gold funda is an ill-fitting lapis lazuli scarab, probably reused; its huge up-curving inlaid wings are supported at each corner over a *tit*-amulet by a small squatting female figure, named by an inscribed gold plaque at each side of the scarab as Isis and Nephthys. Above the scarab, flanked by two uraei, is an inscribed panel naming Wendjebauendjed surmounted by a winged sun-disc. The space between its wings and those of the scarab is filled by two heraldically opposed flying vultures, each holding a *djed* which defies gravity to meet the scarab's head. All the details of the inlaid surface are repeated in the gold of the underside by rather poor chasing.

The second pectoral is of cruder workmanship. It too is suspended by a double string of long barrels but they are cornelian and gold. Beneath a cavetto cornice and bar representing heaven all four surrounds have block-decoration. In the centre, set in a gold funda supported by a *djed* is a composition scarab flanked by two gold plaques naming Wendjebauen-djed. Above and below are stretched the wings of two standing god-desses, Isis and Nephthys, the symbols for their names on their heads; the space before their faces is filled by an *udjat* fronted by a uraeus. Most of these details are roughly chased on the gold of the underside.

The Osirian triad of Isis, Osiris and Horus is the subject of a superb pendant ornament inscribed with the name of Osorkon II, possibly from his tomb at Tanis which Montet found sacked. From the centre of a gold plinth, whose outer faces are block-decorated, rises a tall lapis lazuli block capped by a gold cavetto cornice on which squats the cast gold figure of Osiris wearing an *atef*-crown, his hands on his knees. He is flanked by two superbly modelled solid gold striding figures of his falcon-headed son Horus wearing the double crown and his sister-wife Isis in horns and disc, each with an arm raised in protection. Behind the figures are three rings for suspension.

Small rigid gold pendants in the shape of the human-headed *ba* with outstretched wings, its surface a network of inlaid cloisons, is another non-prescribed funerary amulet found as early as the burial of Tutankh-amun with glass inlays. Pendants in this form were still produced in the Late Dynastic Period but often with semi-precious stone as inlay.

One of the most important prescribed funerary amulets was the heart scarab, usually inscribed with Chapter 30B of the *Book of the Dead*, intended to bind the heart to silence when it was weighed in the balance to ascertain the worthiness of its master to enter the Egyptian paradise. The prescribed material was a dark green stone of doubtful identity and sometimes the spell is one of the other chapters of the *Book of the Dead* intended to prevent the deceased losing this most important of organs. One of the earliest is a human-headed green jasper scarab set in a gold funda around whose plinth runs an early version of the spell. It came from the burial of the 17th Dynasty King Sobkemsaf II, which was robbed in antiquity and is now in the British Museum. The three wives of Tuthmosis III each owned a dark-green schist heart scarab set in a gold mount with a ring at each side so that a plain gold wire might be hooked into it. Tutankhamun's heart scarab, however, was incorporated into an inlaid gold kiosk-shaped pectoral. The block-decorated frame is broken at the top and, beneath large cloisonné pendant wings which flank a sun-disc, the central green stone scarab with vertical cloisonné wings is supported by a kneeling Isis and Nephthys wearing shift dresses with a highly-coloured intricate cloisonné pattern. At each top corner the frame is supported by a uraeus crowned by a sun-disc, its tail coiling in a tight spiral to fill the triangular space. The inlaid hieroglyphs in vertical gold plaques contain the god-desses' words of greeting to Tutankhamun. The inlays are cornelian and polychrome glass.

The practice of inserting heart scarabs into a pylon-shaped kiosk soon devolved to non-royal burials. Two gold examples which once contained glass inlays came from the burials of the Apis bulls at Saqqara but name the vizier of Ramesses II, Paser. One in the form of a solid plaque has the

180

113b

65d

181 Polychrome glazed composition pylon-shaped pectoral with incorporated heart scarab in a barque, blessed by Isis and Nephthys and flanked by a Girdle Tie of Isis and a *djed*. The underside of the scarab bears Chapter 30B of the *Book of the Dead* – the heart scarab formula – for a woman called Ptahemheb. H 9.7cm

Probably from Memphis. 19th Dynasty (*c.* 1275 BC)

inset scarab flanked by the figures of Isis and Neith, their arms raised in adoration; in the other, which is openwork, the scarab is flanked and supported by Isis and Nephthys. For commoners the scarab was usually inset into a solid but highly coloured glazed composition plaque with cavetto cornice decorated with figures of protective deities inlaid in different coloured glazes.

At Tanis the mummy of Psusennes wore no less than four pectorals in the form of a large, dark stone scarab between vertical wings inlaid with striated strips of blue, green and red glass standing on an inlaid *shen* and supporting a cartouche with Psusennes' name inlaid with red jasper and polychrome glass. The details of the top surface are repeated by chasing on the underside and all the scarabs bear a long hieroglyphic inscription, three of them spells for the protection of the heart, including Chapters 125 and 126 of the *Book of the Dead*, the fourth a generally protective text. For three of these pectorals the means of suspension is a double string of long drop beads of feldspar and red and green jasper and single and double drops of gold; the fourth hangs from a long loop-in-loop gold chain. Amenemope had three heart scarabs, two of green stone, one of them mounted, and one of lapis lazuli. That of Sheshonq, however, is once again in a framed openwork inlaid gold pectoral, suspended by a flat gold ribbon with a flat chased gold *menkhet* counterpoise attached. The piece is pylon-shaped with block-decoration on all four surrounds and a cavetto cornice incorporating a winged sun-disc; from its lower edge hangs an articulated gold rectangular section, decorated with incised *djeds* and *tit*-amulets. At the centre of the frame is a large, dark-green stone, winged heart scarab, its underside set to be visible at the back of the pectoral, incised with Chapter 30B of the *Book of the Dead*. The wings, which have cloisons for individual feathers, are supported at either side by a kneeling

181

57

195

Isis and Nephthys. Above and below is a horizontal cartouche, one with the royal prenomen, the other with the nomen, and the whole is surmounted by large pendant wings incorporating a sun-disc. The inlays, all of polychrome glazed composition, are now much decayed.

Wendjebauendjed owned two heart scarabs, one inset into a pectoral, the other on an articulated gold chain. The former, suspended by means of nine long gold tubes, one slightly curved for the back of the neck, has an inlaid base-bar from which rise two palm columns each capped by a crowned uraeus. They support two bars, one representing heaven, the other with block-decoration. The central feature is a large heart scarab set in a gold mount, its underside incised with two of the chapters concerning the heart from the *Book of the Dead*, to which are attached two large vertical gold wings inlaid with composition, moulded to give a radiating effect. An arrangement of an *udjat*-eye on a basket fronted by a *nefer*-sign helps to fill the gap above each wing. An articulated chain made from long gold tubes, including one curved for the neck, is also used to suspend an unmounted 30 green feldspar heart scarab; its underside is incised with Chapter 26 of the *Book of the Dead*, not for Wendjebauendjed but for one of the Ramesside pharaohs. Perhaps this royal heirloom was a gift from his royal master Psusennes.

Specific amulets were also prescribed by the *Book of the Dead*. One which was of particular importance was the heart amulet, the *ib*, mentioned in 32i Chapter 29B; it resembles a pot with lug handles and a rim. At Tanis Psusennes owned a set of nine, graded in size, all of lapis lazuli, some bound with gold; one is on a long loop-in-loop gold chain, another on a gold ribbon, all naming him and most having minutely and exquisitely incised figures of the three forms of the sun-god. Amenemope had two of lapis lazuli and one of rock-crystal, superbly carved with the head of a baboon wearing a pectoral minutely incised with the royal names. This amulet, like those of the leg with foot, hand and face, not only endowed 62d–f the deceased with their particular bodily functions – intelligence, movement, manual dexterity and sight – but could actually act as a substitute should the particular limb or faculty be lost or destroyed.

Another piece of amuletic jewellery was the *sweret*-bead, which was strung on a cord, either alone or flanked by two spherical or cylindrical beads of green material. It is depicted in friezes of objects painted inside coffins of Middle Kingdom date and illustrated being worn on anthropoid 182 coffin lids; actual examples have been found on mummies. Its function is

182 Detail of the painted decoration inside the inner wooden coffin of the physician Seni, showing broad collars with matching counterpoises and a cornelian *sweret*-bead flanked by two ball beads on a cord. H (frieze) *c.* 15cm
From el-Bersha. Middle Kingdom (*c.* 2000 BC)

183 Group of name beads: **a** green glazed composition with prenomen cartouche of Shabaka. L 5.8cm. 25th Dynasty (*c.* 716–702 BC); **b** red glazed composition (?), with cartouche of Shabaka. L 5.8cm. 25th Dynasty (*c.* 716–702 BC); **c** cornelian *sweret* incised with the name and title of the Treasury Superintendant Amenhotep. H 4.5cm. New Kingdom (*c.* 1370–1200 BC); **d** blue-grey and yellow glazed composition, with prenomen cartouche of Amenophis III. 18th Dynasty (*c.* 1390–1352 BC); **e** blue and black glazed composition with the title of the High Priest of Amun in a cartouche. H 6.3cm. 21st Dynasty (Pinedjem I, *c.* 1054–1032 BC)

far from clear but it may not be without significance that beads of similar shape but made of glazed composition in a mould, with a curious jagged-edged back, bearing the names of kings and gods, date to the Third Intermediate Period and later, when the *sweret* no longer appears. Senebtisy's innermost anthropoid coffin and that of Princess Neferuptah had inset into them at the neck a real *sweret*-bead flanked by two glazed composition cylinders; another cornelian *sweret* was found inside Senebtisy's coffin. Around the necks of each of the wives of Tuthmosis III had been a cornelian *sweret* threaded on a plain gold wire closed by twisting one end around the other.

Jewellery of a non-amuletic nature was also made expressly for the burial. Either it is of cheap or fragile materials which could not stand normal wear and tear or else it lacks fastenings or, in the case of collars, counterpoises so they could not have been worn in life. On Senebtisy's body lay three broad collars. One is of copper, the conventional details of semicircular terminals, rows of beads and outermost row of pendants incised in attached gold leaf. The other two, one falcon-headed, the other with semicircular terminals, both of gold leaf on plaster, have rows of cornelian, green jasper, glazed composition or gold leaf on plaster beads and an outermost row of gold leaf on plaster pendants. None have any means of suspension or a counterpoise; this, and the use of gold leaf, shows that all three were purely funerary in function. Found lying at her wrists and ankles were matching funerary bracelets and anklets, again without means of fastening, made from glazed composition cylinders strung between rectangular wooden spacers overlaid with gold leaf. Hor, the 13th Dynasty king buried at Dahshur, must have worn a funerary diadem, but all that remains from it is a gilded wooden inlaid papyrus-head knot. He also owned matching bracelets and anklets of beads and spacers closed by a locking pin; here again the gold elements were merely gilded wood and these pieces must also have been intended as jewellery for the tomb.

Epilogue

It is a curious fact that during the course of the Ptolemaic Period ancient Egyptian jewellery with its characteristic forms and idiosyncratic use of materials and colours virtually ceased to be manufactured. Apart from fossilised representations on temple walls, where even Roman Emperors continued to be depicted in the dress and jewellery of native pharaohs a millennium earlier, it survived only in funerary form, depicted being worn on anthropoid coffins, in funerary papyrus vignettes or in representations on pieces of funerary equipment such as bronze situlae. This explains why as late as the second century AD the stucco coffin of the Greek Artemidorus, with its un-Egyptian encaustic portrait panel inset at face level, still wears a gold collar with falcon-headed terminals as prescribed by Chapter 158 of the *Book of the Dead*. Contemporary gilded stucco coffins with modelled heads wear diadems studded with rosettes just like the one worn by the mummy of Tutankhamun some fifteen centuries

Left 184 Late Period jewellery: **a** gold foil figure of Maat on a loop-in-loop gold chain, perhaps a judge's insignia. Saite or later (after 600 BC); **b** gold foil plaque incised with amulets, jewellery and ritual objects as painted inside Middle Kingdom coffins; intended to be stitched onto mummy wrappings. L 4.7cm. Late Period (after 600 BC); **c** gold foil barrel bead with applied wire decoration. From Kawa. Meroitic (*c.* 300 BC or later); **d** hollow gold ram's head and fish, gold openwork bead, length of loop-in-loop chain and gold wire Heh amulet. Ptolemaic Period (*c.* 300–100 BC); **e** sheet-silver aegis of Bastet or Sekhmet as a pendant. W 4.3cm. 3rd Intermediate Period (*c.* 1000–800 BC); **f** gold plaque with repoussé Hathor head inlaid with enamel and backed on glazed composition. H 5cm. Meroitic (*c.* 300 BC or later)

Right 185 Shield ring of Amanishakheto, the aegis topped by a bearded male bust wearing the double crown, probably the Nubian god Sebiumeker. The ring hinged behind the crown is plain. W 3.6cm
   From the pyramid of Amanishakheto, Meroe. Meroitic Period (late 1st century BC)

earlier or are behung with solid pectorals incorporating a scarab like those favoured by commoners a millennium before.

Thus it is that the coffins of Hornedjitef (EA 6678) and Horsanakht (EA 52949), both of Ptolemaic date, wear pylon-shaped pectorals containing the figures of funerary deities which hang from elaborate straps. In the vignette of the Weighing of the Heart in their funerary papyri Men (EA 10098/6) and Kerasher (EA 9995/1), of contemporary date, wear respectively a bead necklace and *Bat*-pendant, and a broad collar, as well as bracelets and armlets. However, scarcely any actual examples of such pieces have survived which are firmly datable to the Ptolemaic or Roman Periods. Virtually the only representatives of contemporary Egyptian jewellery are amulets, which are usually of glazed composition, small and increasingly debased in iconography.

Of course, jewellery was still being made and worn in Egypt during the Graeco-Roman Period, but nothing any longer marks it out as being Egyptian in origin. The forms, the materials are typically Hellenistic and unless the provenance of a particular piece is known to be Egypt then there is nothing to distinguish it from any other piece originating from the eastern Mediterranean area. Only the lingering interest in the motif of the serpent, whether wrapped around the finger as a ring, or coiled up a forearm as a bracelet, hints of Egyptian influence.

161

If Egyptian traditions in jewellery-making survived at all at this period they did so in the Sudan where the Meroitic culture at first retained a memory of pharaonic forms and decoration. However, as the links between Meroe and Roman Egypt grew more and more tenuous this memory was transmuted into something completely idiosyncratic and eventually quite un-Egyptian.

185

Egyptian craftsmen undoubtedly continued to manufacture jewellery from precious metals, precious and semi-precious stones and many other materials. New influences and styles, however, now transformed their products, and thus a jewellery-making tradition whose roots stretched back some four thousand years into the remotest history was finally brought to an end.

Right 186 Detail of a painted and gilded stucco mummy case with a Greek epitaph naming Artemidorus, incorporating an encaustic portrait of the deceased. The only jewellery worn is a falcon-collar of gold, the birds wearing double crowns. H 1.67m
From Hawara. Roman Period (early 2nd century AD)

Bibliography

There are surprisingly few books dealing specifically with ancient Egyptian jewellery and the most recent of them were both written two decades ago. The *Cairo Catalogue Général: Bijoux et Orfèvreries* was published as long ago as 1927 and contains no hint of the treasures of Tutankhamun or the gold of Tanis. Apart from Aldred's *Jewels of the Pharaohs*, Wilkinson's *Ancient Egyptian Jewellery* and Vilímková's more prescribed *Egyptian Jewellery*, there are useful and instructive sections in *L'or des Pharaons*, *Jewellery through 7000 Years*, *Jewellery of the Ancient World*, *Official Catalogue, the Egyptian Museum Cairo* and *Africa in Antiquity 2: the Catalogue*. Although published well over half a century ago, Williams's *Gold and Silver Jewelry* and Schäfer's *Ägyptische Goldschmiedearbeiten* still contain useful information.

For the chapter on materials the author is particularly indebted to Harris's *Lexicographical Studies*, Lucas's *Ancient Egyptian Materials and Industries* and the various entries in *Lexikon der Ägyptologie*. For the chapter on craftsmen and techniques Lucas, the *Lexikon* and Drenkhahn's *Die Handwerker und ihre Tätigkeiten* have proved invaluable.

ALDRED, C., *Jewels of the Pharaohs* (London), 1971

ANDREWS, C. A. R., *Catalogue of Egyptian Antiquities in the British Museum VI; Jewellery I* (London), 1981

DRENKHAHN, R., *Die Handwerker und ihre Tätigkeiten im alten Ägypten*, Ägyptologische Abhandlungen, Band 31 (Wiesbaden), 1976

HARRIS, J. R., *Lexicographical Studies in Ancient Egyptian Minerals*, Deutsche Akademie der Wissenschaften zu Berlin Institut für Orientforschung, Veröffentlichung Nr. 54 (Berlin), 1961

HELCK, W. AND OTTO, E. (eds), *Lexikon der Ägyptologie* (Wiesbaden), 1975–86

Jewellery Through 7000 Years, exhibition catalogue, British Museum (London), 1976

LUCAS, A., *Ancient Egyptian Materials and Industries* (London), 4th edn revised, 1962

OGDEN, J., *Jewellery of the Ancient World* (London), 1982

SALEH, M. AND SOUROUZIAN, H., *Official Catalogue, The Egyptian Museum Cairo* (Mainz), 1987

SCHÄFER, H., *Königliche Museen zu Berlin, Mitteilungen aus der Ägyptischen Sammlung, Band I, Ägyptische Goldschmiedearbeiten* (Berlin), 1910

VERNIER, E., *Catalogue général des Antiquités égyptiennes du Musée du Caire: Bijoux et Orfèvreries* (Cairo), 1927

Tanis, L'or des Pharaons (Paris), 1987

VILÍMKOVÁ, M., *Egyptian Jewellery* (London), 1969

WENIG, S., *Africa in Antiquity, The Arts of Ancient Nubia and the Sudan, II, The Catalogue* (The Brooklyn Museum, NY), 1978

WILKINSON, A., *Ancient Egyptian Jewellery* (London), 1971

WILLIAMS, C. R., *The New York Historical Society, Catalogue of Egyptian Antiquities, Gold and Silver Jewelry and related objects* (New York), 1924

CHRONOLOGICAL TABLE

	PHARAOHS	OTHER ROYAL AND NON-ROYAL PERSONS
PREDYNASTIC PERIOD Badarian culture Naqada I culture Naqada II culture (*c.* 3200 BC)		
EARLY DYNASTIC PERIOD 1st Dynasty (*c.* 3100-2890 BC)	Menes (*c.* 3100 BC) Djer (*c.* 3000 BC)	
2nd Dynasty (*c.* 2890-2686 BC)		
OLD KINGDOM 3rd Dynasty (*c.* 2686-2613 BC)	Djoser (*c.* 2650 BC) Sekhemkhet (*c.* 2640 BC)	
4th Dynasty (*c.* 2613-2494 BC)	Sneferu (*c.* 2613-2588 BC)	Nofret Queen Hetepheres
	Khufu (*c.* 2588-2563 BC) Khafre (*c.* 2553-2528 BC)	Iry Nebemakhet
5th Dynasty (*c.* 2494-2345 BC)		Kaemrehu Nefer Serefka Wepemnefret Khnumhotep and Niankhkhnum Ti Kairer
6th Dynasty (*c.* 2345-2181 BC)	Teti (*c.* 2345-2323 BC)	Mereruka Queen Iput Ankhmahor Ptahshepses
	Pepy II (*c.* 2277-2183 BC)	Ibi Pepyankh ('Black Heni') Hemre (Isi)
1ST INTERMEDIATE PERIOD 7th-10th Dynasties (*c.* 2181-2040 BC)		
MIDDLE KINGDOM 11th Dynasty (*c.* 2133-1991 BC)	Mentuhotep II (*c.* 2040 BC)	Baqt III Meketre Wah Queen Nofret Ashayt
12th Dynasty (*c.* 1991-1786 BC)	Ammenemes I (*c.* 1991-1962 BC) Sesostris I (*c.* 1971-1928 BC) Ammenemes II (*c.* 1929-1895 BC)	Senebtisy Khety son of Duauf Antefoker Amenemhat Ita Khnumet Qemanub Itaweret
	Sesostris II (*c.* 1897-1878 BC) Sesostris III (*c.* 1878-1843 BC) Ammenemes III (*c.* 1842-1797 BC)	Sithathoriunet Sithathor Mereret Wahka II Neferuptah
	Ammenemes IV (*c.* 1798-1790 BC) Sobkneferu (*c.* 1789-1786 BC)	
2ND INTERMEDIATE PERIOD 13th Dynasty (*c.* 1786-1663 BC)	Hor (*c.* 1750 BC)	Nubhotepti the Child
14th Dynasty (*c.* 1715-1650 BC)		
15th Dynasty (*c.* 1648-1540 BC)	THE HYKSOS RULERS	
16th Dynasty (*c.* 1650-1550 BC)		
17th Dynasty (*c.* 1650-1550 BC)	Nubkheperre Inyotef VII (*c.* 1650 BC) NUBIAN PAN-GRAVE CULTURE Sobkemsaf II ↓ (*c.* 1590 BC)	Queen Sobkemsaf

	PHARAOHS		OTHER ROYAL AND NON-ROYAL PERSONS
NEW KINGDOM			
18th Dynasty (c. 1550-1295 BC)	Ahmose (c. 1550-1525 BC)		Queen Aahhotep
	Hatshepsut (c. 1479-1457 BC)		
	Tuthmosis III (c. 1479-1425 BC)		Queens Menwi, Merti and Menhet
			Amenemheb
			Puyemre
			Menkheperresonb
			Iamunedjeh
			Rekhmire
	Amenophis II (c. 1427-1400 BC)		Kenamun
	Tuthmosis IV (c. 1400-1390 BC)		Sobkhotep
			Menna
			Hapu
			Amenhotepsise
	Amenophis III (c. 1390-1352 BC)		Nebamun and Ipuky
	Akhenaten (c. 1352-1336 BC)		
	Tutankhamun (c. 1336-1327 BC)		Huy
	Horemheb (c. 1323-1295 BC)		
19th Dynasty (c. 1295-1186 BC)	Sety I (c. 1294-1279 BC)		Kairy
	Ramesses II (c. 1279-1213 BC)		Paser
			Neferrenpet
	Sety II (c. 1200-1194 BC)		Queen Tausret
20th Dynasty (c. 1186-1070 BC)	Ramesses III (c. 1184-1153 BC)		
	Ramesses VI (c. 1143-1136 BC)		
	Ramesses IX (c. 1126-1108 BC)		
	Ramesses XI (c. 1099-1070 BC)		
3RD INTERMEDIATE PERIOD			
21st Dynasty (c. 1069-945 BC)	THE TANITES	THE THEBANS 'King' Pinedjem I (c. 1054-1032 BC)	
	Psusennes I (c. 1039-991 BC)		Queen Mutnedjmet Wendjebauendjed
		Smendes II (c. 992-990 BC)	
	Amenemope (c. 993-984 BC)	Pinedjem II (c. 990-969 BC)	
22nd Dynasty (c. 945-715 BC)	Sheshonq I (c. 945-924 BC)		Nemareth (Nimlot)
	Osorkon I (c. 924-889 BC)		
	Sheshonq II (c. 890 BC)		
	Osorkon II (c. 874-850 BC)		Hornakht
	Takeloth II (c. 850-825 BC)		
23rd Dynasty (c. 818-715 BC)	Osorkon III (c. 777-749 BC)		Queen Kama
24th Dynasty (c. 727-715 BC)			
25th Dynasty (c. 747-656 BC)	Pi(ankhy) (c. 747-716 BC)		
	Shabaka (c. 716-702 BC)		
	Shebitku (c. 702-690 BC)		
26th Dynasty (664-525 BC)	THE SAITE PHARAOHS		
	Psammetichus I (664-610 BC)		Ibi
	Psammetichus II (595-589 BC)		
LATE DYNASTIC PERIOD			
27th-30th Dynasties (525-343 BC)			
	PERSIAN KINGS (343-332 BC)		
	MACEDONIAN KINGS (332-305 BC)		
	Alexander the Great (332-323 BC)		
GRAECO-ROMAN PERIOD			
	PTOLEMAIC KINGS		
	Ptolemy I (305-282 BC)		
	Ptolemy II-XII (284-51 BC)		Horsanakht
			Men
			Hornedjitef
			Kerasher
	Cleopatra VII (51-30 BC)		Queen Amanishakheto
	ROMAN EMPERORS (30 BC-AD 323)		
			Artemidorus
	ISLAMIC CONQUEST (AD 641)		

Sources of the illustrations

1 Cairo Museum, **a** CG 52001; **b** CG 53136, 53123 (photo Jürgen Liepe)
2 BM EA 1168
3 The Metropolitan Museum of Art, New York 26.8.99 (photo Peter Clayton)
5 Cairo Museum, JE 85751 (photo Dieter Johannes)
6 Staatliche Sammlung Ägyptischer Kunst, Munich, ÄS 2455
7 Musée du Louvre, Paris E80
8 Cairo Museum, CG 52069 (photo Henri Stierlin)
9 Cairo Museum, **a** CG 52958, 52956, 52955; **b** CG 53018 et al.; **c** CG 52919, 52920–1, 52926–7, 52929–30, 52935–6, 52959–74 (photo Jürgen Liepe)
10 Cairo Museum, CG 52011, 52008, 52010, 52009 (photo Jürgen Liepe)
11 Cairo Museum, **a** CG 53802; **b** & **c** CG 53824–5 (photo Albert Shoucair; courtesy of Thames and Hudson Ltd)
12 The Metropolitan Museum of Art, New York 08.200.31 (photo Peter Clayton)
13 Cairo Museum, CG 52644 (photo Jürgen Liepe)
14 Royal Museum of Scotland, Edinburgh 1909.527.15–19
15 The Metropolitan Museum of Art, New York 16.1.3 (© 1983/88)
16 The Metropolitan Museum of Art, New York 16.1.8–9 (© 1983)
17 BM EA 66827
18 The Metropolitan Museum of Art, New York 40.3.2 (photo Peter Clayton)
19 Griffith Institute, Ashmolean Museum, Oxford
20 Cairo Museum, JE 61884 (photo Lee Boltin)
21 Museum of Fine Arts, Boston
22 Cairo Museum, JE 72332 (photo Albert Shoucair; courtesy of Thames and Hudson Ltd)
23 Cairo Museum, JE 87718 (photo Henri Stierlin)
24 Cairo Museum, JE 72184 B (photo Henri Stierlin)
25 Cairo Museum (photo Peter Clayton)
26 Cairo Museum, JE 90199 (photo Victor R. Boswell Jr, National Geographical Society, for the Egyptian Museum, Cairo)
27 BM EA **a** 65616; **b** 65617
29 The Metropolitan Museum of Art, New York 16.1.14–15 (© 1983)
30 Cairo Museum, JE 87711 (photo Henri Stierlin)
31 BM EA **a** 37532; **b** 51178

32 BM EA **a** 22991; **b** 8309; **c** 7435; **d** 8327; **e** 8332; **f** 3123; **g** 23123; **h** 14622; **i** 8088; **j** 59500; **k** 20639
33 BM EA 922
34 Cairo Museum, JE 85785, 85791, 85796 (photo Henri Stierlin)
35 Cairo Museum JE 85755–6 (photo Henri Stierlin)
36 BM EA 3082
37 BM EA 62150
38 Cairo Museum, CG 52860 (photo Albert Shoucair; courtesy of Thames and Hudson Ltd)
39 BM EA **a** 3077; **b** 24787
40 BM EA **a** 20760; **b** 41515
41 BM EA **a** 7539; **b** 68510; **c** 65818; **d** 7540; **e** 7396; **f** 67404; **g** 7519
42 BM EA **a** 63487; **b** 24312
43 Cairo Museum, CG 52003 (photo Henri Stierlin)
44 BM EA 20871
45 BM EA **a** 65815; **b** 59850; **c** 66620; **d** 57880; **e** 2977; **f** 54644; **g** 29220; **h** 54555; **i** 54594; **j** 22594; **k** 53906; **l** 63476; **m** 65110
46 Cairo Museum, JE 61876 (photo courtesy of the Griffith Institute, Ashmolean Museum, Oxford)
47 Cairo Museum, Carter 269 i/j (photo Editions Gallimard)
48 Cairo Museum JE 61972; 61970 (photo Albert Shoucair; courtesy of Thames and Hudson Ltd)
49 BM EA **a** 63213; **b** 63211; **c** 58026; **d** 62567
50 BM EA 40928
51 *In situ*, Saqqara
52 Cairo Museum, JE 30199 (photo Jürgen Liepe)
53 *In situ*, Deir el-Gebrawi
54 *In situ*, Theban West Bank
55 BM EA 920
56 Mrs Davies' copy, BM EA
57 Cairo Museum, JE 85788, 85799 (photo Henri Stierlin)
58 Cairo Museum, JE 61892 (photo Henri Stierlin)
59 Staatliche Sammlung Ägyptischer Kunst, Munich ÄS 2495b
60 BM EA 3074
61 See 39a
62 BM EA **a** 62444; **b** 57803; **c** 57773; **d** 57812; **e** 54747; **f** 14703; **g** 57710
63 Cairo Museum, Carter 256 g
64 Cairo Museum, CG 52975(?) (photo Victor R. Boswell Jr National Geographical Society, for the Egyptian Museum, Cairo)
65 BM EA **a** 59194; **b** 57699–700; **c** 57698; **d** 7876
66 Museum of Fine Arts, Boston 68.836 (photo Peter Clayton)
67 Cairo Museum, CG 52575–6 (photo Jürgen Liepe)
68 Cairo Museum, JE 86038 (photo Henri Stierlin)
69 Eton College, Windsor (photo Michael Ballance)

70 BM EA 57323
71 See 69
72 Cairo Museum, CG 52715 (photo Henri Stierlin)
73 Cairo Museum, Carter 44A (photo Editions Gallimard)
74 BM EA **a** 3084; **b** 32220; **c** 24773
75 The Metropolitan Museum of Art, New York 07.227.6–7 (photo Peter Clayton)
76 BM EA **a** 40654; **b** 14457; **c** 34264
77 BM EA **a** 40931; **b** 40930; **c** 62468
78 Cairo Museum, CG 52670 (photo Jürgen Liepe)
79 BM EA 6665
80 Mrs Davies' copy, BM EA
81 Cairo Museum, CG 4 (photo Hirmer)
82 Cairo Museum, CG 52859 (photo Victor R. Boswell Jr, National Geographical Society, for the Egyptian Museum, Cairo)
83 The Metropolitan Museum of Art, New York 31.10.8 (photo Peter Clayton)
84 The Metropolitan Museum of Art, New York 68.136.1 (photo Peter Clayton)
85 Mrs. Davies' copy, BM EA
86 Cairo Museum, JE 36279 (photo Carol Andrews)
87 BM EA **a** 63709; **b** 63438
88 Cairo Museum, JE 60684 (photo Peter Clayton)
89 BM EA 67
90 The Metropolitan Museum of Art, New York 26.8.117a (© 1983)
91 BM EA **a** 58518; **b** 67399–67400; **c** 54315; **d** 54459; **e** 14346; **f** 54137–8; **g** 2864
92 Cairo Museum, JE 61961A,B (photo Henri Stierlin)
93 Cairo Museum, CG 52397–8 (photo Henri Stierlin)
94 Cairo Museum, CG 52323–4 (photo Albert Shoucair; courtesy of Thames and Hudson Ltd)
95 BM EA 24907
96 BM EA **a** 29264; **b** 29258; **c** 37221; **d** 16443; **e** 68531; **f** 64297; **g** 64162; **h** 64186; **i** 65535; **j** 2895; **k** 17038; **l** 59306; **m** 63347
97 BM EA 3359
98 BM EA 1171
99 Cairo Museum, JE 72171 (photo Jürgen Liepe)
100 Museum of Fine Arts, Boston 13.3086
101 BM EA 30841
102 The Metropolitan Museum of Art, New York 26.8.135, etc (photo Peter Clayton)
103 The Metropolitan Museum of Art, New York 26.8.70/58.153 (photo Peter Clayton)
104 Museum of Fine Arts, Boston 21.307
105 BM EA 59334
106 BM EA 649

107 Cairo Museum, 11/11/20/17 (photo Jürgen Liepe)

108 Cairo Museum, **a** CG 53096–9; **b** CG 53069, 53083; **c** CG 53076, 53079–82 (photo Albert Shoucair; courtesy of Thames and Hudson Ltd)

109 Cairo Museum, Carter 320 C (photo Henri Stierlin)

110 The Metropolitan Museum of Art, New York, The Theodore M. Davis Collection. Bequest of Theodore M. Davis, 1915 (30.8.66); Gift of Edward S. Harkness, 1926 (26.7.1346,.1348)

111 The Metropolitan Museum of Art, New York, Rogers Fund and Henry Walters Gift, 1916 (16.1.3)

112 Cairo Museum, CG 52002 (photo Henri Stierlin)

113 BM EA **a** 54460; **b** 3361

114 The Manchester Museum, 5966

115 Cairo Museum, CG 52004 (photo Editions Gallimard)

116 Cairo Museum JE 61897 (photo Henri Stierlin)

117 Cairo Museum JE 61893 (photo Henri Stierlin)

118 Cairo Museum Carter 267A (photo Henri Stierlin)

119 Cairo Museum JE 61885 (photo Lee Boltin)

120 Cairo Museum, JE 72172 (photo Henri Stierlin)

121 BM EA 14456

122 BM EA 37891

123 The Metropolitan Museum of Art, New York 08.200.29 (photo Peter Clayton)

124 The Metropolitan Museum of Art, New York 16.1.16 (photo Peter Clayton)

125 The Metropolitan Museum of Art, New York 26.8.41 (photo Peter Clayton)

126 BM EA 37984

127 Cairo Museum, CG 52068 (photo Editions Gallimard)

128 Cairo Museum, JE 85759 (photo Henri Stierlin)

129 Cairo Museum, JE 85762 (photo Henri Stierlin)

130 Cairo Museum, JE 72189 (photo Henri Stierlin)

131 Cairo Museum, JE 85772 (photo Henri Stierlin)

132 Cairo Museum, CG 52089 (photo Jürgen Liepe)

133 Cairo Museum, CG 52070, 52072 (photo Jürgen Liepe)

134 The Metropolitan Museum of Art, New York 26.8.121 (photo Peter Clayton)

135 The Metropolitan Museum of Art, New York 26.8.125–8 (photo Peter Clayton)

136 BM EA 14594–5

137 Cairo Museum, JE 85760 (photo Henri Stierlin)

138 Cairo Museum, JE 62360 (photo Henri Stierlin)

139 Cairo Museum, **a** Carter 256 ww; **b** JE 62370 (photo Lee Boltin)

140 Cairo Museum, CG 52642 (photo Editions Gallimard)

141 Staatliche Sammlung Ägyptischer Kunst, Munich Äs 2495a

142 Cairo Museum, JE 85781 (photo Henri Stierlin)

143 The Metropolitan Museum of Art, New York 16.1.10a–11a (© 1983)

144 The Metropolitan Museum of Art, New York 16.1.7 (photo Peter Clayton)

145 BM EA 6665

146 BM EA **a** 14349; **b** 4159; **c** 49717; **d** 14345; **e** 36466; **f** 65316; **g** 37308; **h** 2933

147 Musée du Louvre, Paris N728

148 BM EA **a** 24777; **b** 68868; **c** 54549; **d** 71492; **e** 53893; **f** 32723; **g** 37644; **h** 36468

149 Cairo Museum, **a** JE 62432; **b** JE 62428; **c** Carter 256ff (3) (photo Lee Boltin)

150 Cairo Museum, JE 85222A (photo Henri Stierlin)

151 Cairo Museum, JE 87702 (photo Henri Stierlin)

152 Staatliche Sammlung Ägyptischer Kunst, Munich Äs 2446b

153 Staatliche Sammlung Ägyptischer Kunst, Munich Äs 2446d

154 Cairo Museum, CG 53070 (photo Editions Gallimard)

155 BM EA **a** 24774; **b** 30478; **c** 30477

156 BM EA 2572

157 BM EA **a** 30484–5; **b** 30486–7; **c** 3363; **d** 30482–3

158 BM EA **a** 59416–7; **b** 14696; **c** 14695

159 BM EA **a** 65330; **b** 26976; **c** 33888; **d** 65798; **e** 23426; **f** 59782

160 BM EA **a** 65279; **b** 3081; **c** 59418

161 BM EA **a** 54583; **b** 54533; **c** 15715; **d** 2965; **e** 58141; **f** 16977; **g** 54458; **h** 16521; **i** 2923; **j** 2922; **k** 54547

162 Cairo Museum, JE 72334 (photo Albert Shoucair; courtesy of Thames and Hudson Ltd)

163 Cairo Museum, CG 52672 (photo Albert Shoucair; courtesy of Thames and Hudson Ltd)

164 Cairo Museum, JE 87715 (photo Henri Stierlin)

165 BM EA 68502

166 Staatliche Sammlung Ägyptischer Kunst, Munich Äs 5301

167 Cairo Museum, CG 52671 (photo Henri Stierlin)

168 Rijksmuseum van Oudheden, Leiden Ao 11a

169 BM EA 14693; 66840–1; 66718

170 Rijksmuseum van Oudheden, Leiden Ao 2b

171 *In situ*, Theban West Bank

173 Cairo Museum, JE 87709 (photo Henri Stierlin)

174 BM EA 10098/1

175 BM EA 14355

176 Cairo Museum, Carter 261 P1 (photo Lee Boltin)

177 Cairo Museum, JE 85813, 85819, 85814, 85820 (photo Henri Stierlin)

178 Cairo Museum, JE 61946 (photo Albert Shoucair; courtesy of Thames and Hudson Ltd)

179 Cairo Museum, JE 85785 (photo Henri Stierlin)

180 Musée du Louvre, Paris E6204 (photo Henri Stierlin)

181 BM EA 7865

182 BM EA 30842

183 BM EA **a** 65831; **b** 65832; **c** 30643; **d** 65231; **e** 48951

184 BM EA **a** 48998; **b** 14380; **c** 63616; **d** 65280; **e** 3360; **f** 15031

185 Staatliche Sammlung Ägyptischer Kunst, Munich Äs 2446c

186 BM EA 21810

The maps (4, 28) and the line drawings (51, 53, 54) are by Christine Barratt

Indexes

References in italic type are to those illustrations not specifically mentioned in the text.